CH

PRAISE FOR *MEAN MEN*

"Mark Lipton's unsettling masterpiece makes a compelling case for why, all too often, mean men get ahead in business and politics. He shows why their unhealthy nastiness and selfishness is too often confused with healthy competence and drive. He documents the damage they do and, thank goodness, shows that leaders don't need to be mean to get ahead—how some of our best (such as Mark Zuckerberg) have matured into caring and giving people and how such wisdom has helped them build great and civilized organizations." —Robert Sutton, professor of management at Stanford University and author of *The No Asshole Rule* and *The Asshole Survival Guide*

"*Mean Men* is a book whose time has come. More than ever, in this 'Trumpian age,' it's important to decipher the darker side of leadership. Mark Lipton provides a penetrating analysis of what can go wrong in the leadership equation. He helps us understand why Lord Acton's statement that 'Power tends to corrupt, and absolute power corrupts absolutely' is even more relevant in this day and age." —Manfred F. R. Kets de Vries, distinguished clinical professor of leadership development and organizational change at INSEAD, France, and author of *Riding the Leadership Rollercoaster*; *Leaders, Fools and Imposters*; *The Neurotic Organization*; *Unstable at the Top*; and *Prisoners of Leadership*

"Like a kid afraid to see what was in the dark basement but compelled to do so, I kept creeping into Mark Lipton's incredible world of *Mean Men*. What I found was spellbinding and intellectually vital. What I left with is renewed hope that all of us can be leaders who can make the world better, day by day. This is an enduring volume." —Sydney Finkelstein, Steven Roth professor of management and director of the Tuck Leadership Center at the Tuck School of Business, Dartmouth College, and author of *Superbosses: How Exceptional Leaders Master the Flow of Talent* and *Why Smart Executives Fail*

"What's worse than an asshole, or the worst sort of asshole? The guy who is abusively *mean*. Mark Lipton's engaging book gets into the head of mean men, why our entrepreneurial culture is spawning them, and how we might get back to true leadership and civil cooperation." —Aaron James, professor of philosophy at the University of California, Irvine, and author of *Assholes: A Theory* and *Assholes: A Theory of Donald Trump*

MEAN
MEN

ALSO BY MARK LIPTON

Guiding Growth: How Vision Keeps Companies on Course

MEAN MEN

The PERVERSION
of AMERICA'S
SELF-MADE MAN

MARK LIPTON

Voussoir

Published by Voussoir Press, New York
www.marklipton.com

 Edited and Designed by Girl Friday Productions
www.girlfridayproductions.com

Editorial: Leslie Miller and Nicole Burns-Ascue
Interior Design: Paul Barrett
Cover Design: Anna Curtis

Image Credits: Cover image © kpatyhka/Shutterstock; Author photo: Val Allard

ISBN (Hardcover): 978-0-9986130-1-7
ISBN (Paperback): 978-0-9986130-0-0
e-ISBN: 978-0-9986130-2-4

First Edition

Printed in the United States of America

To Valerie, who inspires me every day

CONTENTS

PROLOGUE

NOBODY LIKES BEING FIRED. BUT when Zynga laid off over five hundred employees in the spring of 2013, it's a good bet that some of those let go by the social game-maker were happy to move on.

Zynga's CEO, Mark Pincus, was not a fun guy to work for.

Pincus became a billionaire during the minibubble for overhyped social media companies in 2010 and 2011. But by 2013, he was fighting to keep his company afloat. And for those who knew him well, there was a poetic justice to his fall.

Mark Pincus was *mean*.

Pincus, a serial entrepreneur with a Harvard MBA, led Zynga to financial success in the early years with social media game apps like FarmVille that leveraged Facebook's social network to grow an ever-expanding subscriber base. While Wall Street sung the praises of Zynga's unique business model, both Pincus and Zynga were raked over the coals by the trade press. Innovative, yes—but Pincus and Zynga were using these first-generation social gaming apps alongside predatory lead generation tactics to manipulate their users into unknowingly signing up for subscriptions. Pincus exposed his growing estrangement from ethics in his 2009 speech at the Y Combinator Startup School in Berkeley where he admitted doing "every horrible thing in the book to just get revenue right away."[1]

Pincus made no apologies for his behavior. Taking a cocky stance in interviews, he noted proudly the multiple times his belligerent attitude got him fired from previous jobs. Internal reports from Zynga's current and former employees painted a picture of an ethically bankrupt organization where the unofficial motto was "Do Evil" (the inverse of Google's "Don't Be Evil"), and the basic MO was to straight-out steal other companies' game ideas and focus on lead generation analytics.[2] On the outside, there seemed to be no limit to Zynga's growing power to not only steal more effectively from competitors and manipulate its users, but also leverage the law to its advantage. They had cash, and cash talked.

Meanwhile, inside the company, Zynga had established its reputation as a meat grinder for employees. Their mission? Make a profit. Even before the mass layoffs, a steady stream of high-profile talent was leaving. One former employee called it the "worst possible work environment and culture imaginable . . . CEO says stuff like, 'When you come to the conversation understanding that I'm always right you'll have a better outcome.'"[3]

Zynga's downward spiral at the hands of an unethical, arrogant, and abusive leader shows why these particular men are a real and growing problem: these guys don't just make life miserable for those around them—they damage or destroy entire companies, nonprofits, sports teams, music bands, movie studios . . . the list goes on. More than that, these "leaders" have become twisted icons for success in contemporary American society. Happiness is no longer a goal in and of itself. Ethics mean nothing compared to the win. Power, at any cost, at all costs, is what makes the nation tick.

Which is the culture that brought Mark Pincus back to Zynga. In early April 2015, he announced his return to the CEO role. That's right, the man the analysts blamed for the deep slide in virtually every measurement of the company's success was back in the saddle. Why? He was still so loaded with shares of Zynga he had weight to swing around. And he had a board that allowed back a former CEO who had proved himself ineffective. But the rest of the world took notice: the day after Pincus's announcement, Zynga's stock tanked more than 10 percent. He didn't last long. By March 2016, Pincus handed over the reins to board member Frank Gibeau, but only after laying off more than a thousand employees and putting the company's tony headquarters on the market. By the time Pincus left the second time around, Zynga's stock had fallen 85 percent since its peak in 2012.[4] Why does corporate America refuse to learn its lesson? Why do we tolerate, even celebrate, these "bad boys" even after they have proved toxic to both company culture and long-term success?

Because America loves a winner, especially the guy who's forged his own path. The tech entrepreneur. The Hollywood mogul. The rags-to-riches politician. The driven athlete. In 2016, a self-proclaimed winner and real estate mogul won the US presidency and was named *Time's* Person of the Year. Pass any newsstand and you'll see their faces—mostly male, white—on magazine covers. Social media eats them up; they're the darlings (and demons) of Twitter. But there is another side to many of these talented individuals, a side too many of us like to ignore. These "leaders" are often just out for themselves. They step on others to get ahead. They are deceptive and ruthless. They have explosive tempers and abusive personalities. In a word, they are *mean*.

In fact, a disproportionate number of them share characteristics of a dark personality disorder that compels people to behave badly even as it drives them to create and excel. Pincus is but one example; the behavior seems rampant in entrepreneurial spheres where individual talent and ambition reign. The same men who flourish in challenging circumstances may also be mean: they are abusive to employees or colleagues, unprincipled in their pursuit of success, and devoid of empathy; they're pathological liars, unable to feel remorse, and incapable of taking responsibility when they fail; and they're arrogant and prone to see others strictly as tools for their own advancement.

Does this constellation of traits sound familiar? Mean men are everywhere, and too often the full extent of their behavior is hidden from view. What's more troubling is that even when they're outed, we too often fail to hold them accountable. They are instead *rewarded* in an America enthralled with competition, risk-taking, efficiency, and monetary success. Pincus gets a second try at the brass ring, and Trump gets 306 electoral votes. In the face of their abusive behavior, their subordinates, suppliers, and entourages are cowed, while board members, investors, voters, and even the media look the other way. And in doing so we simply create more mean men, teaching them in every instance that mean is not only tolerated, it's celebrated. Before we reach the point of no return, we must uncouple "mean" from our definition of American success—before these men don't simply populate entrepreneurial firms and our government but become the new American heroes for a generation of fledging leaders.

This book goes beyond the now-familiar stories about famous mean men, such as Apple visionary Steve Jobs, to expose the bad behavior of mean men in nearly every entrepreneurial sector of American society: Silicon Valley, Wall Street, Hollywood, professional sports, and even religion. In writing this book, I dove into recent groundbreaking social science research as well as interviews, court documents, and media accounts to reveal a veiled world of fear, bullying, cheating, and worse. I drew on my four decades of experience as an organizational consultant. And I have tapped my professional network of psychiatrists and consultants for their stories of men who were in charge and mean. Yet this is not just a book about a problem; it is meant to serve as a call to action, to move us toward a nation where good guys—you know, guys capable of empathy—really do finish first.

And yes, I did say "guys" intentionally. All but one of the people profiled in this book are men. In the beginning, that was a decision born out of research. Nearly all the studies that have been done on entrepreneurs and personality-disordered executives focus on males. Yet along the way I discovered something even more intriguing—and controversial—behind the skewed results. More on that later.

Though I am a researcher, this isn't an academic issue—it's a national phenomenon. I want to paint a clear picture of the psychology shaping modern America so that all of us can work to take our country down a different path. So let us begin. Let us take a deep dive into what and who a "mean man" is and look at the path of destruction he leaves in his wake. After all, each one of us is caught up in the churn.

CHAPTER ONE

MY OWN INTRODUCTION TO "MEAN"

"Fighters, fanatics, men with a lust for contest, a gleam of creation, and a drive to justify their break from the mother company."

—Supply-side economist and investor George Gilder on entrepreneurs

"The way of the entrepreneur is a long, lonely, and difficult road. The men who follow it are by necessity a special breed. . . . As a group, they do not have the qualities of patience, understanding, and charity many of us admire and wish for in our fellows. . . . The men who travel the entrepreneurial way are, taken in balance, not remarkably likeable people."

—Orvis F. Collins and David G. Moore in *The Enterprising Man*

AARON HAD FELT THE ENTREPRENEURIAL fire in his belly since he was a teenager. Street-smart but fairly unsuccessful in school, he managed to get into a private college yet quit after his sophomore year and started working in the service department of a computer hard-drive manufacturer outside San Francisco. After two years there, he became restless again. His idea-generating mind was producing a new business scheme every month, and he was anxious to see if he could make them work. He kept his day job but began filling his nights and weekends with different schemes, trying to find the right "angle" to chase each successive idea. He didn't want to be a world-changer or solve a vexing problem. He wanted to get rich.

Aaron was twenty-four when he met Lisa. She was twenty-one. His work ethic impressed her, reminding her of her hardworking father. They married less than two years later, shortly before Aaron decided to leave his job. "I work with idiots," he said to her before he quit. "They don't know how to think *big*."

Lisa was tolerant, even supportive, of Aaron's "hobbies," but she was dubious of his capacity to create a lasting business. She wanted security for them and their children, soon to be on the way. Ten years later, having blown through three consecutive partners in as many start-up initiatives, Aaron finally had a success on his hands. His fourth venture fit an important niche in the transforming digital consumer electronics industry. Riding the wave of disruptive innovation from merely portable to minuscule music players, he found his calling in the sometimes-shadowy world of gray-market electronics.

That's about the time he hired a consultant to help fuse his thinking with the ideas of his junior partner, an engineer who owned less of the firm but had still invested heavily to become part of Aaron's "adventure." A series of strategy conversations among the two and their CFO were facilitated to find the intersections where they came close to agreement. As the consultant worked with them, it was impossible not to notice Aaron's aberrant behavior and the effect it had on most everyone around him.

While the business was growing steadily, and Aaron had hired talented and competent people, it quickly became clear that he wanted to control virtually everyone and everything. What's more, he had a hair-trigger temper. The normally charming CEO was developing a reputation for morphing without warning from a Jekyll into a Hyde.

"Screams that could peel paint off the walls" was how one staff member described the outbursts. Few were spared his earsplitting and caustic attacks—neither partners, staff, nor family. Just when it seemed Aaron would reach the point of physical violence, he'd stamp off like a frustrated beast.

Aaron refused to acknowledge the impact his behavior had on others, or even concede that his screaming was in any way inappropriate. For him, it was as if the outbursts never happened. He never flat-out denied them. Instead, he deftly shifted the blame onto others. His confidence was such that others believed him, wondering if *they* actually triggered or fanned the tirades. Confused and frustrated, his forty employees were more than ready to bolt.

And yet . . . the other Aaron was *so* compelling—he had an entrancing side as attractive as his controlling side was ugly. When he sensed that an employee was on the verge of quitting, he would go to them and talk them out of it—calm their fears, dissipate the frustration. This was the side of Aaron that enticed customers and investors and endeared him to his children. His wife felt as though she got whiplash dealing with the dichotomies in his personality: he could switch at will from being a screaming bully to being a sweet and vulnerable "big boy."

During meetings with the consultant, Aaron spent time talking through his plans to grow the business and the need for him to think beyond "the next big deal." While he rarely discussed what his life was like growing up, he did offer that his late father, a prominent attorney, had believed Aaron was a "loser." Aaron knew he had been a perennial disappointment to the respected litigator, and he'd never been able to show him the successful business he had built.

After the consultant worked with the firm for a year and half, the rest of the senior leadership team came to realize that Aaron had created very different stories about the exact nature of the business for different groups—employees, investors, suppliers. Whispers started among business associates, friends, and family. The sources of his supply chain of "surplus products" salvaged from manufacturers were murky at best. And on more than one occasion, his secretary opened his briefcase to find it packed with wrapped bundles of crisp fifties. Aaron's spending habits became increasingly ostentatious, his purchases screaming out, "Look at me! I'm the success that no one thought I'd be."

The consultant transitioned from being the firm's strategy consultant to being Aaron's executive coach, since that's what Aaron and the business needed most. But even in that role, the experienced consultant had sufficient insight to know he'd never have much impact. Aaron needed serious help, and of a different kind. The coach recommended that he see a mental health professional. Aaron rejected the idea, and the engagement was then terminated.

The coach's last memory of Aaron is of him reaming out a sales manager. The two were in the office hallway, and the decibels traveled across the entire floor of the hulking former manufacturing plant in Oakland. After subjecting himself to Aaron's ranting, the manager went into the men's room, apparently seeking refuge. Aaron followed, screaming, not skipping a beat. His coach found out later that Aaron had yelled at the sales manager for ten minutes through a locked stall door until the employee managed to escape.

In the end, Aaron's business and marriage crumbled. But he would not be deterred. Instead, he sought out fresh opportunities and, with his charm and the promise of success, attracted new partner-investors (and romantic interests). Did they know of his past? Absolutely. But he always managed to win over those essential to making each successive new firm take flight, until once again, the walls began to crumble.

WHY MEAN MEN?

When Walter Isaacson published his biography of Steve Jobs, the media was abuzz about the book's juiciest takeaway: Jobs had been a titanic jerk. Isaacson's book was filled with nearly unbelievable tales about tantrums, stony coldness, double-crosses, and controlling behavior. It was such a juicy story that the film version hit theaters only four years later, a film featuring a Jobs who "has betrayed his friends, alienated his allies, and mistreated his loved ones," forcing the viewer to challenge "some deeply cherished myths about the correlation between virtue and success," as the *New York Times* reviewed it. Of course, the viewer isn't trapped in this ethical space for long. The *Times* concluded, "Jobs's behavior also confirms equally deep assumptions about the ultimate virtue of ruthlessness in the capitalist economy."[1]

I wasn't surprised by any of this. In fact, I knew that some of the worst stories about Jobs didn't even make it into Isaacson's book (or the film). More broadly, I wasn't shocked that a top entrepreneur could behave so badly, because I'd quietly been collecting my own stories about guys like Jobs, men like Aaron, for years. Steve Jobs, I knew, was just the tip of a toxic iceberg when it came to twisted people in high places. And by the time the Isaacson book came out, and way before the Trump phenomenon, I had already begun exploring the question of what makes these mean men tick.

In fact, you can trace a long lineage of entrepreneurs who shared characteristics with Aaron, or Pincus, Jobs, or Donald Trump. American icon Henry Ford, father of the assembly line, was also known for his outsized flaws and extreme behavior. Yet just as Ford vehicles are with us today, so, too, are many of his "leadership" traits, characteristics that fit a pattern we see with men born a century later and running companies in the here and now: a quest for total financial control, complete domination of product design, the need to claim credit for success without any personal responsibility for failures, and difficulty working with other executives or partners. You could even add emotional manipulation and rage to the list.

The consequences of Ford's controlling, abusive personality are also familiar: in his day, Ford undermined his company's growth just as some modern entrepreneurial CEOs have destroyed not only their organizations but people's lives. Many of these same companies would never have experienced such incredible growth without the entrepreneurial drive of their founders. But too many businesses stumble badly thanks to the dark side of the men who built them.

Henry Ford occupied the executive suite well before the rise of organizational psychology and management theory, the disciplines that make me tick. But research over subsequent decades would confirm what is common sense (spoiler alert!): a controlling, abusive leadership style isn't deeply hurtful to just people; mean men are also bad for the bottom line. A desperate need for control prevents collaboration and delegation, stifles creativity, and drives away the talented stars companies should want to hold on to. Mean destroys community and divides organizations and social groups.

Business leaders know that encouraging employees to innovate and iterate is hugely important for long-range success, once considered essential for only consumer-products companies but now critical for all industries, with the advent of ubiquitous market disruptions. It was important for car companies in the 1920s facing fierce competition and fast-changing public tastes; it's even more important today that these companies redefine themselves as "mobility" providers. But creativity matters for just about any organization—corporate, nonprofit, or governmental—since creative solutions can improve efficiency and keep down costs while opening up promising avenues for expansion. Customers could have any color, Ford famously said, as long as it was black. Controlling leaders not only squelch creativity—they risk alienating the very customer on whom they depend.

My research was originally focused only on founder entrepreneurs. I sifted through a few decades of data to understand the typical personality characteristics and quirks that motivated men to start businesses in particularly competitive industries. In my work on executive leadership effectiveness, I was naturally drawn to these guys. But it didn't take long to realize that other professions and roles exhibited the same underlying requirements.

As practiced in the United States, entrepreneurship or entrepreneurial leadership is all about standing alone. It requires aggressiveness and innovativeness in the face of possible failure. It adheres to the assumption that standout personal achievement is valued over the success of a group, with vision and leadership seen as virtues of the *individual*. Especially as Americans, we like to see ourselves as born mavericks and innovators, never satisfied to live with the status quo.

Politicians and professional sports figures need entrepreneur-like thinking and a personality that influences them to behave in ways that get them noticed, garner a following, and break through the competition. Many others began to fit into a broader definition of entrepreneurial leadership (though I hesitate to use the word "leadership"), in that they have taken risks to forge their own path and operate with a high level of autonomy. They exhibit a style and personality common to that of the entrepreneur. Those with this entrepreneurial style bring their outsized energy and drive to many sectors of society wherever individual initiative and risk is rewarded. Unfortunately, a subset of those are mean men who also bring a unique set of risks and drawbacks.

If they're so awful, why am I so interested in mean men?

A big reason is that I've seen them in action up close, and I've seen the enormous damage they inflict on both people and organizations. Their behavior is appalling, and it's wrong. But more than that, I know it doesn't have to be this way. Contrary to the popular wisdom, mean doesn't "get results," and it doesn't "work." In fact, a growing body of compelling research shows just the opposite. It is the leaders who support and empower people, act with authentic leadership, and inspire trust who get the best results in the long term. This is true across the board— in business as well as social and political realms.

DISCOVERING THE DARK SIDE

The idea behind this book began decades ago, during the explosion of Internet-related start-ups that turned Lower Broadway in Manhattan into Silicon Alley. As more and more founder-CEOs arrived on the start-up scene in New York City, I heard the same sentiment expressed regularly, if sotto voce, about many of these entrepreneurs: "I don't trust him." "He's ruthless." "He's got an evil side."

But the public loved these guys. It didn't matter whether he was touting a half-baked business model or the next Facebook; it didn't matter whether the fellow in question had a history of creating successful firms or whether the ink was barely dry on his college diploma. Tech entrepreneurs were the era's golden boys, able to capitalize new businesses with nothing more solid than a well-sold vision. Tech would change the world, we were told, and many of us were drawn in by their promise. We were attracted to their quirky awkwardness, combined with an infectious enthusiasm and a magician's ability to poke holes in any skepticism. These were, after all, good times. But this was still the late 1990s. We were drunk on the chance to be part of the Next Great Thing.

I certainly was. I've had a day job as a professor of management and the chair of graduate management programs at The New School, a New York–based university with a reputation for being innovative. In my consulting practice, I focused on CEO leadership development. I helped entrepreneurs build high-functioning executive teams, and I facilitated intensive sessions with those teams as they developed strategies. The tech wave was a boon to me personally and seemed to hold so much promise.

It also marked the beginning of my journey into mean, though I didn't know it at the time. Initially, I channeled my research during this first eruption of digital start-ups into studying the degree to which vision mattered in companies and testing new ways for executives to develop this essential leadership competency. I published a book on the topic. Yet even as I was studying and writing about vision, I was keeping a mental file of my impressions of the entrepreneurs I was working with and of the outrageously negative behaviors common to many.

My own impressions were echoed by others. By those who worked for entrepreneurs, those who advised them as consultants and investors, those who were part of their families. From each, I heard chillingly similar themes about a different side of the iconic self-made man.

I heard about an obsessive need for control, a need so strong that it undermined their ability to delegate key tasks to others. Worse, it led them to micromanage everyone in their world and to explode in anger when people took their own initiative. I heard about their distrust of others, at times bordering on paranoia, even as they started and presided over ventures that required empowering others, building strong teams, and entering into high-stakes partnerships.

I heard about out-of-control arrogance and about dismissive, condescending behavior by overly self-confident self-starters who believed so deeply in their own worldview and talents that they viewed others as mere tools to achieve their goals, rather than as colleagues with their own good ideas.

I heard about impulsive decisions and extreme risk-taking, often with disastrous results, as entrepreneurs, convinced of their own genius and ignoring counsel, followed their "gut."

And I wondered, was there a dark side to entrepreneurship? Did the role of entrepreneur attract a particular personality . . . or personality *disorder*? Why did many of these men, who initially seemed emotionally mature and charismatic, come to turn on those they were close to, the people they said they trusted?

Of course, not all entrepreneurs I worked with or studied had this dark side, but proportionately, there seemed to be a meaningful critical mass. When I mentioned what I was observing to colleagues, friends, and a host of people who worked in and around innovative new businesses, they all nodded knowingly. They were seeing what I was seeing. The more I realized I was striking a similar chord, and that there was a pattern here, the more I had to follow the trail.[2]

That was my introduction to mean men, but you've probably had your own. That's because they don't exist just in the tech sector. Mean men work in politics, the media, sports, law, and medicine. Large corporations and government agencies tend to have higher "organ rejection rates" for folks like these, but if the 2016 election results remind us of anything, it's that you can still see them there. My findings hold for others who take initiative and risk to meet a need in society, whether that's to provide goods and services, for social improvement, or for entertainment. Think of the star athlete who's turned his talent into a brand, the surgeon with an expanding practice and a patented new technique, the bestselling author cranking out global hits, the politician always on the hustle.

Surprising as it may be, the dark side is even common in the non-profit sector, within organizations dedicated to making the world a better place. During my years researching and working with nonprofit entre-preneurs, I heard story after incredulous story of founders clinging to control when their organizations desperately needed fresh leadership. When new CEOs appeared, these same men found ways to sabotage their success. Entrepreneurial leaders can be profoundly effective, char-ismatic, and admired, or equally charismatic and diabolical. They don't always use their powers for good.

MYSTERIES OF THE ENTREPRENEUR

In a grainy 1977 mug shot, a young man smiles confidently at the camera, his tinted glasses more nerd than wise guy. For good reason. The photo is of Bill Gates, Microsoft cofounder and now global philanthropist. He'd been arrested for a traffic violation in Albuquerque, New Mexico. According to media reports, that was not his only arrest from his younger years.[3]

Famed Harvard professor and psychoanalyst Abraham Zaleznik once said, "To understand the entrepreneur, you first have to understand the psychology of the juvenile delinquent."[4] And he was onto something, correctly identifying a go-it-alone, rebellious, risk-taking streak found in many successful entrepreneurial men.

Zaleznik's wry observation was corroborated in 2013 when a group of European scholars examined data from a massive longitudinal Swedish study. The study traced individuals from childhood, through adoles-cence, all the way to adulthood, and it examined the career paths they pursued. Gates's "criminal" career notwithstanding, data showed nei-ther teenage crime nor adult crime was relevant as a predictor of later career choices; there was, however, a strong correlation between early antisocial rule-breaking and an entrepreneurial bent.[5] One explanation suggests that when a bright, creative mind and rule-breaking tendencies come together early in life, a pathway toward entrepreneurship is likely. In fact, this groundbreaking study found that antisocial rule-breaking was the strongest predictor among all variables measured for determining if someone would work in an entrepreneurial career by middle age.

Entrepreneurs are often described as particularly action-oriented, and at least in adolescence, they may have a certain drive to behave in antisocial ways that play as rebellious and nonconformist to others. While on the whole they aren't necessarily personal disasters, nor do they all fit the criteria for personality disorders, studies show that entrepreneurs are prone to drama, or at the very least seem to attract it. As in a compelling detective story where the author puts a body on the doorstep in the very first paragraph, entrepreneurs present most things in their lives as a problem to be solved, a danger to be faced, or a bad guy to overcome—and they already have the solution, where they are the savior, ready to go.

PROFILING THE FUTURE ENTREPRENEUR

What might we see if we comb through the early years of entrepreneurs? For many, a person with an unhappy family background, an individual who feels displaced, a misfit in his environment. He perceives his broader world as hostile and turbulent, populated by people he thinks want to take control away from him. He exercises an innovative rebelliousness as a means to adapt as well as to demonstrate his ability to break away, to show independence of mind. We might also see someone who demonstrates remarkable resilience in the face of setbacks. The entrepreneur has an enviable ability to start all over again when disappointments and hardships wreck his plans.

The entrepreneur is not the only one who finds himself at odds with his environment. As a young man, he is also perceived by others as out of place, frequently provocative and irritating because of his seemingly irrational, nonconforming actions and confrontational ideas. To be fair, these same traits may also account for his many productive contributions later in life.

Yet for all we do know, there is still so much more to learn about the psyche of the entrepreneurial leader. My formal research revealed how incomplete our understanding is of these lone rangers. Yes, the media covers this crowd nonstop, and academics have also put them under a microscope, but all this scrutiny still hasn't given the broader public a full picture of some of the most driven and successful people in America.

Both as a researcher and as a business consultant, I wanted to get to the root of these collected observations about the entrepreneurial profile. For too long these outsized entrepreneurial leaders have been poorly understood and as a result have not been called to account for their more outrageous behaviors.[6] Researchers had observed entrepreneurs' decisions and strategies and what goes on in their organizations. And they'd categorized a cluster of personality traits that a suspiciously disproportionate number of these leaders exhibit. But no one yet had connected all the dots. *Why* do "mean" entrepreneurs and entrepreneurial leaders behave the way they do?

ARE MEAN MEN A MODERN INVENTION?

Mean men are not new, of course. They've been with us through the entirety of human history. Henry Ford, Andrew Carnegie, Cornelius Vanderbilt, Benjamin "Bugsy" Siegel, P. T. Barnum, Benjamin Franklin— heck, going back to the 1400s, even Pope Sixtus IV fits the bill. But on the data front, we now have the tools to drill into the dark side of ambition and success, revealing insights about mean men that weren't available just a decade ago.

What's also new, and just as revelatory, is that a growing body of meticulous research now has documented the effect of mean men on those around them. This research allows even the most data-driven to go beyond the myth that "mean works," and it can stop us from supporting powerful tyrants who may not be popular but are respected because they get results.

Bob Sutton, the insightful and plainspoken Stanford University management professor, writes convincingly in *No Asshole Rules* about, well, organizational assholes.[7] You know the guy—he's the one who makes your life miserable, ruins every meeting, takes credit for every idea, belittles and besmirches. We all know *that* guy. But that guy isn't really the issue. No, the meanness that is the focus of this book goes beyond the type of behavior that Sutton writes about to describe entrepreneurial leaders who are shrewdly manipulative in ways that "asshole" simply doesn't capture. As we'll see, many of these mean men are just as charming as they are horrific. Mean is worse than ineffective; it's downright destructive.

As more and more Americans genuflect to those scrappy, aggressive, and self-absorbed entrepreneurs who find prestige—however fleeting their success may be—that adulation carries a greater impact. Our condoning mean in the realm of office politics (and national politics) is creating a *culture* of mean, which is a noxious, systemic issue that cannot be solved by teaching people how to deal with the jerk in the next cubicle.

The problem of mean men is also growing. That's because America has become a "free agent nation," to use Daniel Pink's phrase,[8] allowing more people to rise on their own, achieving success and claiming power positions without first being socialized appropriately. These changes in the economy and our cultural norms, combined with a generational shift in the expectations around organizational life, have not transformed only modern companies. They have revolutionized the way many industries do business. And in the wake of some of these shifts, we are groping to redefine civil behavior when the natural law of the corporate jungle is to grow or die.

While we imagine that leaders have had their rough edges sanded down by PR firms and executive coaches, freewheeling organizational structures and 360-degree evaluations, risk-averse in-house counsels and social media trolls, the truth is quite different. Where powerful but calm, rational men like Barack Obama once stood as one archetype of success, our expectations for our leaders are changing. Structurally, there are fewer checks than ever on bad behavior by *driven* and *successful* men, the kind who wrestle bears.

The abusive behavior of mean men gets excused in any number of ways, but perhaps no excuse is more common than the idea that mean is how you get stuff done. This excuse has spawned endless clichéd phrases. "You can't make an omelet without breaking a few eggs," after all. Effective leaders, it's said, aren't afraid to make "heads roll" or have "sharp elbows." Some leaders revel in their tough nicknames: "Neutron Jack," "Chainsaw Al," "The Enforcer," "The Exterminator," "Rahmbo," "The Steamroller." In fact, conventional wisdom seems to support being as mean as you can get, just short of landing in prison.

What's more, our vision of the self-made man is now tied to our feelings about who and what is successful in American terms. Even as researchers, organizational experts, and top executives call for more generosity, consumers and fans and voters send conflicting signals about the reward of generosity, empathy, and concern for the collective group.

Cornell economist Robert Frank reminds us that many employees are subject to counterintuitive, if not just screwy, organizational reward systems that feel zero-sum: in promotion decisions, only one person advances while the rest are left behind. In forced-ranking performance evaluations, for every employee who earns a five, another must be given a one. In competitive bonus pools, more money to stars means less for the rest of the team. We throng to watch people get canned on *The Apprentice* and watch aspiring entrepreneurs battle it out on *Shark Tank*. Poll numbers rise every time a politician bashes a competitor or bucks the party or strikes a blow against "political correctness" by tossing out some outrageous racist or sexist sound bite. These situations pit people against one another, encouraging them to undercut their colleagues. What's this team business? Get ahead, *win*. Though a Wharton study found that "giving" results in higher unit profitability, productivity, efficiency, and customer satisfaction, along with lower costs and turnover rates in business, most corporate cultures reinforce the opposite.[9] And our social structures are starting to reflect the same change.

In fact, one of the most difficult arguments against the culture of mean is that meanness is so often rewarded. Males considered "agreeable" earn much less money than their tougher counterparts. A 2011 study by Cornell and Notre Dame researchers found that agreeable men earned roughly 18 percent less than men considered disagreeable.[10] Men who are kinder, more trusting, and more cooperative take a big pay cut while those who are more competitive, arrogant, and manipulative and who don't value relationships snicker all the way to the bank. And we seem to be training up the generations that follow to feel the same way. A study of college students found that it was the classmates described as less trusting and more arrogant who were recommended for management positions. Is this what's meant by "tough capitalism"? Have we really become a culture where "my way or no way" gets rewarded more? Where walking away from the table isn't a last-ditch option, it's a sanctioned first step? Do we value one histrionic quarterback with a good arm more than the team?

Enablers of mean men often can't see clear downsides to their behavior. Yes, abuse may occur. Tantrums may happen. Underlings may quit in tears, one after the other. Competitors and detractors may be derided and humiliated. "Truth" might become entirely subjective. But putting up with all that is seen as worth it given the result: the IPO, winning the election, the blockbuster hit.

In fact, though, mean men pose far greater risks than most of their enablers realize. Their impact on their firms, specifically on the employees and investors, is becoming increasingly clear to researchers and laypeople alike. What's more, they are destructive to business, but also to our greater society. If we are to be a nation of small businesses and entrepreneurs who will innovate our way to a brighter future, what is the greater American risk if the price is bullying, abuse, and even violence?

IT'S NOT "JUST" BUSINESS

As I said at the beginning of this chapter, my story began during the dot-com consulting days in the Silicon Alley of New York City, watching those brash young-Turk CEOs push people around. The lens through which I was seeing "mean" was limited to technology start-ups but soon expanded. Images were forming in my head, but I needed a clearer picture of the bad behaviors I was seeing in the course of my work.

Then I was offered a coveted scholar-in-residence position at the Austen Riggs Center, ranked among the top-ten psychiatric centers in the United States. This was the moment to test the convictions about my mean-man research: I would need to take a six-month sabbatical, close down virtually all of my consulting practice, and move to Norman Rockwell's hometown of Stockbridge, Massachusetts.

As psychiatric centers go, Austen Riggs breaks the stereotypical mold. I trust that all fine psychiatric hospitals have brilliant people trying to help those in great psychic pain. But unlike others in its rarified group, it's small and not affiliated directly with a medical school. There are no "locked rooms." Despite their small size, they maintain an active research agenda and offer cutting-edge programs that attract clinicians from around the world. But most important, Riggs focuses on "treatment resistant" psychiatric disorders. The upshot of this distinction is that the overwhelming majority of their patients have failed to find lasting relief from their disorders. In too many cases, Riggs is the final stop on a long tour of facilities and the patients' last, best hope. Their clinicians take on tough, complex cases and use an array of strategies to help their patients find relief.

It may sound peculiar, but for a transdisciplinary researcher like me, this is about as good as it gets. The offer from Riggs was a singular opportunity to learn about psychopathology, dig into two decades of research about the inner drama that gets played out in so many entrepreneurs' heads, and determine if there is an untold story lurking in the data. At Riggs, I'd be given full access to the wickedly smart staff, clinical privileges to read case workups prior to patient case conferences, and an open invitation to attend all patient case conferences. It was an extraordinary opportunity to see firsthand some of the most complex psychiatric disorders and learn how to map their potential origins.

My first week there, I asked Dr. Gerard Fromm, then director of Riggs's research and professional development division, the Erikson Institute, why he chose me over others to be the Erikson scholar-in-residence. "We have a good measure of self-interest in what you're probing, Mark," he told me. "Because some of the patients who come to us for help are from very high-achieving families, often with driven fathers whose stress plays itself out in their relationships with their spouses and children. The more you can answer your questions, and understand what's behind their behavior, the better we may be able to understand the parental influence that perhaps helped to shape these patients and what they are now struggling with."

This was my first aha moment. As obvious as it may seem, I honestly never considered the effect of these mean entrepreneurial men as fathers. My focus until that moment was on the collateral damage to employees. I had heard plenty of carping from venture capitalists and angel investors over the years about "the totally crazy SOB we sunk our money into." But I walked out of Jerry Fromm's office wondering about the broader impact these grown men were making way beyond their employees and investors, permeating their families and leaking out to affect us all. This was the moment *Mean Men* truly began to take shape.

HEROES BEHAVING BADLY

We love our entrepreneurial men—the same way we've loved our cowboys, our patriots, and our rebels. They're our heroes. Our media and education systems hold up the entrepreneur as the salvation to a troubled economy, the fount of organizational innovation, and the symbol that often represents capitalism at its best. We write books on how to be breakout entrepreneurs, trying to distill replicable lessons from their huge wins in the marketplace, so that the rest of us can harness that intangible energy, that entrepreneurial spirit, and bring it to bear at work, at home, in our lives overall. And to be clear, that entrepreneurial spirit can indeed work to spur innovation and pioneer new ideas.

We're also clear on what is good about the entrepreneurial style of leadership. But here, we're interested in how it becomes mean. In the chapters that follow, I'll identify the *drives* that create the "entrepreneurial personality" and then show how they can lead innately to particular *behaviors*. These actions go to the core of an entrepreneur's *character*, which is formed very early in life and influenced, in part, by the genetic cards he is dealt. And while all entrepreneurs want to succeed, and most want desperately to learn the keys to success, some are trapped by a paradox. These men are psychologically predisposed to personality dysfunction that keeps them not only blind to the ways their behaviors can be harmful to others but also self-implosive.

As I analyzed decades of data to create a "profile" of the classic entrepreneur, one insight caught me thoroughly by surprise: Scrutinizing the constellation of behaviors associated with entrepreneurs (the what) and the drives that direct and sustain these actions (the why), a pile of puzzle pieces starting fitting together . . . and a vivid, disturbing pattern began to emerge. Put together, these drives and actions became the clinical definition that profiled a dark psychiatric disorder. They didn't even need to fall to the extreme in order for this to be true.

The following chapters re-create this journey and give you the opportunity to arrive at the same conclusions. The story begins with a list of the most prominent drivers for entrepreneurs as defined here—the stuff that gets them up in the morning, guides their actions by day, and sustains those actions day after day. We'll see how these drivers usually foster an entrepreneur's success . . . and just as likely how they can undermine it. Linking the "what" to the "why" brings us into the world of personality and the disorders displayed when there's too much of an otherwise good thing.

These observations of entrepreneurs are drawn from many sources: from eminent psychiatrists and psychologists to investigative journalists, and my own independent research. Ultimately, of course, I challenge you as the reader. Consider entrepreneurial types you have known, or know of, or that you hear about in the news today. Then look at the underlying factors I'll lay out for you and decide for yourself if it's just a coincidence. And when these factors are at their extreme, I'm confident you'll be able to make an educated clinical conclusion, too.

CHAPTER TWO

THE HERO'S PERSONALITY

DECADES AFTER THE REAL ERA of *Mad Men* there was Peter Arnell, the legendary advertising impresario who helped shape brands the likes of Pepsi, Samsung, DKNY, and Bank of America, and the boss from hell.[1] One former employee, who spoke to me for this book on the condition of anonymity, described Arnell as punishing a personal assistant by making him spend a meeting sitting under a desk. Other employees and clients spoke of Arnell excoriating office workers and provoking tears for mundane tasks or utterances.

"He has this remarkable capacity to be both the most intoxicating character—lovable, brilliant, seductively intellectual—and then turn on a dime and be staggeringly cruel," a former business associate recalled in a *Newsweek* feature on the "brand guru."[2] "He is unencumbered with any sense of morality. Until you experience it firsthand, it's just completely and utterly unfathomable."[3]

Yuck. And the obvious question is how exactly did Peter Arnell *get* this way? What drove this sick behavior? Arnell's early life story is classic among a certain strand of entrepreneurs: he overcame obstacles through sheer grit and brilliantly invented a new life that left his past far, far behind.

Arnell grew up in Sheepshead Bay in Brooklyn. His maternal grandfather, Nathan Hutt, was a Jewish immigrant from Russia and a fishmonger who raised Peter and his sister, along with his wife, after Arnell's father abandoned the family. As a child, Arnell also had a weight problem. "I was always the fat guy," he said. "And fat guys always did well in school. I did well. That's how I got attention."[4]

Arnell was influenced by Hutt's strong work ethic—sometimes rising before dawn to work with him at Manhattan's Fulton Fish Market. Arnell graduated from Brooklyn Technical High School, studying architecture, and later had the good fortune to hook up with postmodernist architect Michael Graves. He met Graves at a lecture and talked his way into an internship at Graves's offices.[5]

Peter Arnell was on his way.

He got into advertising after he met a Princeton architecture student, Ted Bickford, and they started a print design shop together in SoHo. Their big break came when the fashion designer Donna Karan asked them to design an ad for her. Later, they designed the iconic DKNY logo, with the Manhattan skyline in the distance. By the mid-1980s, the Arnell-Bickford agency was on a roll, with clients that included Bank of America, Chanel, Condé Nast, and Tommy Hilfiger. Arnell, still in his late twenties, was driven to succeed—growing the firm to book millions of revenue. And he liked the finer things in life, too, eventually acquiring an eight-thousand-square-foot penthouse in Tribeca and an estate in tony Katonah, New York.

Yet even as Arnell won more accolades for his work, stories began to circulate about his volatile temper and his misogyny. The harsh reality of working for Arnell would eventually be exposed in detail by a sexual harassment suit brought against him in the 1990s. The suit was novel at the time because it didn't accuse Arnell of making unwanted sexual advances to the plaintiffs, but rather of verbally abusing them during "fits of rage" simply because they were women. "Mr. Arnell constantly degraded and abused me and other female members of my staff in front of other male employees" is how one plaintiff put it. "On numerous occasions, I heard Mr. Arnell say, 'Those women out there are [expletive deleted] useless,'" another former employee detailed in the deposition. And also, "While yelling at me from a distance of approximately one inch from my face, Mr. Arnell asked me how I could be so [expletive deleted] stupid to ask a caller to leave his beeper number."[6]

In responding to the plaintiff's allegations, Arnell's lawyer pointed out his behavior was "not illegal" and claimed his "right to free speech."

The essence of Arnell's defense: "As case law demonstrates, words like 'stupid,' 'useless,' 'worthless,' and 'incompetent' constitute nonactionable, protected opinions."[7]

In 2007, when Arnell made *Gawker*'s "Worst Boss of the Year," one employee/reader gave a complicated review of the ad man, finding the ability to forgive him his considerable faults: "It's all true. Arnell is a difficult boss as well as a sadist with a lower case, sans serif 's.' He's also a crude bully, a terrible coward and famously insincere. But, in his favor, when he's not pretending to kiss the ass of the insipid rich, famous and powerful, he shows a refreshing contempt for authority and takes an anarchistic delight in creative destruction. His saving grace is that the man is ultimately an aesthete. Of his many fetishes, his love of beauty has compelled him to create some of the most beautiful advertising work in the last twenty years."[8] (These same rationalizations would later be applied to Steve Jobs.)

Arnell's career would eventually hit major turbulence after controversial design work on the Tropicana and Pepsi brands, and later, through a fallout with Omnicom, the company that bought his advertising firm in 2001.[9]

Arnell's behavior begs two questions: Why would someone so successful be so mean? And what drives a guy like this? The answer can be found in the List of Ten, a group of common characteristics that decades of research strongly suggests entrepreneurial leaders share. We can all think of successful entrepreneurial examples, from the triumphant nerd turned billionaire to the working-class Joe who rose from nothing to command a vast empire. But while the various types of entrepreneurs and the fields they work in are varied, their behavior patterns are not. On first glance, the list might seem overwhelmingly positive in that many of these characteristics would seem to increase an individual's potential. What's wrong with ambition and drive, you might ask? The answer is nothing—in moderation. The trouble comes when an individual is all about the need to achieve and when ambition eclipses empathy. In fact, when too much of one or more of the characteristics on this list is "expressed," to use the psychologists' term, it can lead to diagnosable personality problems.

THE LIST OF TEN: CHARACTERISTICS OF AN ENTREPRENEURIAL PERSONALITY

1. NEED FOR ACHIEVEMENT

You don't climb from a broken home in the depths of Brooklyn to the pinnacle of the advertising world unless you simply *must* succeed. A deep need for achievement was among the first variables ever associated with entrepreneurs—it's the stalwart anchor of entrepreneurial traits. Arnell has it in spades, as do most of the other men discussed in this book.

The need to achieve was first researched in depth by the psychological theorist David McClelland, who spent most of his career trying to understand what motivates us as human beings.[10] McClelland's question was simple: Why do some of us strive to excel, while others try to skate by? Unconvinced these differences were simply personal idiosyncrasies, McClelland sought to lay out underlying laws of behavior that could explain and even predict individual choices and life trajectories. McClelland viewed human motivation as the result of three basic needs—the need to achieve, the need for power, and the need to affiliate with others.[11] The relative importance each of these holds for an individual determines how strong their drive to succeed will be.

The need to achieve can be boiled down to a strong desire for success and realizing it through challenging situations. It starts developing early, kids picking it up through life experiences and by reading the value signals of our culture. Troubled or stable, healthy or dysfunctional backgrounds can also shape this desire. Individuals who are forced to master problems on their own earlier on in life tend to exhibit a higher need to achieve in adulthood. That certainly jives with Arnell's situation as a boy who was abandoned by his father, and we saw how a rough upbringing shaped Aaron as well. We'll see similar backgrounds in other entrepreneurs later in this book.

McClelland's findings have largely stood the test of time. In 2004, a group of psychologists confirmed that the need for achievement is closely associated with the choice of an entrepreneurial occupation and with success in entrepreneurship.[12]

It's not hard to imagine how this trait can take a wrong turn. The desire can be so powerful that high achievers see others as mere tools rather than people. Individuals might feel they are above the rules, given the grand importance of what they are doing. The most published organizational psychologist in the history of the field, Edwin Locke, sees the need for achievement as nothing less than the moral authority to do what you must to satisfy your personal needs.[13] In short, the individual has a moral obligation, or passion, to achieve his dreams. Locke (standing on Ayn Rand's shoulders) implies that one's own happiness is the highest moral purpose. This *obliges* entrepreneurs to put their work before other priorities because acting in their own interest is conflated with what is right. Whether the entrepreneur is in business or politics or another sector, they come to see their life's work and mission as so important that all else must be secondary.

2. DRIVE

Needing to achieve—and achieve *big*—is one thing, but doing so is quite another. That's why drive is such an all-important factor for entrepreneurs. At its root, drive is composed of three elements: proactivity, ambition, and energy. Entrepreneurs are not ivory-tower intellectuals, content to sit and dream. They're action-oriented, with a compelling need to make things happen and to make their vision real. Proactive rather than passive, they become impatient for results. Entrepreneurial ambition focuses on the operational challenges and on outlining the specific steps needed to move toward a high-level goal.

Energy is the third essential ingredient of drive. Any person trying to propel themselves to the height of their field needs to have a high level of raw endurance. They need to be able to work the long hours, tolerate physical discomfort, and stay focused with no sleep, little food, and zero downtime. Bringing organizations from idea to working reality—often referred to as "standing up" a firm—takes enormous amounts of effort. Drive, including high energy and stamina, is critical to managing these demands. Those with drive go further in life and work. But a determination to make things happen, and *now*, can lead these types to rush forward with such intensity that they dismiss the feelings of others, intrude on their turf, ignore the potential contributions of others, or just shove them out of the picture altogether.

In fact, drive, particularly for entrepreneurial personalities, is embodied by a strong desire for mastery and can mask underlying insecurity. Karen Horney, the prominent twentieth-century psychologist who developed an essential theory of neurosis, first showed how the incessant drive to be the best is closely related to doubt.[14] Raging drive, in some cases, owes something to the fear of amounting to nothing. Simply put, some ambitious people are neurotically obsessed with impressing others. In many of these cases, while they appear confident, they lack independence and self-esteem. Their drive to succeed is simply about trying to look good in other people's eyes.

3. AUTONOMY

A familiar reason people strike out on their own is that they can't stand working for others or depending on a team for results. If you create your own company or make it as a star athlete, you may feel accountable only to yourself. It's common to hear stories of highly successful people who are incapable of sharing responsibility and want to make everything happen themselves.

Autonomy, in other words, is a key entrepreneurial trait. Those craving autonomy not only are drawn to careers where they don't have to follow the normal rules, but they also tend to prefer working on their own without direct oversight from others.[15]

Nobody succeeds entirely on their own, of course, but there are various spheres where the individual, not the group, may *seem* to be the central player: politics; medicine; sports; the creative arts like music, acting, or directing; and business entrepreneurship. In fact, while the history of technology start-ups *looks* like a parade of partnerships—Steve Jobs and Steve Wozniak (Apple), Bill Gates and Paul Allen (Microsoft), Larry Ellison and Robert N. Miner (Oracle), Mark Zuckerberg and Dustin Moskovitz (Facebook)—none of those "partners" stayed together.

It's a phenomenon not only with business entrepreneurs, of course. We can see prescient examples in politics. Shortly after the election of New York City mayor Bill de Blasio, the two most powerful Democratic politicians in New York State—de Blasio and Governor Andrew Cuomo—diverged to stake out extreme positions. Instead of working together, the two started a public "war of independence," and their tension and one-upmanship hurt the same voters who had put them there. While neither man may make the cut as "mean," they are both clearly entrepreneurial actors where party affiliation is outweighed by their strong needs for autonomy.

And there's the rub with entrepreneurs: they deeply desire autonomy and work in fields that reward individual initiative, yet they ultimately need others to bring their success to scale. Any enterprise that is likely to generate major wealth, political power, or fame is just as likely to entail constant interaction with others. Entrepreneurs need to hire, organize, and inspire a collection of people with diverse points of view. Particularly key is recruiting others with complementary skills and then trusting them to do their jobs. Successful entrepreneurs are able to call up collaborative skills and behaviors to a point, and many can create their own organizations and sustain them—sometimes for years. But being a brilliant creator is not enough. The entrepreneur also needs to be a savvy politician, a charismatic speaker, an inspiring coach, a bit of a technical expert, and an efficient administrator. Building a company, winning the Super Bowl, and passing new laws all require nurturing a set of *inter*dependent relationships and interaction. *Positive* interaction. But the prevailing need for autonomy can get in the way. The emphasis on rugged individualism is so prevalent in Western culture in general, and in the United States in particular, that working with others is often diminished as an important entrepreneurial characteristic.

4. NEED FOR CONTROL

In addition to a high need for achievement, the best organizational builders also exhibit a strong need for power. That power takes different forms: personal power to direct others and socialized power to organize a team toward a larger goal. Research holds that those individuals who possess a high need for both achievement and power, and who exhibit a high degree of self-control, are the most successful entrepreneurs in society, so long as their need for power is directed toward positive social outcomes.

But many entrepreneurs are preoccupied with the need for power over others. This affects their ability to take direction or to give it properly, which in turn alters their aptitude for getting along with others. Some have what I call "authority ambivalence." They are filled with fantasies of grandiosity, power, influence, and authority, but they simultaneously feel helpless. As their fantasies become real, they develop a painful fear that their continued desires for "more" and "better" will spiral and put them ultimately at the mercy of others—the very people they are often intent on controlling.

Control issues are deeply embedded. Strong managers can identify in positive and constructive ways with authority figures, even looking to them as role models. Many entrepreneurs are less adaptable. Those with high needs for control are suspicious about authority and often lack finesse when confronted by themes of dominance and submission. For them, structure can be stifling. They can work with others in structured situations only if they both design and run the game. It's no wonder that successful entrepreneurs sometimes get forced out by investors, that star athletes often have conflicts with coaches and teammates, or that little gets done when the politicians in the US Congress are unable to collaborate. If there's any doubt the world of politics can mimic the characteristics and compulsions of corporate entrepreneurs, we need look no further than Michael Grimm.

Dogged by a potentially devastating tax fraud and campaign finance investigation near the end of his first term, the New York City congressman was accustomed to high levels of control when he was an entrepreneurial businessman. His 2014 reelection campaign tested him, with the charges causing an increasing degradation of his credibility, and the local press was all over him. On January 28, 2014, Grimm lost it with a local TV reporter who asked him about the charges. On camera, Grimm threatened to both break the reporter in half and throw him off the balcony on which they were standing. Though Grimm won the election, he later pled guilty to federal tax evasion. Going into his second term as a convicted felon, he refused to resign, but the party finally persuaded him to quit in early January 2015.

The dark side of an overwhelming need for control is obvious. Pejorative terms such as "control freak" and "micromanager" have long been part of our lexicon, and nobody likes to work for, or with, these kinds of people, though we'll often dismiss obsessive control in the face of perceived "genius" or talent. Trust, too, is a factor here, since for any act of delegation in a relationship, the decision to keep a tight grasp on control is really about *trust*—or, more accurately, *distrust* of others. Delegation is always, at its core, an act of trust.

5. INTERNAL LOCUS OF CONTROL

Believing deeply in their destiny and future is crucial for entrepreneurs, as is believing in their own ability to influence the world around them. This internal sense of self-determination makes success seem more likely and increases motivation. A strong need for control, combined with an internal locus of control, can shape an entrepreneur's domineering style. They may enjoy the power to direct and even intimidate, to evoke obedience if not respect. Tough and unsentimental, they may see themselves as effective leaders because they coerce performance from subordinates. They get stuff done.

But the threat of external control can preoccupy many entrepreneurs. The fear of someone dominating them or infringing on their will often creates a sense of impotence. Unfortunately, the conflict does not remain internalized. Those deeply concerned about being in control don't admire or tolerate autonomy in others; they want people who will do their bidding.

6. IMPULSIVITY

In a fast-moving, competitive world, being quick on the draw can translate into a decisive edge. But impulsivity is also dangerous. The absence of careful planning and an inability to delegate can introduce a serious threat to any venture—whether a company, a campaign, or the building of a celebrity brand. Impulsive entrepreneurs may find it difficult, if not painful, to differentiate between day-to-day operational decision making and more strategic actions. His penchant for relying on "hunches" makes for a time horizon that is biased to the short term.

Impulsivity for the entrepreneur reflects a shortsighted fixation on immediate gratification that reaps collateral damage. High levels of impulsivity may make someone more likely to cleverly manipulate or deceive others for personal gain. At the extreme, those with impulse drives may act out toward others or may have compulsive needs for gambling, shopping, or sex.

7. SUSPICION OF OTHERS

Entrepreneurs have a disproportionate tendency over the general population to distrust those in the world around them, and this can easily
extend to those who work for them. They fear becoming victims, and in
reaction, they develop their own means for monitoring their environment, keeping watch for signs that confirm their suspicions. Suspicion of
others is closely related not only to impulsivity, but also to the desire for
autonomy and the need for control we've already discussed.

Distrust, and the simultaneous monitoring for threat, can serve the
powerful entrepreneur as it may relate to some business needs—competitor moves, supplier manipulation, radical changes in customer preferences, for example. Intel's tough former CEO and idol of Steve Jobs,
Andy Grove, made this argument in his book *Only the Paranoid Survive*,
and his huge success suggests that maybe there was something to the
idea.[16] But the picture looks darker to the extent that distrust of others
isn't motivated at its core by business needs but by the need for self-
protection and a fear of being victimized by someone else. In the face of
ongoing suspicion, the people around the entrepreneur suffer deterio-
rating morale as his need for control trumps the imperative of organizational effectiveness and wounds the enterprise. In order to alleviate the
entrepreneur's ever-present suspicion, those around him become sycophants, the last people someone in power needs giving them advice.

Biographers and journalists have long noted Rupert Murdoch's nearly
obsessive control needs and suspicious nature. James Murdoch may have
been easy for his father to control, but if the senior Murdoch had put in
place a more independent, seasoned executive, he or she may well have
steered News Corp clear of the massive wiretapping scandal of 2011. But
in 2014, Murdoch the father transferred "future leadership of two publicly held firms worth a combined $80 billion to his two sons, almost as
casually as if they were the keys to the family station wagon."[17] The message was self-evident: the family legacy was to remain intact, regardless
of what might have been best for public shareholders.

A ranking executive at the firm subsequently told the *New York
Times*, "How did you think it was going to turn out?"[18]

Finally, in June 2015, eighty-four-year-old Rupert announced his
diminishing role by solidifying his sons' authority, with both sons
expected to take over the most important executive roles in the company.

These moves may not have been the best for the long-term growth of a $78 billion worldwide monolith but, for better or worse, he retains the control he's had for the past sixty years.

8. PREDISPOSITION TO TAKE RISKS

Richard Cantillon, the eighteenth-century Irish French economist, laid claim to the term "entrepreneur" by defining it as a "bearer of risk."[19] And risk-taking was one of the first characteristics ever investigated in relation to entrepreneurs, as economists theorized that it was the primary differentiator between entrepreneurs and non-business-owning managers.[20] If everyone had the same comfort with risk, many more people might be their own boss. There is now a large and nuanced literature about risk-taking and entrepreneurship, but one thing is clear: those who strike out on their own, and aim high, tend to have a reasonably strong appetite for risk. What's tricky, though, is having the right level of appetite. Some successful entrepreneurs get as far as they do because of their willingness to put everything on the line (and refusal to take credit for failure). Yet this same risk-seeking can lead to their undoing where a more measured taking of account would prevent high-stakes losses.

9. SELF-CONFIDENCE

To get ahead, entrepreneurs must believe they can deal with the world, meet life's challenges, overcome obstacles, and achieve the goals they set for themselves. All this boils down to good old-fashioned self-confidence, typically developed from early childhood experiences in which one undertakes independent projects, masters difficulties, and succeeds. Yet the line between self-confidence and arrogance is famously thin.

As far back as 1921, the economist Frank Knight argued that the function of entrepreneurs was to "specialize in risk-taking."[21] But studies of entrepreneurs find that, in general, they're as risk-averse as everyone else. However, when it comes to starting a business, they are daring. Does this contradict the rule that came before about their predisposition to take risks? It is very much consistent, because self-confidence influences entrepreneurs' behavior so powerfully. A study in the *Journal of Business Venturing* found entrepreneurs to be overconfident about their ability to prevent bad outcomes and also overconfident about the prospects of their business. The examination of approximately three thousand entrepreneurs found that 81 percent thought their businesses had at least a 75 percent chance of success, and one-third thought there was *no chance* they would fail, data that bear no relation to reality.[22]

Marked overconfidence is a genuine psychological hazard. And whether it's due to ignorance or to some psychological disorder that denies real risks, overconfidence indicates that an entrepreneur may not be in touch with reality. Overconfidence also tips easily into arrogance, which usually combines excess self-confidence with a gross underestimation of risk, including of one's competitors.

In today's start-up culture, this tendency for false, self-focused optimism is intensified by other factors. Developing new products and finding seed funding often gives early-stage positive feedback to entrepreneurs—possibly false feedback that underestimates the risk. Amplifying this is the "fail fast, fail often" mind-set that gives many entrepreneurs gold stars for trying to develop the Next Big Thing. But two comprehensive studies show that practice does not make perfect. One study found that around 80 percent of entrepreneurs with unsuccessful businesses would go on to fail again. The other, a study of German entrepreneurial ventures, concluded past failures made entrepreneurs *more* likely to fail than those trying their hand for the first time.[23]

Not surprisingly, we also hold these con(fidence) artists in some esteem; there are parts of them, alluring parts, that we admire and even wish to emulate. They are independent and usually self-made. The same men who are willing to risk everything and, in truth, *do* have outsized talents can prove to be horrendous bosses and partners. Now a philanthropic hero, Bill Gates in his earlier CEO years rarely let his employees forget that he was smarter than they were, while Steve Jobs was inclined to let an underling know what a "stupid shithead" the employee was for not living up to Jobs's expectations. Then there is the oft-told joke about Oracle's Larry Ellison: "*Question:* What's the difference between God and Larry Ellison? *Answer:* God doesn't think he's Larry Ellison."

10. NEED FOR APPROVAL

Given the nine characteristics noted already, the need for approval may seem counterintuitive. *These guys,* you may think, *probably don't care what others think of them.* But entrepreneurs often reveal a great need for admiration and applause and an overriding concern about being heard and recognized. Entrepreneurs don't seek direct approval so much as they search for more oblique approval. Alex Preda, a behavioral finance scholar at King's College, writes that "talent for persuasion is key: after all, the public must be convinced to part with their money on the basis of the simple promise that an idea will yield profit in the future."[24] Influencing others to give them something, whether it's investment capital, accolades, or votes, is the entrepreneur's way of reaffirming his self-esteem. Raising money to start a business or fund a nonprofit requires selling an imagined future—you have to influence others to buy into your dream. Running a successful campaign requires getting voters to buy the vision, which must embody the personification of the candidate.

"Some entrepreneurs I have known hear an inner voice that tells them they will never amount to anything," notes leadership scholar and psychoanalyst Manfred Kets de Vries. "But regardless of who put this idea into their minds, these people are not retiring types who take such rebuke passively; they are the defiant ones who deal with it creatively through action. . . . They will ride to the top in spite of all the dangers; they will get the applause; they will find a way to master their fears."[25] An entrepreneur's need for applause fights their inner feeling that they might be insignificant, nothing.

TEN + T: THE AMPLIFYING EFFECT OF TESTOSTERONE

In some ways, entrepreneurial leaders are almost superhuman—more driven, more confident, more independent—than most of us mere ordinary mortals. It's no wonder that these people play such a profound role in shaping society and get so much media attention. They are the real-life action figures of our time. It's also no wonder that so many of them are male, given how testosterone amplifies many of the traits we've been discussing.

As a steroid hormone, it affects much of the neurology and physiology of both genders (from aggressiveness to bone mass). However, genders do not produce testosterone in equal amounts and hence are not influenced equally by the hormone. Levels are typically seven to eight times greater in adult males than in females, and men produce far more of it—on average twenty times the daily amount—than women.

Research has found a close relationship among testosterone, certain personality traits, and occupation. Known simply as "T" among endocrinologists, testosterone is associated not only with physical characteristics such as strength and size, but also with psychological tendencies such as aggressiveness, risk-taking, and persistence. Testosterone amplifies most of the characteristics on the List of Ten. One exception is its effect to mitigate or help regulate the need for approval and to keep it in check. What's more, evidence links T with antisocial behaviors like violence and aggression, as well as with less socially toxic behaviors such as assertiveness and fearlessness. Actions related to dominance- and status-seeking have been associated with testosterone in both men and women. A drive to dominate seems to be associated with the need for achievement and esteem from others—needs that we already correlate strongly with entrepreneurship. High T is closely associated with the need for independence, greater self-centeredness, and being more action-oriented, restless, and nondeferential.

Researchers at the University of Western Ontario have gone the furthest in declaring an empirical association between key behaviors related to entrepreneurship and those affected by T. Simply put: men with higher levels of testosterone are more likely to behave entrepreneurially, and they have a higher propensity to have had an entrepreneurial experience.[26]

THE ROUGH ROAD TO THE LIST OF TEN

Before condensing my findings into a neat numbered list, I was still at Austen Riggs with two research goals in mind. First, I needed to dig deep into the literature on the entrepreneurial personality. Piece of cake. The second goal was to learn as much as possible about psychopathology from the ever-helpful Riggs clinicians. I was both annoyed and surprised when I got bogged down on that first goal. It turned out that analyzing the available research on entrepreneurial personalities was no easy task.

The annoyance: By that time, most psychologists studying the entrepreneurial personality had been hammered by a strongly leveled critique of their work by one William Gartner, a professor of entrepreneurship at

Clemson University. Gartner, among others, was reacting to the approach researchers had taken to create the most accurate personality profile. In essence, scholars had found a startling number of traits and characteristics attributed to entrepreneurs. When you put them all together, they portrayed a person full of contradictions. In effect, there was enough shoddy and uncoordinated research that the end result described a generic "Everyman," not the archetypal entrepreneur.

One cause of the problem was that researchers never agreed on the fundamental definition of "entrepreneur." When you're measuring something, everyone needs to be on board with precisely the same understanding of what the "it" is that's being measured. Makes sense, right? Added to this uncertainty was biting criticism of the research designs and analysis of the data emerging from these ambitious studies. Years later, a new crop of highly skilled researchers entered the field, but they too persisted in focusing their research such that they missed the whole. "Something gets lost," Gartner noted, "when the focus of research on entrepreneurship sticks too closely to the 'esoteric knowledge' of a narrow disciplinary perspective. A finding can be right and interesting to a scholar within a specific theoretical perspective, but, wrong or obvious" to the public.[27]

Gartner's words struck a deep chord with me. I was coming at this with my experiences of mean entrepreneurs and looking for some rationale to contextualize my understanding. But then an article by Mark Singer in the *New Yorker* put me back on the path. Singer chronicles the method used by Michael Zinman to build a fine collection of books . . . okay, not mean men, but no matter. The advice holds. "You don't start off with a concrete theory about what you're trying to do," says book dealer William Reese. "You build a big pile. Once you get a big enough pile together—the critical mess—you're able to draw conclusions about it. You see patterns. . . ."[28]

And so I broadened the scope of my work, staying open to ways to understand the mean men. I went for the "critical mess." This was when I expanded my view of "entrepreneurs" beyond only business founders. There were other professions where the entrepreneurial *personality* flourishes.

My experience at Austen Riggs gave me two critical insights, first of which was that few disordered personalities are disordered in only one way. The second aha was the List of Ten and the startling place to which it led. Psychopathology was *the* topic of my conversations daily with psychiatrists and psychologists. As we will see in the next chapter, any overblown personality characteristic can start creating problems when combined with certain others. The epiphany was that this unique and specific collection of personality characteristics, the List of Ten, had the potential for defining one particular personality disorder that could explain it all. Before we go further, let me be clear that this book is not meant to "diagnose" any of the public figures or disguised fact-based cases. Not only is this practice frowned upon by both the American Psychiatric Association and the American Psychological Association, but in a time when facts have come to have less meaning than ever before, I have no desire to contribute through armchair diagnoses.[29] While *Mean Men* stops short of pinning a psychiatric disorder on any one person, to you, the reader, I say this: study the self-made men you know and certain entrepreneurial figures in the public eye and compare their behaviors, motivations, and actions to the List of Ten. Because whether someone is tagged with a clinical diagnosis is really not the point. The List of Ten is important because we must recognize the abnormal extremes of these otherwise common personality traits in order to combat the behaviors they engender, and tear down these false heroes before they establish a new normal from which there is no return.

EVERY MEAN MAN NEEDS SOMEONE TO ABUSE . . . AND SOME OF US NEED *HIM*

Identifying mean men and understanding the roots of their behavior is critical for all of us, whether we are part of the corporate world, work in the nonprofit sphere, or simply exist in modern society—its own type of organizational environment. That's because too many of us fall victim to their mind games and abuse. While he was alive, critics cavalierly compared Jobs to a sociopath in trying to explain his lack of empathy or compassion. Apple workers were his human objects, mere tools to get things done. But for every critic, there is often a disciple. To explain why employees and coworkers put up with him, some of these critics invoked Stockholm syndrome, saying his employees were captives who had fallen in love with their captor.[30] "Those who know anything much about his management style know he work[ed] by winnowing out the chaff—defined as those both not smart enough and not psychologically strong enough to bear repeated demands to produce something impossible (such as a music player where you can access any piece of music within three clicks) and then be told that their solution is 'shit.' And then hear it suggested back to them a few days later," the British technology analyst and historical commentator Charles Arthur remarked in the *Register*. "That's not how most people like to work, or be treated. In truth, Steve Jobs wasn't an icon to any managers, apart from sociopathic ones."[31]

Were all the people who stuck with Jobs at Apple really sociopaths? Of course not. But these employees, like others who endure the abuse of mean men, probably had characteristics that amplified their vulnerability to manipulation and control. (Truthfully, the stock options probably didn't hurt either.)

What kinds of people, exactly? For starters, individuals with psychological scarring or high levels of stress are particularly liable to fall under the spell of mean men. They're also most likely to stick with these individuals over time. Meanwhile, people who feel alienated and marginalized can be powerfully drawn to the grand sense of purpose conveyed by "leaders" such as these. Many felt the 2016 election gave proof to this idea, with a highly energized, economically disenfranchised group of voters powerfully drawn to "make America great again" as defined by Donald Trump. But the psychological underpinnings of this common dynamic explain why many of us continue to embrace mean.

DANCING A PSYCHOLOGICAL TANGO

Psychoanalyst Hans Kohut asserted that some individuals have what are known as *mirror-hungry personalities*, in that their narcissism hungers for reactions from others. Our mean man needs that feedback to tell him he is not only accepted, but admired, and he sees validation in the "mirror" reflection of other peoples' responses to him.[32]

But no matter how positive the response, his own sense of worthlessness means he cannot be satisfied, so he continues to seek new audiences who will give him the attention and recognition he craves.

To become attractive to more and more people, our mean man works to convey a sense of grandeur, omnipotence, and strength, and in doing so becomes attractive to those *seeking* this idealized source of strength. The mean man carries a sense of conviction and certainty that is manna to those who are plagued by doubt.

It is in the follower's reaction that we recognize a complementary theory that explores how these men attract what are called *ideal-hungry followers*. It may explain why so many of us are not only willing but eager to follow and idealize the mean man.

He comes to the psychological rescue of his followers, taking the form of whoever the followers need him to be. In serving as their hero, he protects them from confronting themselves and their fundamental inadequacies and alienation. Marc Galanter of New York University conducted systematic studies of "charismatic religious groups" (aka cults). He found that psychologically wounded individuals are particularly attracted to charismatic leader–follower relationships. The lonelier and more isolated the individuals were before joining, the more committed they would be to the movement and the recruitment process. Instead of relying on their individual judgment, they tended to follow without question the dictates of the leader.[33]

If this makes the followers sound like they are under a spell, that's not quite accurate. Nor would the organizations, sports leagues, or political groups these men rule be deemed "cults" in any way. But understanding the average person's willingness to tolerate and endure such treatment is essential if we are to understand the potential long-term impact these men may have.

CONFLICT-AVERSE—TO A FAULT

Mean men draw most of their power of attraction and fascination from the emotional dependence of their followers. Driven by their need for the mean man to fit their ideal, the followers establish what psychologists call a *fusional relationship*, in which at least one individual avoids conflict at virtually any cost because they see the relationship as utterly conditional. We know that won't be the mean man.

Most of us instead go through a process of *differentiation*. You and the other person in the pair each take responsibility for knowing what you want and how to get it. You know how to negotiate with each other about what you are both able and willing to provide. But when the relationship is fused, there is a dependency that precludes raising disagreements or expressing needs. You're walking on eggshells.

Recall that one overriding need of our mean man is to be in control. If he can develop and maintain *un*differentiated relationships with others, the odds of his staying in control improve. If he is successful in this strategy, his entourage will be stocked with these desirables, sustained by their inability to break the connection once their dependency has been established.

IT'S A FAMILY THING

Psychoanalyst and Columbia University medical school professor Ethel Person looked to the Freudian theory known as *seduction of the aggressor* to explain our attraction to mean men.[34] According to Person, masochism could be the result for the small percentage of the population with unresolved childhood development issues in adulthood. And the mean man becomes the trigger for their masochism.

Putting Freud aside, what might this look like? Some people with parental scarring will attach themselves to people they actually fear, then try to overcome this fear by "taking" their abuse. An employee may "need" the experience of an abusive boss to show that they will not be fazed by the harsh treatment. While it may seem that the mean man is the "seducer," he is in fact sensitive to the particular needs of these followers. He doles out abuse, and the trigger gets pulled for the abused to want to satisfy him.

But even those of us with a healthy developmental scorecard—loving parents, a happy childhood, healthy boundaries, and comfort in our own skin—will still often put up with mean. As mean becomes normalized in organizations and in society, our tolerance increases. (Google "normalization Trump" and see how many articles pop up.) "That didn't take very long," writes Tom Toles in the *Washington Post*. "The specter of Donald Trump moving into the central position of American power seemed troublesome for a minute there, but it is amazing how adaptable people are!"[35] We stop calling these mean men or their behaviors to account. And this is what must change.

CHAPTER THREE

THE PSYCHOLOGY OF MEAN

DOV CHARNEY, THE CONTROVERSIAL FOUNDER of American Apparel, was born and raised in Montreal, Canada. His mother, Sylvia, is a painter and sculptor, and his father, Morris, is an architect. Like Peter Arnell, Dov Charney had to overcome an early obstacle in life—in Charney's case, a learning disorder. He has said that he was "functionally illiterate" until he was thirteen and that it wasn't until he got to junior high that a teacher worked with him for two hours a day, teaching him how to read and write.[1]

He graduated high school after eleventh grade but attended Choate Rosemary Hall boarding school in Connecticut for an additional year. It was there that his entrepreneurial drive kicked in. He started importing Hanes and Fruit of the Loom T-shirts to Montreal, purchasing them in bulk quantities in the United States and selling them for a profit. By his own account, he later rented a moving truck to move thousands of shirts at a time across the border, all while still being too young to buy a beer. Now there's an entrepreneur.

In 1987, Charney enrolled at Tufts University. During his freshman year, his T-shirt company trade name, "American Apparel," came to be— the brainchild of his partner, Bob Smith.[2] Yet Charney's partnership with Smith wouldn't last. Smith found him too difficult to deal with, the first of many similar complaints about Charney in coming years; his need propelled his success while his other entrepreneurial traits, like a desire for control, drove people away.[3]

Charney dropped out of Tufts as his business picked up, and he moved to South Carolina to begin manufacturing T-shirts. By the mid-1990s, while in his twenties, Charney had built American Apparel into a budding company that catered to young urban people. He had grandiose dreams from the start, once proclaiming that he wanted to be remembered as one of the great CEOs of our time and of his generation. Charney would also conflate American Apparel with the very soul of the nation, saying, "We'll be a heritage brand. It's like liberty, property, pursuit of happiness for every man worldwide. That's my America."[4]

But from its earliest years, Charney's business was a rocky ride, with big ups and downs. He filed for bankruptcy in 1996. And even as Charney's company bounced back and soared, success that led to millions of dollars in earnings and accolades, bigger problems followed for Charney. Remember, chronic overachievers are strong-minded and stubborn, and they don't like to conform. They prefer to work solo rather than with a team. They take outsized risks. While strong overachievers can be very creative and think outside the box, their knee-jerk inclination may be to *stay* outside the box, in ways that can lead to trouble.

And that's not all. As we see in later chapters, an entrepreneur's ambition and drive may come from a dark place of ego and hubris as they chase after an ephemeral pursuit of glory. They don't want to be just a strong CEO; they want to be the *best* CEO of their generation.

These grand dreams—along with a deep need for approval—are often linked with persistent feelings of powerlessness. Though powerlessness is a painful emotion for anyone, for entrepreneurs it tends to trigger a proclivity toward impulsiveness and a quest for control. They are prone to action—often rash action—and fits of rage when they can't have control of events, a condition clinically known as *intermittent explosive disorder*. Though the labeling is self-evident, those with high impulsivity–triggered IED have recurrent aggressive episodes way out of proportion to any given stressor that triggered them. And it's not just through screaming fits that they channel their rage (like Aaron from chapter 1); high levels of impulsivity can play itself out through pathological gambling, sexual compulsion, and stealing, to name only a few.

Dov Charney is a perfect illustration of all this. Thanks to the multiple lawsuits that piled up against him over the years, I uncovered details of how he has dealt with stress and worked with others. It isn't a pretty picture. Charney was prone to legendary and dangerous fits of rage. One lawsuit plaintiff, former store manager Michael Bumblis, claims that Charney grabbed his throat and began choking him during a store visit. Why? Because Bumblis was improperly storing inventory on the store's second floor.

Charney also inspected one of the dressing areas in Bumblis's store and, finding dirt and dust on the floor, reportedly grabbed the dirt and "managed to push his dirt-filled hand into [Bumblis's] face with such force as to cause [his] head and neck to snap backwards."[5] Bumblis was fired from American Apparel.

Charney's fits were an ill-kept secret. "I've witnessed a lot of people get verbally accosted by the CEO," said one former employee.[6] Another offered this unsolicited advice to American Apparel: "CEO should probably stop berating employees during the conference calls."[7]

Charney's impulsivity also manifested itself in compulsive sexual behavior, which would later spur some of the infamous court action against him. Female former employees described "sexually offensive conduct" by Charney and a sexually hostile work environment. One suit said that photos from vintage adult magazines were "posted in plain view in the American Apparel stores."[8] Another said that Charney regularly used disparaging terms such as "cunt," "slut," and "whore" in front of both male and female employees.

This from a well-known CEO who, in 2004, was named Entrepreneur of the Year by the staid accounting firm of Ernst & Young.[9]

Mary Nelson is one of the many former employees who have filed suit against Dov Charney and American Apparel. In Nelson's case, she named Martin Bailey, chief manufacturing officer at American Apparel, as a defendant as well. The lawsuit was filed in 2005 with Nelson alleging that while she worked for American Apparel as a sales manager, "throughout her employment with American Apparel, Charney subjected Ms. Nelson to a hostile work environment . . . [when] Charney regularly made unwelcome, inappropriate comments and/or suggestive nonverbal signals to Ms. Nelson."[10]

More specifically, the lawsuit's allegations claim that Charney told female workers to "grow a dick." He would drop his pants in front of Ms. Nelson to reveal his underwear. He would touch his penis in her presence and note that "there are a lot of girls out there that need this cock." He also asked her to masturbate with him. The court filing continues with accusations of Charney's lewd comments that get only more repulsive.[11]

Nelson won a $1.3 million settlement from American Apparel. In 2014, Charney was fired by the board—twice.[12] In 2017, both Amazon and Forever 21 were in the bidding for Charney's former company as it went to auction. American Apparel filed for bankruptcy for the second time in November 2016, $177 million in debt.[13]

HOW THEY GET THIS WAY: SOME BASIC VOCABULARY

You cannot help but look at a guy like Charney and wonder how someone who acted this outrageously got so far. Just as you wonder the same thing about Peter Arnell. Both men have striking contradictions: driven, smart, strategic—yet also easily unhinged and downright *mean*. Something doesn't add up.

Dealing with the complexity of these characters demands going beyond naming these men jerks or assholes and figuring out how to get along with them. Determining where this bad behavior comes from, not just the *what* but the *why*, requires some foundational knowledge of personality psychology. (Don't worry, I'll make it easy.)

Think about someone you hold in high regard or that you are close to. How would you describe that person? Most people would list positive adjectives or descriptive words like "friendly," "generous," or "warm." These are all examples of *traits*, or fairly stable characteristics that together make up our individual personality. In psychology, we use the "trait approach" to help us predict and understand long-standing patterns of behavior that generally hold true regardless of time and place. Where certain personality traits consistently occur together, they may constitute a personality disorder.

We know, for example, that someone with the trait of deceitfulness will probably have other related traits beyond deceit. If these pile up in the wrong way, they could indicate a disorder. If the person is lacking in empathy and remorse, and is manipulative, aggressive, and irresponsible in addition to being deceitful, then we will probably see trait-induced behaviors indicating a recognized personality disorder.

The current bible for diagnosing personality disorders—*DSM-5*—identifies four trait-related features required to establish a disorder:[14]

1. Distorted thinking patterns
2. Problematic emotional responses
3. Over- or underregulated impulse control
4. Interpersonal difficulties

We can say that Peter Arnell and Dov Charney share some odd and unflattering characteristics that provoke lawsuits from employees (who tend to win or settle for damages to their advantage), but their "meanness" is by no means identical, given the greater constellation of so many other factors that define personality traits.

Patterns of personality are made up of not only our specific traits, but also the *dimensions* or strengths of each trait. Dimensions have low and high poles, indicating how strongly they are expressed. You may be more generous than average, or less trusting than most. Like the size of our noses, our height, or our physical strengths, there are no absolute cutoff points. An *abnormal trait* is simply a statistical deviation from the average and does not necessarily indicate disease or dysfunction. For example, virtually all basketball players are abnormally tall (compared with the population). Deviant personality traits are also relative to what is considered "normal."

In the 1930s, anthropologist Ruth Benedict described cultures in Melanesia, where paranoia, theft, and lying were considered not just statistical norms, but laudable traits. While these traits are undesirable in our frame of reference, Melanesians have a different frame of reference. Benedict believed that each culture chooses from "the great arc of human potentialities" only a few characteristics that become leading personality traits of persons living in that society. (Benedict may have been prescient in foretelling the shift in "laudable" traits we may now be experiencing in modern American culture).[15]

For example, firefighters and police officers tend to score very high (they are "deviant" or abnormal in this sense) on dimensions that measure exploratory behaviors in unique situations, traits they need to do their jobs. In the same way, missionaries and relief workers are abnormally high on dimensions of sentimentality and cooperativeness. In both cases, these specific personality traits and the dimensions, or strength, of each trait happen to be aligned with what the situation requires. And in neither case would we consider their deviance to be bad; rather, we would consider their service work beneficial and positive.

We must also consider that personality traits represent our behavioral tendencies both in circumstances involving reward (praise, affection, money, position) and nonreward (criticism, coldness, nonrecognition). Therefore, seeing someone's reactions in these contexts gives us the key to unlocking their personal temperament. But there's more to it than that. Asking a person who grew up in a gang-infested neighborhood about their attitude toward fighting and using a weapon may not give us a reliable measure of how aggressive they are. They may have adopted some aggressive behaviors to cope with their environment and, lucky for them, it kept them alive and continued to reinforce behaviors that were outside their natural characters. We all learn adaptive behaviors that are outside the comfort zone of our personality traits.

Notwithstanding, not only are traits stubbornly stable over time, but they are essential to organizing the way we think and, ultimately, the ways we act and react to our world. The same traits get played out across different situations. While we may adapt specific behaviors to a situation (like aggression in the kid from a gang-infested neighborhood), traits are notoriously difficult to influence; instead, they are intrinsically and chronically rigid, repetitive, and predictable. Though the number of possible human traits cannot be counted, psychologists commonly use sets of anywhere from three to sixteen commonly recognized definable traits in discussing personality dimensions. There are psychological models and theories that take into account many more traits as well.

Regardless of how they are measured or the number we study, traits are the bedrock of our personality, formed early in life and interwoven with our values, beliefs, and assumptions about the world. They're quite enduring in guiding the ways we behave and how we think. Traits operate independently of the other traits, and each trait is assumed to be measurable in some way. Finally, based on their dimensions—is it a strong or a weak part of the person's personality—we are able to determine deviation, the statistical difference in measurement of how one person's set of traits may vary from another's. In terms of the entrepreneurial leader, how this applies will quickly become apparent.

THE DISORDERED PERSONALITY

When clusters of *particular* personality traits occur simultaneously, it signals that a personality *disorder* may be evident. And sometimes such disorders are simmering among those at the highest reaches of organizations.

Take Noel, a senior executive, who was forced to resign from his position in a fast-growing start-up. Persistent difficulties with top management compromised his ability to perform effectively. But it was his long-standing interpersonal problems that grated on many who crossed his path. Superficially charming, he often manipulated the affections of others to get what he wanted, and withdrew his attention when he found other people no longer useful. Friends and colleagues eventually avoided Noel.

"All is fair in business" was his rallying cry, and if people were "stupid," well, that just wasn't his fault. Asking subordinates to manipulate the sales numbers to increase his bonus was in keeping with his mantra: you are guilty only if you get caught, and the law is for stupid people.

Noel was the child of wealthy parents, attended an Ivy League school, and according to him, was a frat boy who drank heavily while underage, used illegal drugs, vandalized neighbors' homes, hired hookers, and bragged all the while that he was never caught. He married a family friend because "it was good for business." Over the years, he had a number of extramarital affairs for which he professed no regret. After he was fired, he fell into a depression—which he eventually overcame. Back on his feet, he moved into an arena where men like Noel often thrive, up to a point: entrepreneurship.

Noel would ultimately be diagnosed by his psychiatrist as having psychopathic personality disorder. With his sense of inflated grandiosity and a pervasive pattern of taking advantage of and manipulating other people, disregarding ethical considerations and moral norms, and showing little if any remorse for his actions, he seemed to fit the type.

So what's the difference between a guy like Noel or perhaps Dov Charney—men who have or may have a personality disorder—and more psychologically healthy people? Basically, it's that the traits of the latter individuals tend to be more *adaptive*. Healthy people may have a high level of ambition or drive, but they also have an ability to rein that ambition in, to adapt that trait to the circumstances when it's prudent. Not so for those with a disordered personality, since their ambition or drive may be such that it doesn't adapt to reality or convention. The internal censor or sense of restraint doesn't kick in, as it would for healthy people. And that's how they get into trouble.

Life is often easier for healthy people. Having control over a reasonable level of adaptiveness allows us to size up situations in life with greater objectivity. Simply put, those with greater adaptiveness are happier, healthier people. Oh, and they're a lot easier to work with or for, too. They don't give two of their female employees vibrators, as yet another lawsuit against Charney alleged that he did. Or say things like: "I frequently drop my pants to show people my new product."[16]

Characterizing and cataloging personality disorders has been the lifework of Theodore Millon, former Harvard and University of Miami professor and author of at least nine books on the subject. Millon, deceased in 2014, continues to rank among the most influential psychologists in the world when it comes to this niche of psychology. He managed to take complex disorders and distill them down to understandable traits, and equally important, he conceptualized the notion of personality disorder in a way that's clearer than any I've examined.

Millon showed how personality disorders are made up of maladaptive traits, and he offered two explanations for the sliding severity of a disorder. An individual would move closer to pathology as a) the intensity of certain maladaptive traits increased, or b) the number of maladaptive traits went up.[17]

You have probably heard the throwaway cliché of insanity, described as expecting a different result from doing the same thing over and over again. While grossly oversimplified, it is true that most people are good at establishing coping strategies to get what they want. If it doesn't work out by trying option A, then we strategize an option B or C and so on. Individuals with personality disorders aren't able to develop alternate strategies and tend to stick with option A, their preferred option, even if it doesn't result in the desired outcome. When option A doesn't get them what they want, their stress level rises, and they feel out of control and vulnerable.

Personality-disordered individuals are therefore "adaptively inflexible." Psychologically healthy people know *when* to take initiative and change something in their lives; beyond this, they also know *how* to adapt and what options the world offers them. "Normal" implies not only a readiness to be flexible in interactions, but also an accuracy in judging that any initiatives or reactions taken are proportional and appropriate to the circumstances around them. If, for example, the boss wants something done in a particular way, most people will follow directions without much fuss. In many ways these situations are almost scripted—we know what to do and how to behave in a seemingly limitless number of situations.[18]

But personality-disordered people are limited by far fewer alternative strategies in their repertoire. To make matters worse, they impose strict, irrational conditions for implementing these alternatives, almost as though factors (and this often means other people) in their environment will somehow knowingly conform to *their* needs. Eventually, they erupt, thrown into crisis mode by the frustration of being unable to bend reality (and others) to their will. While most of us often find life enjoyable and seize opportunities to learn new and more adaptive strategies, the disordered individual derives far less enjoyment from these circumstances. In fact, new situations that require rather quick adaptiveness can be living hell for them, and they react with seemingly inexplicable behavior.

A personality disorder also prompts *maladaptive* behaviors, ways of coping with situations that an individual thinks will reduce his anxiety but in fact result in dysfunctional and nonproductive outcomes. Another way of understanding personality disorders is to see them as exaggerations of the personality traits that, to varying degrees, are present within us all. The *magnitude* of each trait along the continuum, not simply its characteristic, coupled with a low ability to adapt, tends to spell trouble.[19]

Put another way, think of each trait as being monitored on the temperature gauge in a car. For most people, most of the time, a collection of traits will hover somewhere in the middle, or in the "normal" range. There are times when one or more traits will heat up and brush periodically against the red zone. If a defined set of traits is imagined in the higher midrange for longer periods—close to the hot red zone but not in it—and they are the traits related to the List of Ten, then it may identify our signature mix that predicts the "entrepreneurial personality." This could indicate a relatively well-adjusted entrepreneur.

But what if several of the traits within this defined set are *always* in the red zone, consistently on the hot end of the scale? In a car, this means you're overheating, and you'd be wise to pull over to take stock and check under the hood or go visit a mechanic. The same is true in people. If an entrepreneur is unable to regulate, to adapt the extent to which a set of these traits have effectively taken over his personality, then it may be the signal of a disordered personality.

Contrast the entrepreneurial "healthies" with those farther into the red hot zone. Those in the red zone have crossed the border into the realm of lying, manipulation (if not downright cheating), and perhaps even criminality (though they may never have been caught). We would suspect that they feel like emotional wrecks. But they are completely unfettered by anxiety and totally unbound by conscience.

While the mean men we discuss here may show some characteristics of a clinical disorder, I will not stretch the definition to the point we can apply it to anyone we find merely objectionable. On the continuum of irritating mean men, at one end of the scale we find the jerks. As jerks become more annoying, they may be assholes as defined by Sutton. But in the worst case, if a cluster of the characteristics in the List of Ten are consistently in the red zone over a long period, then *psychopathy* is, in fact, the personality disorder that describes them. Shocked? Me too. Finding the strong relationship between the List of Ten—specifically, when a disproportionate number of traits on the list are in the red zone—and the personality disorder of psychopathy stunned me. Though psychiatrist and researcher Ethel Person was among the first to see the link between entrepreneurs and psychopathy, I had not expected to find a correlation with a disorder with such dark implications. Perhaps some simple narcissism (which, of course, is never "simple") combined with one or two other traits? Sure.

When I had this realization, my own understanding of psychopathy, a complex disorder that has been researched more fully only in the past decade, was superficial at best. But as I dug into the most contemporary research and matched our current understanding with the traits, characteristics, and behaviors of the mean men observed, I became confident that this disorder was by far the best fit. At this extreme, mean men are remarkably nasty and tend to make others' lives a living hell. The notion that psychopaths choose entrepreneurship as the stage for acting out their internal psychological drama adds a new, and possibly disturbing, dimension to our understanding of the entrepreneurial phenomenon. Yet the data indicate strongly that a magnetic pull on psychopaths toward the career of entrepreneurship is not a random set of events.

And because those with disordered personalities fail to change, the pathological themes that tend to dominate their lives become vicious cycles, a bad one-act play that gets performed over and over. So blind are they to opportunities that may lead to improvement, that repeated dysfunctional themes provoke new problems and repeatedly create situations that remind them of their failures. As the cycle continues with some of the most successful Americans in business today, the meanness does more than affect those who interact with the mean men on a daily basis—it begins to affect and shape our culture at large.

THE MASK OF SANITY

Among entrepreneurs, most fall in the "normal" category, which includes some behaviors we might not see as nice but are not uncommon. The entrepreneurs may be opportunistic individuals and see personal gain as more important than the collective good. They may consider winning as one of the most worthwhile goals in life and shift their logic to gain personal advantage. They work hard, take risks, believe they have influence over much of the immediate world, and have ample self-regard. They're often exceptional salespeople, and they sometimes cut ethical corners.

Take, for example, silver-tongued Hampton Creek CEO and founder Josh Tetrick, the self-anointed king of vegan "mayonnaise."[20] Once a sustainability darling, food-technology company Hampton Creek was selected by famed philanthropist and Microsoft founder Bill Gates as one of three companies "shaping the future of food."[21] In his passionate TED talk, Tetrick implores his listeners to "*feel*, not just hear, what's really going on" in commercial food production, and elicits feeling (if not nausea) by then illuminating the disgusting and rather inhumane conditions of egg-laying hens, complete with visuals. What Tetrick "cares about," he tells us, is not the chickens, but people like "Susan," a girl he met in sub-Saharan Africa whom Tetrick desperately wants "to thrive." His "innovation in the food space" will accomplish just that through "a miracle of nature," he promises.[22]

The challenge of feeding a global population humanely is not a problem Tetrick discovered, though to listen to him you might not know that. Even his company's main product, vegan mayo made with pea protein, is rather derivative. But what Tetrick lacks in originality he makes up for in salesmanship. He loves narrative, he tells us in the beginning of his TED talk, and to listen to him is to believe him. This Southern-born boy can spin a yarn, to the tune of $220 million dollars in investment capital and the nod from Gates. However, as happens with many mean men, the facade (and his vegan cookie dough) is beginning to crumble. In 2016, the company quietly scrubbed its Facebook page of the claims that every jar of its vegan mayo saved 80 gallons of water and every vegan chocolate chip cookie saved 7 gallons of water and 35 grams of carbon emissions.

Turns out those claims weren't true. But it didn't stop there. In August 2016, the Justice Department, together with the US Securities and Exchange Commission, launched an investigation into the company for criminal fraud and securities violations, the company having been accused of buying back its own product from the retail market in order to boost claims of its popularity. "We're the #1 selling mayo in Whole Foods," Tetrick had crowed to investors.[23]

The story was first broken by *Bloomberg*, an inconvenience Tetrick responded to with this written comment: "We're aware of the informal inquiry and we'll be sharing the facts, as opposed to the inaccuracies reported by Bloomberg."[24] Tetrick has his work cut out for him. Former employees have said everyone knew what the company was really up to. And while the CEO claims buybacks were limited and done for quality control, at least one investor and investor liaison disagreed. In 2014, Ali Partovi warned the board and also Tetrick himself, writing in an email, "It's only a question of time before the consequences catch up with us. If an investor discovers it during due diligence, we could lose financing and run out of cash. If they don't, they'll realize they were duped within months, and they might have a case for fraud."[25]

In addition to *Bloomberg*, *Business Insider* published its own piece, interviewing former employees who spoke to the deliberate mislabeling of ingredients as well as to the use of deceptive marketing. While the former employees were bothered by the muddy ethics, they said that Tetrick was more than willing to make the trade-offs. "Hampton Creek's CEO Josh Tetrick knew they were uncomfortable with these practices, but the conversations were overlooked in favor of pleasing investors, fulfilling contracts, and moving fast."[26] There might be plenty for Tetrick to deal with in the months and years to come. A *TechCrunch* article laid out allegations that included exaggerations related to research and development, false claims of Gates as an investor, trumped-up retail partnerships, and even Tetrick's dog contaminating the lab space.[27] Though muddy ethics can be the precursor to more severe disordered behavior, by the summer of 2017, Tetrick has yet to cross that line.

Even as many mean men often appear to act normally, they can be malevolent individuals. The psychiatrist Hervey Cleckley was a top pioneer in understanding people who covered dangerously antisocial behaviors with a mask of normalcy. Cleckley worked at a psychiatric hospital in the late 1930s, and that facility, like others of its kind in the first half of the twentieth century, often had criminal offenders who were believed to have some form of mental illness.

These men seemed "normal" under most conditions. Cleckley watched as they charmed, and then manipulated and took advantage of, other patients, family members, and even hospital staff. As a result, he came to believe the disorder could serve as a cloak, helping those with it live with the trappings of normalcy. Noteworthy, too, was that unlike the stereotypical "common criminal," these men generally came from "good homes" with loving parents and yet still ended up ruining lives without any feeling or display of remorse, shame, or conscience. These patients often made poor life judgments by virtue of *not* learning from their past personal experiences. They continually repeated dysfunctional or unfruitful behaviors; *adaptiveness*, noted earlier, was elusive to them. They lacked insight about themselves and the impact their behavior had on others. What's more, since they were unmoved by the feelings of others, notions of remorse or shame were alien. On the face honest and forthright, especially to those new to them, they were all the same insincere more often than not.

Cleckley's review of his patients' records indicated they could be extremely egomaniacal and virtually unable to experience deep emotions, particularly love and compassion. In fact, they seemed to lack the capacity to feel deeply at all, except in one area. His patients were able to connect intensively with primitive *proto-emotions*—such as anger, frustration, and rage.

He personally experienced these patients as having superficial charm and reasonably good intelligence. They could tell creative, believable stories. They did not seem to show delusional or irrational thinking (which often characterizes a hospitalized psychiatric disorder). And they did not seem anxious or neurotic.

As he noted in his fifth edition of *The Mask of Sanity*, this type of patient "presents a technical appearance of sanity, often one of high intelligence capacities, and not infrequently succeeds in business or professional activities."[28] The book's title captured Cleckley's belief that these men do not show obvious symptoms of mental illness. Such is the clinical and everyday nature of psychopathy.

Cleckley was quite taken by a profound underlying characteristic of the psychopathic disorder in which the language and emotional components of thought are not properly integrated, a condition known as *semantic aphasia*. Individual emotion-laden words are understood, but the psychopathic individual cannot grasp the broader meaning of what he hears. These can be rather simple words that we have experienced deeply: "love," "annoyance," "tenderness," or "fear." Otherwise stated, this individual has a deep-seated inability to understand the *emotional dimension* of language, particularly those aspects associated with attachment (the desire to seek an emotionally supportive relationship) and with empathy. He can say the word "love," for example, but he has absolutely no idea what the word means, and certainly no idea what love feels like.

Cleckley was startled by another characteristic: Nothing about the disorder suggested oddness, inadequacy, or moral frailty. The "mask" is actually one of robust mental health. But behind the mask he found pathological liars, adept at sizing up situations and feigning sincerity. Put these ingredients together, stir until just combined, and you'd have a psychological profile that allowed these men to rise.

No one in the clinical world is more responsible for propagating the concept of psychopathy than Robert Hare. He spent forty years as a professor at the University of British Columbia specializing in forensic psychology and getting inside the head of criminals. Hare was influenced by Cleckley's work and used it to gain insight into men in prison systems. One of his most significant contributions was the first tool to assess psychopathy in a prison population.[29] Although other tests of psychopathy have since been developed, and an increasing number of researchers have expressed reservations about Hare's methodology, his approach has dominated if even for the wild commercial success of his assessment tool.[30] But it is this tool that's at the heart of dissension in the research world. Over the past five years, strong disagreement—and hard data—has surfaced arguing for elimination of lawbreaking or violence as conditions for a diagnosis.[31]

In the early 1990s, Cleckley's observations, and a list he developed of "qualities" of the disorder, were subjected to rigorous theoretical and field testing by Hare, the forensic psychologist. Hare found that his study subjects showed clear traits of egocentricity, a grandiose sense of self-worth, intolerance of boredom, lack of empathy, a tendency to manipulate others, lack of remorse, and a superficial charm and charisma. Imperviousness to shame was later added, to illustrate their lack of internal behavioral controls.[32]

These were *mean men*.

Wait a second, you're saying to yourself, *is this guy really making the argument that some of the most successful men in America today are psychopaths? As in criminals? Worse—Ted Bundy?* Yes, my research would suggest the former, and no, I am clearly not saying the latter. This is but one of the common misconceptions about psychopathy and our more nuanced modern understanding of the disorder. I am distinctly *not* applying this diagnosis to any individual; I am illuminating many of the common misconceptions held about what "psychopathy" is.

PSYCHOPATHY: THE MYTHS

1. PSYCHOPATHY DIAGNOSIS REQUIRES AN ACT OF VIOLENCE AND/OR LAWBREAKING.

Many still equate the psychopath with famous serial killers of yore. The media continues to link the terms "psychopath" and "killer" as almost interchangeable descriptors. But psychopathy can and does occur in the absence of any criminal convictions, and many individuals assessed as psychopathic have no history of violence. Psychopaths, nonetheless, do engage in behaviors that may cause social injury or conflict with the interests of the social order (like hurtful gossip, lying, manipulation, and having no regard for the effects of their actions on the feelings of others). Social harm may be distasteful, but it's generally not against the law.[33]

2. PSYCHOPATHY IS THE SAME AS PSYCHOSIS.

Owing perhaps in part to the similarity of the words "psychopath" and "psychotic," another common assumption is that psychopaths are irrational, out of touch with reality, or both.[34] Fueling this myth is the news media's frequent and inaccurate use of the term "psychopath" when featuring such famous killers as Charles Manson, David Berkowitz, and John Hinckley. These men may very well have been psychotic, but they were not psychopathic. More recently, the term "psychopath" was used incorrectly by at least one political commentator in the context of Jared Lee Loughner, who shot and killed six people and wounded fourteen others, including US Congresswoman Gabrielle Giffords, in Tucson, Arizona.[35]

While psychopathic traits may be seen in some cases alongside psychotic symptoms, those with psychopathy alone generally act quite different from those presenting with only psychosis. Psychopathic individuals are generally rational, free of delusions, and well oriented to their surroundings. Psychotics act very differently than this.

3. PSYCHOPATHY IS SYNONYMOUS WITH ANTI- SOCIAL PERSONALITY DISORDER (ASPD).

Until the most recent version of the *DSM* was released, it was strongly suggested that these terms were synonymous. And today, many still consider their differences to be unremarkable. But the key difference between the two is embedded in the assumption of violence or other criminal activity. A determination of psychopathy includes personality traits *inferable* from behavior. But determination of ASPD hangs directly on the emphasis that the individual in question engages in antisocial, criminal, and—to some extent—violent behaviors. This is not just technical hairsplitting. As diagnostic methods become more precise, criminality and violence have dropped precipitously in importance.[36]

4. PSYCHOPATHS ARE BORN, NOT MADE.

The current understanding is that the interplay between genetics and environment will always influence behavior, and any psychiatric condition, including psychopathy, is neither entirely "born" nor "made." Based on what is now known, it seems very likely that psychopathy has many causal factors, and the influence of one's environment (particularly family setting and dynamics) has been shown to be quite strong.[37]

5. PSYCHOPATHY IS INALTERABLE.

While this belief lacks convincing scientific basis, it is extraordinarily pervasive. So pervasive, in fact, that researchers have not even bothered to test the notion until recently. Initial empirical work now suggests that personality traits in general, and psychopathic traits specifically, do change as one moves through what are known as "developmental transitions." Intentional, motivated change—with the help of highly skilled therapists—is showing some promise in limited clinical settings.[38]

The "messiness" in coming to terms with *psychopathy*—and *psychopaths*—in the last decade has been rooted in debunking the strong reliance on criminal behavior in defining it. Unquestioned assumptions of the past fostered the impression—wrongly—that psychopathic individuals invariably commit crimes. Leading researchers in the field have now pivoted, agreeing that too much emphasis was placed on criminal offender populations when studying psychopathy in the past.

MEAN IN THE CORNER OFFICE

I hope you now see that on the spectrum of psychopathy as a disorder, our interests don't lie with those on the "severely abnormal" end of the scale. Instead, we're interested in the *successful* psychopath.

Most of us have met one of these guys, or at least seen him on the news. On first blush, he seems charming and glib. With a polished ability to take advantage of others, he has figured out the role he needs to play to get what he wants. Aggression that bumps up against abuse, if not outright violence, may be an option, but a psychopath also knows how to manipulate rhetoric, be it a compliment, a white lie, or an exaggerated apology in order to achieve his self-serving goals. To him, the end goal is what matters, making a terrorizing rant or feigned respect equally useful as circumstances dictate.

And what's striking is that, again and again, we find guys like this in the entrepreneurial world and in other positions of power where an entrepreneurial style is called for. Stories of well-known entrepreneurs reveal a pattern of destructive, unethical, immoral, and at times even illegal behavior. While the bad behaviors are typically coupled with superficial apologies, the entrepreneurs in question generally fail to convey a true sense of remorse or regret. On the surface, they typically possess an unrealistic sense of self-importance, and they are invariably shrugged off as just a flaming narcissist.

In fact, it's clear that these entrepreneurial men do manifest behaviors closely aligned with psychopathy. While it may seem outrageous to say, it raises a fascinating question: Could substantial characteristics of the psychopathic disorder survive, if not thrive, in legitimate settings? Answering that question is complicated. What's clear, though, is that many researchers now embrace an expansive view of psychopathy—one that looks beyond the severe cases of fraudsters and killers to individuals who exhibit milder symptoms and can often operate successfully in the world.

Over the past decade particularly, researchers from North America, Europe, and Australia performed some particularly muscular and complex statistical analyses to find that successful psychopaths can indeed exist. For one, psychopathy is undeniably not synonymous with criminality. Of course, quite a few psychopaths find their way into the criminal justice system, some spending significant portions of their lives in prison. But most manage to avoid involvement with the system in adult life. Perhaps their disregard for social norms is so obvious or severe as to land them in jail. Maybe, they just aren't caught for the crimes they do commit. Some control their self-serving behaviors to remain within the bounds of legal behavior—not because committing an illegal act would be wrong, but because it might prove inconvenient. It could interfere with them getting what they want.

Additionally, some psychopathic traits may help make an individual successful (admired or feared but not necessarily liked). Turning on the charm and going to any lengths to achieve often work in high-stakes, pressure-filled environments.

Theodore Millon developed draft criteria for the *DSM-III*, published in 1980. Millon's criteria for psychopathy is strikingly similar to the extremes of the entrepreneurial personality. A random occurrence? You decide.

A pattern is typified by a self-assertive, temperamentally hostile and socially forceful and intimidating manner. There is pride in self-reliance, unsentimentality and hard-boiled competitive values. Malicious personal tendencies are projected outward, precipitating frequent outbursts of explosive rage. Vindictive gratification is obtained by humiliating and dominating others. A rash willingness to risk harm is notable as is a fearlessness in the face of threats and punitive action.[39]

Noel, our unlikable corporate-fired-newly-blossomed entrepreneur, is a case in point. The psychiatrist who diagnosed him with psychopathic personality disorder realized that going by the book—literally, following the assessment criteria in the *Diagnostic and Statistical Manual of Mental Disorders* (*DSM*)—would be problematic. He came from a privileged background and didn't exhibit some of the formal *DSM* criteria for the disorder: "repeated physical fights or assaults," "use of aliases," "a reckless disregard for the safety of self and others," and "evidence of conduct disorder with onset before age 16 years." His behavior was bad, but not so bad that it stopped him from going pretty far in life.

Noel spent time being diagnosed by his psychiatrist. The physician did not reach this conclusion from a fifty-minute appointment but rather through weeks of private-office talking with him and sifting through his background, the inconsistent false truths, and the patterns that developed. And while psychopathy best identified the constellation of personality traits and behaviors that characterized Noel, many cases are far subtler.

Let's go back and scan the List of Ten one more time. Contrast in your mind the entrepreneurial "normals"—those who display healthy doses of each of these characteristics—with those who exhibit far more amplified demonstrations of the same characteristics. This is the mean man we see crossing the border from adaptive entrepreneurial leader into disturbingly abusive entrepreneurial leader. Yet these men elude easy classification as psychopathic because they are highly functional in a great many ways: we see them running companies, making movies, and operating in government.

What we're seeing here is *subclinical psychopathy*. As I noted before, they may appear to the casual observer to be upstanding high achievers, if a bit eccentric. They may lead relatively normal lives, not hurting others in ways that grab public attention. These aren't our superstar mean men. Those afflicted may conduct themselves with decency and propriety in certain spheres, but in "the moral or active principles of the mind they are still strangely perverted or depraved."[40] And their actions cause problems in hidden economic, psychological, and emotionally abusive ways. They do not make warm and loving parents, children, or family members. They do not make reliable friends or coworkers.

To a clinician, "subclinical" means that the pathological behaviors are far less pronounced but the underlying disorder is still clear. A disorder that stays below the surface of clear clinical detection lands in this category when it has few recognizable clinical findings and the patient seems highly functional (never mind what those on the business end of the behavior may be experiencing). It is distinct from a clinical disorder, which has overt signs and symptoms that can be easily recognized.

As we dig deeper into mean men in the pages ahead, keep Millon's description in the back of your mind, along with the List of Ten. You'll find them both eerily appropriate for many of the folks we'll meet. Red zone–level traits and characteristics that correlate strongly with clinical criteria build a compelling case for subclinical psychopathy as one plausible explanation for what lies beneath the personality of some entrepreneurs and entrepreneurial-style leaders, the ones I will henceforth simply call "mean."

THE SIX TYPES OF MEAN

Now that we have a basis in the general definition of *subclinical psychopathy*, let's look at six profiles that gather different bundles of traits to create six flavors of mean you'll recognize. These profiles, fashioned from six of Millon's ten subtypes of psychopathy, hold especially true for a certain type of entrepreneurial leader. Whether it's the do-whatever-it-takes Opportunist or the rageful Hothead or even the audacious Cowboy, my bet is that at least a few of these profiles will remind you of someone you know, either from your own life or from Twitter. . . .

1. THE OPPORTUNIST

This mean man is defined by his arrogance, a callous disregard for others, and his facile deception. He is happy to exploit others to get what he wants and often expects recognition or privilege just for being who he is. Personal integrity is not part of his makeup.

For psychologists, it's important that the Opportunist lacks a "superego," which represents society's standards and determines our personal standards for right and wrong.

His relationships are largely unscrupulous and amoral, and he's not afraid to humiliate or deceive others to get what he wants. In fact, he enjoys the game and maintains relationships only so long as he has something to gain. Not only is he indifferent to the attitudes and reactions of others, but he may prey on the weak and vulnerable, feeding on the emotional turmoil and anger he evokes.

Calling him on his unethical behavior doesn't result in a normal response; sometimes he seems to invite danger, and he's skilled at evading responsibility. Skilled in the nuances of social influence, he uses charm and a studied naïveté to carry off his lies.

2. TWO-FACE

Characterized by friendliness and sociability, with this guy it's all a facade.

New acquaintances love him, but his facade soon begins to crack as he shows a more genuine side of unreliability, impulsivity, deep resentment, and moodiness. He knows how to work a room, seeking attention and excitement with more than a hint of seduction. But whatever connection he makes is shallow and fleeting. Relationships often end abruptly and harshly.

Others may experience him as irresponsible and undependable because his enthusiasm is short-lived, and he seeks excitement in immature ways. All charm on first blush, he is also contriving and plotting; crafty and scheming; insincere, calculating, and deceitful. Rarely admitting responsibility for personal and family difficulties, he shows a clever defensive denial when confronted. He is quick to rationalize his inevitable interpersonal difficulties and project blame onto others. Self-indulgent and demanding of attention, he responds in kind only when it aligns with his needs.

Two-Face is thoroughly unashamed of his deceitfulness. More than other types, his insincerity may seem boundless, as he does everything necessary to get what he needs and wants from others. In contrast to some other types, he seems to ride the high he gets from the tension of the deceit.

As he ages, his need for approval from others becomes less desperate, but he cannot be weaned from the need to manipulate. Lying beneath the surface of his behaviors is a great fear that no one will care for or love him, unless they are made to do so.

While he is adept at concealing his vulnerabilities, he fears looking indecisive or softhearted. So when he is crossed or faced with potential embarrassment, he is quick to anger, which is expressed in vengeful or vindictive ways. He must appear impenetrable and in control at all times.

While both the Opportunist and Two-Face share a certain deviousness, plotting and scheming in their careful strategies to manipulate others, Two-Face genuinely craves attention and approval, something for which the Opportunist has no use. Two-Face wants to hold the respect and affection of even those he pushes out of the way, perennially searching for new sources of love and admiration.

3. THE COWBOY

This thrill junky takes any chance to prove himself and is infatuated with new possibilities and uncharted territory. For this psychopath, risk makes him feel alive. He's not in it to prove he can succeed or for a big score. It's the thrill itself that fuels him.

He responds before thinking and reacts in characteristically unreflective and uncontrolled ways. His behavior goes beyond impulsiveness; he is essentially fearless, unmoved by events or circumstances that most people would find dangerous or frightening.

To others, he can easily look the fool rather than courageous. His need for autonomy and independence can be so strong that he never develops habits of self-discipline. His internal, real world is consumed with doubt about ever truly achieving, and his risk-taking brings an emptiness that constantly tempts him to prove himself against new and exciting ventures.

As an entrepreneur, politician, or athlete, he may be described as dauntless, intrepid, bold, and audacious. In contrast to other types, whose basic motivations are mostly aggrandizement and revenge, the Cowboy is drawn to the adrenaline high, needing more and more stimulation and excitement. His undependable and irresponsible nature aren't enough to land him in psychopathic territory; it is that coupled with his disregard for the impact his behaviors may have on others.

4. MR. DISSATISFACTION

Aggrandizement marks this psychopath. Mr. Dissatisfaction is never happy because he feels that life has not given him his due—he's been deprived of his rightful amount of love, support, and money. He believes, in essence, that he was born holding the trump card, but bad luck has always gotten in his way. His motto? "It's not fair."

Given this underlying pretext, envy and a desire for retribution motivate him to take back what he has been deprived of. Of all the types, he has the most brushes with the law, since he may "take back" through acts of destruction or theft. It is through these acts that he tries to fill the emptiness of his own life, dismissing with a sense of entitlement his violation of the social order. Insatiable and perennially unfulfilled, he never achieves a deep sense of contentment. Although he has little compassion for his negative effect on others, feeling little or no guilt for his actions, he remains at the core insecure about his power and possessions. In the role of entrepreneur particularly, he exploits others to satisfy his desires. Yet nothing is ever enough. Jealous of what others have, he is pushy and greedy, a poster boy for conspicuous consumption.

5. THE HOTHEAD

This subtype is distinguished by his unpredictable and sudden displays of hostility. He is infamous for "adult tantrums" marked with uncontrolled rage and his fearsome attacks on others.

Not unlike the tantrums of children, this explosive behavior is a reaction meant to cope with frustration or fear. While this behavior may have the effect of intimidating others into silence or passivity, that is not the primary intent. Instead, the outburst works to release his own pent-up feelings of humiliation.

Disappointed and frustrated in life, he loses control and seeks revenge for the mistreatment and criticism to which he feels subjected, and he combats a perceived futility. His rages often have no apparent provocation and can well up from inside. He is vigilant around loyalty and hunts for any sign of betrayal.

Because he is unable to resolve the real sources of his resentment and frustration, the Hothead externalizes those feelings and takes it out on others. He is unable to verbalize what he feels and why, though a sense of impotence and failure is at the root of his aggressive acts.

He may find himself in a profession where rash behavior is inappropriate, or he may have his rage normalized and be able to function in society—think of the violent basketball coach, the wall-punching executive, or the ranting politician who "just gets passionate" about his beliefs.

6. THE DOGMATIST

You will recognize the Dogmatist as the most overtly and directly contentious and argumentative of all the types. To him, everything and everyone is an object available for nagging, a sounding board for discharging his minor irritabilities, or even a target for litigious action.

He is relentless in magnifying every minor friction and turning it into a repeated and bitter struggle. He may insist that his argumentativeness is rooted in principles, and while there may be a grain of truth found in his beliefs, the "higher principles" are mostly just opinions. He is unquestionably right; others are unquestionably wrong. Fault-finding and inflexible, he delights in contradicting others. Unlike an intellectual, the Dogmatist is less concerned with the legitimacy and logic of his reasoning than with argument as a tool to frustrate and undermine his opponents.

The Dogmatist's hostile and oppositional style is at the core of his persona. His denigration of anyone in the name of his latest position or cause is well rehearsed and relentless. Criticism of others "is good for them." He believes he takes no personal satisfaction in berating people and has no ulterior motives for imposing his opinions, so he feels unconstrained, in fact duty bound, to say anything "to set people right."[41]

***

Armed with these profiles and a sense of what these men are capable of, we can interact with them in less damaging ways (or choose not to altogether) and analyze their behaviors with a critical and careful lens. Collectively, we can see if the shoe fits, and if it does, that can be our signal to resist normalizing their behavior. Instead of writing off their outrageous acts in the face of genius or profit or windfall success, we can acknowledge what they have achieved without rationalizing the destruction they've left in their wake.

CHAPTER FOUR

ARE ONLY MEN MEAN?

IN 2006, KEN MEHLMAN, THE chairman of the Republican National Committee, asserted that then senator Hillary Rodham Clinton was too angry to be elected president.[1] Of course, labeling women in leadership roles as "angry" is nothing new, nor does it appear to be going out of style any time soon. A decade later, and though the Republican National Committee chairmen may have changed, the criticisms remained the same. In September 2016, Reince Priebus tweeted, among other things, that during a commander-in-chief forum, Clinton was "angry and defensive . . . no smile and uncomfortable . . ."[2] After a long political career, no doubt Clinton is used to such comments, and the reader could practically see her rolling her eyes as she tweeted this response: "Actually, that's just what taking the office of President seriously looks like."[3]

It's been many years since shouting down one's opponents has become normative political behavior, and the manner of debate during the 2016 election season was no exception. So why has Clinton been continually singled out and painted as possessing a destructive and prohibitive trait? While she was being advised by staffers to seem kinder and more approachable, Donald Trump was insulting his way to center stage and cowing his fellow nominees one by "low-energy" one. In the Republican camp, there wasn't enough red meat for one part of the base, the debaters' belligerence and rancor making for must-see TV. Except, that is, for Carly Fiorina, that lone woman in the crowded Republican field, who was chastised for interrupting (by Trump no less) and told to—wait for it—smile more. Or FOX News anchor Megyn Kelly, who, after pulling no punches in a debate questioning Trump on his poor treatment of women, had her tough journalism chalked up to menstrual rage by the unamused candidate: "She gets out, and she starts asking me all sorts of ridiculous questions and, you know, you could see there was blood coming out of her eyes, blood coming out of her wherever. . . ."[4]

As we've already seen in the anecdotal evidence thus far, meanness often gets results—for men. Mean men are often perceived as powerful, persuasive, competent, and in control. Their very meanness may in fact help them claw their way to the top and convince those around them that they deserve to act as they do. Political affiliations aside, Trump's success is the very best recent example of this: every news story about his ruthlessness seemed to only bolster his appeal. Not even racially charged language, accusations of fraud, testimony from women he allegedly victimized, his own infamous *Access Hollywood* remarks, or reports of past civil rights violations could dent his popularity. "That's called business," he said during the first presidential debate, failing to refute the fact that he gleefully profited from the housing crisis of 2008.[5] To the charge he hasn't paid income tax in decades, he responded, "That makes me smart," and the public seemed to agree.[6] His winning of the presidency surprised many, but perhaps it shouldn't have: for men, the odds are on meanness winning.

The comments of the Republican National Committee chairmen serve to illustrate that, within professional arenas, expressing anger or seeming "mean" has a much different effect for women. The media has seized on these comments precisely because the problem isn't so much about anger or meanness per se, but that Clinton and her peers were being accused of behavior that isn't befitting a woman. During Clinton's first run, columnist Maureen Dowd of the *New York Times* categorized the "woman problem" in this way:

> *They are casting Hillary Clinton as an Angry Woman, a*
> *she-monster melding images of Medea, the Furies, harpies. . . .*
> *This gambit handcuffs Hillary: If she doesn't speak out strongly*
> *. . . she's timid and girlie. If she does, she's a witch and a shrew.*[7]

If for the moment we allow anger to stand in for meanness, we'll see that research backs up this observation. Theorists who look at emotion at play in society now suggest that displays of certain emotions, including anger, can communicate both competence and an entitlement to elevated social status position. A number of studies meant to explore the dynamics of anger expression between genders were unambiguous in their findings: men who blew up at work were rewarded for it. They were more likely to be hired and given more autonomy, and also had more power and status conferred upon them than men who were sad rather than angry.

But as Clinton's experience suggests, professional women who express anger suffer for it. Rather than anger, modesty and kindness are expected from our ladies, and we punish them if they fail to conform to this prescriptive stereotype. Groundbreaking studies by Victoria Brescoll and Eric Uhlmann, professors at Yale and Northwestern, respectively, found that female professionals who express anger don't get the same boost in status enjoyed by angry men. Bottom line: women are conditioned away from mean.[8]

Something even darker showed up in these studies. Both anger and pride were the only emotions most people believe men naturally express more than women. In essence, men get a free pass on displaying anger due to our own cultural bias. We see male anger as a more natural response to objective, external circumstances. When women show anger, it seems out of context, and thus we naturally presume it's a product of her personality. Her anger is viewed as internally caused ("She's an angry person" or "She's out of control") rather than externally instigated ("The situation was frustrating"). Or, as Lisa Feldman Barrett put it in a *New York Times* article describing her study of this phenomenon, "She's a bitch, but he's just having a bad day."[9]

Brescoll and Uhlmann's study went even further in explaining the gendered status of mean. The expression of anger by men *increased* their potential to be conferred higher status by others. Angry men were more likely to be seen as leaders. However, professional women who expressed anger were dinged professionally and earned lower wages. Angry women were also seen as less competent than angry men and unemotional women.

Unlike with men, a woman's occupational rank (whether CEO or trainee) in no way influenced the level of status conferred on her. Angry women were consistently seen as out of control. Interestingly, the study showed that when women were able to provide an *external* reason for their anger, they didn't suffer the same loss in perceived status and competence. But men don't have to worry about explaining the root cause of their anger because the sense is they just don't get out of control. This despite what we've seen of many mean men—that they seem intrinsically angry and oftentimes completely unable, or unwilling, to rein in their outbursts. And no wonder—it yields them results. According to Uhlmann, "For men, it seems to be advantageous to get angry without providing justification."[10] In short, not only do men get to explode without reason or provocation, when they do, they are held in high esteem, are perceived as more competent, and even earn higher salaries.

To me, the research helped answer a compelling question that arose while writing this book. From my personal consulting work to the stories gracing the news, examples abound of mean men. Where, I wondered, were all the mean women? Try as I might, I had incredible difficulty finding examples of powerful women who exhibited the same set of traits that make up a mean man.

WHERE ARE THE MEAN WOMEN?

In the course of my research, I found one woman who appeared to fit the bill. Linda Joy Wachner was born in the post–World War II boom in New York City to older parents. Though she had a sister, she was already grown, and Wachner spent a good deal of time alone. At the tender age of eleven, scoliosis required her to spend a year immobilized in a body cast before having surgery for her condition. Instead of wallowing or engaging in self-pity, Wachner seemed only to steel her resolve to make a name for herself. She decided to follow in the footsteps of her father and uncle in the garment business. She started as a buyer and worked her way up until she became the first female vice president of Warner's, the lingerie division of Warnaco.

In 1986, Wachner successfully pulled off a leveraged buyout of the company. She was at the time the only woman to have done so.[11] Success at this level, she claimed, required toughness. Her aggressive, no-holds-barred manner drew complaints from men and women who considered her manners unladylike. But her supporters at the time cried foul, arguing that Wachner, in essence, merely adopted the same businesslike style that has allowed so many men to reach the same heights. Wachner justified her actions in a *Ms.* article, saying: "To get a company turned around before it bleeds to death, you have to have a certain posture in the way you go about things. I'm tough, but I'm fair."[12]

But there's another side to this story. The same drive to win that propels some to unimaginable heights of power and wealth can just as easily result in out-of-control behavior with disastrous consequences. Is Linda Wachner a rare *female* example of what happens when lack of self-discipline and arrogance converge in a leader?

Colleagues and business reporters at the time commented on Wachner's lust for money, her abrasive style of management, and her all-encompassing hunger for power. Like other egocentric leaders obsessed only with the bottom line, she drove away key management talent. When she was at the peak of her career, Wachner was typically depicted by the media as a hard-charging, foulmouthed boss, who won praise from investors by cutting deals and building a stable of brand names that brought in billions in sales revenues. Customers and stock-holders loved her; competitors feared her. She became one of the high-est-paid executives in her time, earning more than $158 million in salary, bonuses, dividends, and special stock deals in a six-year period.[13]

Like many leaders made golden through financial success, Wachner soon proved she was willing to do whatever it took to keep the profits high. Even when her team warned against it, Wachner carried through on a plan to dump name brands on discount retail outlets. No longer exclusive to high-end retailers, the labels in question suffered a status drop in consumers' eyes. And their suppliers didn't stand for it. Calvin Klein filed a lawsuit against Warnaco for breach of contract in selling their products to unlicensed retailers.

While Wachner won in court, the lawsuit and her hubris assured her downfall. She lost trust with suppliers including Klein, who said Wachner was his "personal enemy." And while Wachner declared the outlook sunny, debt mounted. Warnaco posted losses of $334 million in 2000 and was forced to file for bankruptcy protection. Three years later, Wachner was let go, but she went kicking and screaming, demanding a quarter of a billion dollars in severance. More ethics violations surfaced, with the Securities and Exchange Commission charging Warnaco execs includ-ing Wachner of defrauding investors. Wachner settled for $3.5 million in Warnaco stock and $200,000 cash to leave the company, but then was forced to pay more than $10 million along with two former colleagues to settle the federal fraud case.[14]

Wachner would do anything to get ahead, and few survived at Warnaco unless they bought into her rules for success—or at least appeared to. In *Power, Ambition, Glory*, Steve Forbes and John Prevas compared her to Alexander the Great; for both leaders, they argue, "it was all about the conquest." In the end, her hubris and limitless greed brought down both the leader and the company, with a former employee opining to the *New York Times* that "she was the main reason it (the company) fell apart. There is some genius there, but she could not run a $2 billion corporation by herself."[15]

COMPLICATED PICTURE

If Linda Wachner were a man, would I have automatically characterized her as mean? Does she fit the criteria of the List of Ten? In truth, because she isn't a man and because of how women with a more masculine style, including anger and lone-wolf leadership, are judged, that answer is complicated. What I know is that the real world presents professional women and women leaders with a dilemma. On the one hand, appropriate anger can get others to become more responsible or unequivocally communicate someone's incompetence. But if women are to maintain their status in any social system (politics, organizational life, or entrepreneurship, to name only three), then they may have to suppress some of their emotions to be seen as rational. Strategically, women have to figure out how to express anger without incurring the social penalty that men seem to escape.

Stanford researcher Larissa Tiedens argues that anger is a status emotion and that women who express it are often labeled with personality-based explanations.[16] When others attribute a woman's anger or meanness to internal causes (e.g., "such a nasty woman"), it helps us to explain the lower status they confer on her, as Hillary Rodham Clinton has found. They are rated as less socially skilled and therefore less hirable for jobs that require social interaction skills than are men who behave identically. Women who demonstrate assertiveness, competitiveness, independence, and courageousness (what social psychologists call "agentic factors," or traits that demonstrate personal agency) often experience backlash and have to manage the ensuing catch-22. Women leaders have to walk some impossibly fine line between appearing incompetent and nice and competent and cold. If she shows anger without attributing it to some external factor, she is the ice queen, the ballbuster, the dragon lady, the bitch.

Experimental studies consistently find that, unlike men, when women try to negotiate greater compensation, they are disliked. When they succeed in a male occupation, they are disliked. When they fail to perform the altruistic acts that are optional for men, they are disliked. When they criticize, they are disparaged. Is there a pattern here? Are the same behaviors that enhance a guy's status the ones that make a woman less popular? In leadership roles, women may find themselves in a never-ending double bind of figuring out how to direct, command, and control their followers without appearing to do so.

IF WOMEN CAN'T GET ANGRY, WHAT DO THEY GET?

Neither men nor women have been well served by the gender socialization of anger. It's also pervasive, starting when we're young. Men are encouraged to be more overt with their anger from the time we're kids. If boys have a conflict on the playground, they can fight it out. To do so might even seem more masculine or "manly." Girls are encouraged to keep their anger under wraps. They are quick to receive the message that overt anger is unpleasant and unfeminine. But those feelings have to go somewhere; for girls, anger may manifest not in playground fisticuffs but through sulking or destructive gossip. On the positive side, this conditioning against anger also makes women proactive and more likely to use more problem-solving approaches in resolving conflict, traits that might constitute anti-mean behavior.

So are women just better human beings, more prone to generosity and agreeableness than they are to getting ahead, making the deal, crushing the competition? The research suggests to me that while inherent goodness isn't gendered, how we react to and reward the expression of mean traits reflects a gender bias in society.

Women still feel anger—they are simply conditioned to not express it, or cannot express it in the same ways men can. There are many ramifications of this. For decades, sociologists have wondered why women suffer depression at a higher rate than men, as much as twice as much according to some epidemiological studies.[17] Recently, scholars turned their attention to what is known as the gendered-response hypothesis. According to this theory, women don't suffer more stressful situations than men do, nor are they somehow biologically more vulnerable to its effects; rather, women simply express the effects differently.[18] A growing body of work finds that women tend to respond to stress by *internalizing* problems (resulting in effects like depression), while men *externalize* behaviors as a response, resulting in antisocial behavior like extreme anger and substance abuse.[19]

It's important to note that internalizing anger is not synonymous with suppressing it; in fact, research shows women and men are equally likely to suppress that type of negative emotion. While they may manage the anger differently—women are more likely to talk it out with others while men are more likely to use substances to dull the effects—those are simply different ways of coping. Ironically, research has revealed women are angrier, reporting more persistent and more intense anger than their male counterparts.

Would we have more mean women if we gave the same allowances for powerful women to express their anger? Maybe or maybe not. What we do know is that women are powerfully conditioned away from mean, while men quickly realize that mean works in some contexts. As a society, we need to take a hard look at the behavior we reward and that which we punish—and the monsters we're creating as we do so.

CHAPTER FIVE

THE MAINSTREAMING OF MEAN

MEAN MEN ARE HARDLY A new phenomenon, and the tyrannical boss has been a familiar archetype in American culture ever since the invention of the modern industrial-era workplace. In fact, in many ways organizational culture is far more touchy-feely now than it used to be—much as corporeal punishment in schools is out, along with spanking your kids.

Yet powerful forces have been at work in American society that have fueled bad behavior in high places, allowing more mean men to get to the top and stay there, even as they create misery all around them.

These forces can be roughly divided in two baskets: First, thanks to changes in the economy and business, those with entrepreneurial traits can rise to leadership roles without having to "pay their dues" in large organizations and play by someone else's rules. Second, thanks to a combination of economic and cultural changes, men in particular feel more license to exhibit outsized personality traits, including very negative ones. They can now more easily get away with bad behavior, so long as they get results.

Let's dig into both of these baskets.

FREE-AGENT NATION

It's unlikely that a guy like Aaron could ever have become a boss fifty years ago. Why? Because he wouldn't have been able to start his own thing so easily by raising a bunch of venture capital and putting together a business. The Aarons of yesterday rarely became entrepreneurs. Instead, succeeding in business typically meant climbing to the top of a big corporation, learning to subordinate yourself to others along the way.

That wasn't true in business only, by the way; it was true in lots of sectors. Top athletes were essentially owned by teams. Film directors, screenwriters, and actors were on the payroll of Hollywood studios. Nearly all journalists worked in news organizations. Politicians were beholden to party bosses, and so on.

Today, there's a "free-agent nation," in which more and more people are in charge of their own careers and destinies: Sports stars jump from team to team in search of the highest pay. Directors and actors have their own production companies. Outsiders are "in" in political circles. And almost any twenty-five-year-old with a good tech idea can raise millions of dollars, skipping the humbling dues-paying that used to be part of growing up.

The transformation of the business sector has been especially profound, and the explosion of entrepreneurship in the past few decades reflects a number of changes in the economy. First, the shift away from a manufacturing to an information and services economy has greatly lowered the costs of producing goods as well as shortened the time frame for scaling up a large business. Back in the industrial age, creating many kinds of goods required building factories filled with machinery and lots of workers, all dependent on a supply of raw materials. Now we live in an age where high-value goods, and great wealth, can be created by smaller groups of technologists sitting in front of computers, like the programmers and designers working at Zynga who created games like FarmVille. And when actual physical goods do have to be produced—for example, iPhones—it's possible to do so more cheaply and flexibly than ever. You no longer have to build your own factory; you can outsource production to somebody who already has that factory in a place with rock-bottom labor costs.

What's more, the creation and production of new goods can now happen with remarkable speed. Zynga was founded in April 2007 and launched its first game just three months later. After FarmVille was launched in 2009, within six weeks it had ten million users, a number that quickly doubled.

High-end services, like the advertising campaigns created by Peter Arnell, are another example of how wealth can be created out of thin air by a bunch of smart people sitting at their desks. Consulting services are another example. Sixty years ago you couldn't build a big business by sending management experts around to companies to, well, just listen and talk.

A second shift is marked by the easy availability of capital. A single individual with a good idea can now mobilize tens of millions of dollars to pursue his vision in a way that was extremely rare before the rise of the modern venture capital industry. In turn, that industry has emerged because there is exponentially more cash sloshing around today with owners looking for a higher rate of return.

In short, for those who have the gumption to think big and do their own thing, the barriers to entry are lower than ever. And they keep falling as innovation rushes forward. The Internet companies that dot-commers started in the 1990s were much cheaper to scale up than the software companies created by Bill Gates, Larry Ellison, and others in the 1980s. In turn, the companies created during the latest tech boom—like Facebook, Twitter, and Zynga—have been even cheaper to start and scale because of developments like cloud computing and other advances that fuel faster growth.

But it's not just technologists who can start businesses more cheaply. The explosion of the franchise model has made it less expensive to start businesses in a number of sectors, from restaurants to retail to private education. And let's not forget the many new people who chart their own path by starting new ventures in the lucrative financial industry by managing a bit of that vast sea of cash slopping about. A generation ago, ambitious people who went into finance spent their careers in big companies like Merrill Lynch and Prudential. Now a great many of them start their own hedge funds and mutual funds—or firms that sell niche information to such funds or to the public.

All these shifts have created a society that rewards entrepreneurial personality traits as never before. Back in 1956 when William H. Whyte wrote his bestseller *The Organization Man*, the List of Ten traits could be a serious liability for an ambitious young man. If you graduated from business school in, say, 1960, the vast majority of your career opportunities were in large corporations, where you'd be expected to take orders from others, follow rigid procedures, and check your impulsivity—behaviors that are difficult for entrepreneurial types. And if you couldn't learn to subsume yourself to the group, becoming just another man in a "gray flannel suit," chances are you didn't have much of a future in business.

An earlier and extreme example of the alignment of work with the organization is that of American icon Henry Ford and his company's famous "Sociological Department." Staff from the department, dubbed "social workers," were sent to employees' homes to make sure Ford's workers were not "living in sin," engaging in premarital sex, drinking, smoking, or making purchases on installment plans. Employees were expected to produce their bankbooks to prove they were saving enough of their earnings, and their marriage certificates to prove they were adhering to Ford's "Rules of Living," a pamphlet distributed by these "social workers" that laid out acceptable and unacceptable behaviors for his employees. Any worker who got divorced, used alcohol or tobacco, committed adultery, or took in boarders was disqualified from the higher pay scale.[1]

Today, entrepreneurial personality traits are still a liability for large organizations, regardless of what many firms say publicly to attract young talent. The difference is that now entrepreneurial people have many more choices outside of large organizations, enabling them to do their own thing. They jump into powerful roles without ever having learned how to work within groups and teams. Since some do find instant success, many entrepreneurs never see the need to learn these group skills that used to be essential.

If freedom from constraint is one aspect of a free agent nation, fear is another. Those climbing to the top outside of established institutions are on their own. They have no one to catch them if they fall. Stakes that high can intensify the need for control, as entrepreneurial leaders try to cope with risk and uncertainty. It's scary for the young film-school grad to fund and produce their first indie, with the pressure to sell distribution rights at film festivals. There's a fear factor for the talented grad athlete from a prominent university to go pro, where they may be permanently sidelined by an injury within a few short years. And it's a risk to go into politics; first, they have to win, all the while knowing that their entire life's history will be combed through by journalists looking for the scoop and that every verbal gaffe is a Twitter moment waiting to happen.

THE INDISPENSABLE INNOVATOR

Another, and related, shift that's taken place in the economy is that creativity has become far more valued. While innovation has always been crucial to business success, sheer brawn played a much bigger role during the industrial era. An "organization man" might be extremely valuable, but systems were designed so that he was replaceable. Wealth was created by mobilizing and managing armies as opposed to leveraging the sheer brilliance or luck of a few individuals. And because the pace of change and innovation was slower, top people didn't need the kind of creative firepower that can turn organizations on a dime.

Now we live in a time where ideas are all-important, where the 140-character update can form the basis of entire new industries or change an election. But the lower entry barriers to creating goods and services means that it's not enough to have just *one* big idea. You need to keep having lots of new ideas to stay ahead of the competition and to avoid being left behind by successive, fast-moving waves of disruption. If you can't innovate your way through disruption in an increasing number of industries, then just leave the keys on the desk, call the investors, and turn out the lights for the last time.

These trends have put more power in the hands of those super-creative individuals who do have brilliant ideas, and a steady stream of them. They have more power for three reasons: first, because ideas are more valuable in a knowledge economy; second, because it's easier than ever for individuals to finance and build companies to monetize ideas or other forms of talent; and third, keeping creative founders around is often crucial to a company's ability to innovate.

In other words, it's not simply that creative people can more easily end up in leadership positions regardless of their maturity or emotional intelligence. It's that it's harder to live without these guys—no matter how loathsome they are. Steve Jobs is the classic example: his genius powered Apple to one success after the other to the point that it was hard to imagine Apple succeeding without him (and in fact he was brought back to reinvigorate the company). That wouldn't have been the case if Jobs had started a company making widgets in 1947.

Common sense suggests that the more indispensable a leader is, the more flexibility he'll have to do as he pleases. In some cases, this can be for the good. Tim Cook's credibility earned from successfully leading

Apple and having the supreme support of his board was no small factor in his coming out as a gay man and working to set an important tone for inclusion across corporate America. On the other hand, Michael Jeffries, the former CEO of Abercrombie & Fitch who had a knack for offending a wide swath of individuals and advocacy organizations, had an enormous amount of autonomy from his board[2] . . . as long as he was delivering the revenue, profit, and constant growth. Only when the money train stopped was he fired. As we'll see later in the book, a big reason mean men are finally ousted from leadership positions where they've abused their power is not because their overseers have suddenly developed compassion for subordinates or concern for brand tarnishing if the rambunctious CEO behaves inappropriately and gets himself considerable negative news. It's because they stop being so indispensable in bringing ideas and strategic savvy to the company. Peter Arnell is a perfect case in point. He finally got derailed not because of years of abusive behavior, and not because some boneheaded ideas cost his clients tens of millions of dollars, but because he had the temerity to publicly insult his clients before the dust cleared. As we will see in later chapters, Dov Charney's demise was not due to any decrease in his ability to innovate or identify an emerging style; he got the boot when his board thought he was just too toxic for some groups of investors and the nature of the lawsuits against him was finally starting to impact the brand. His meanness became an economic issue.

HOW MARKET VALUES BEAT HUMAN VALUES

The increased focus on the bottom line continues to empower successful leaders, at least as long as they keep being successful. The rise of "shareholder capitalism," in which activist investors throw around their money and weight, has produced an obsessive attention on quarterly earnings and profits. Leaders who deliver good results are worshipped, warts and all; those who don't may not last very long. Politicians deliver pork and favors to their largest contributors and stay in office. Athletes keep working if they win another Tour de France or Super Bowl, but when they don't win, they quickly fade from memory.

Much has been said about the consequences of the shift to a leaner, meaner brand of capitalism focused on near-term profits—how it's been bad for workers, how it's reduced investment in long-term research, how it's fostered risk-taking and led to various forms of corporate misconduct, and how it's given rise to the Royal CEO. Closely related is how the bottom-line obsession gives more license to abusive leaders who might not have been tolerated in an earlier era but today are allowed to do whatever they want as long as the stock price keeps going up. The rising value of a company gives stockholders incentives to look the other way when bad behavior prevails. There is also the fear that removing an abusive leader could hurt a company's stock price, regardless of the longer-term value destruction they may be creating.

Of course, it's a whole different story when a mean leader starts to lose money. Suddenly, those previously overlooked sins get greater attention. After Dov Charney was fired by American Apparel's board, many observers concluded that his multiple personal missteps were not the reason, but rather the company's abysmal performance in the years leading up to his removal. "The combination of being a virtual outlaw and losing money is not a combination which you can persist with for long," John C. Coffee Jr., a professor at Columbia Law School told the *New York Times*. "I think your margin for error shrinks once you begin to lose money, and you have all your constituencies concerned about the future. It's realpolitik."[3]

Today's narrow focus on profits isn't the full story, either, in terms of the shift to a meaner form of capitalism. We've also seen a broader triumph of market values over human values, with measurable business outcomes like greater efficiency and productivity pushing aside fuzzier ideals such as empathy for others or loyalty to workers. Modern analytics don't measure being a civil and compassionate human being. But it might not matter if what can't be measured is not highly valued in the first place.

EXTREME INDIVIDUALISM

This country has always worshipped the triumphant individual. Think of the redundant plots of Horatio Alger Jr.'s popular nineteenth-century stories: A fatherless, penniless boy—possessed of great determination, faith, and courage—seeks his fortune. With the world out to get him, tempt him, divert him, or separate him from his small savings, our hero prevails in the end. Alger's stories gave America a righteous ideal: a society in which imagination and solitary strength summoned its just reward. The key virtue was self-reliance. The admirable man was a self-reliant man. Ultimately, it was about being your own boss.

But prior to the 1960s, American individualism seemed to operate within clearer limits than today. Yes, you could make your own way, but it was within the context of being part of society rather than harboring a disregard for it. You were still expected to defer and conform to higher edicts: from the church, the state, and the moral standards of your community. While it's important to note that those standards tended to ignore or withhold the rights of many, there was at least the facade that we had a collective standard of virtue or social responsibility, and for much of the population it was a powerful facade. We've seen a big break from that in the past half century. "Do your own thing" came to have more traction than "Do the right thing," as just about every institution that once pushed Americans to look beyond themselves has seen its influence decline sharply. Religion, with its call to personal restraint and probity, has dwindled significantly in influence. Government is no longer trusted. The population's mobility has created a massive shift in the notion of communities of people living and growing together over decades. Communities no longer have the cohesiveness that once allowed them to impose common standards.

As Robert Putnam cogently argued in his book *Bowling Alone*, the steep drop in social capital and the collective force that guided our behavior has been shifting markedly in our country. Let's be clear: on many accounts this moves us forward. Larger, important questions that simmered on the back burner when the collective wasn't ready to face them have been allowed to heat up in this new environment and demands for social change are less easy to ignore: rights and tolerance for those in the LGBTQ population, police violence against innocent blacks, our assumptions about guns or who gets to vote. The trend toward individual, rather than unified, thought has produced many positive results, allowing a greater range of freedom of expression and true diversity, inclusion, and tolerance. It's easier to be who you are and live as you please, without shaming or bias. But the downside has been less regulation of any number of negative human behaviors, and we've seen the rise of a far more violent, ruder, crasser, greedier, unethical America than our grandparents could have imagined. The media is fragmented, polarized, and ignored—in contrast to the days when Walter Cronkite spoke to the nation with enormous moral authority.

The rise of mean must be understood within the context of that shift. The growing embrace of libertarian ideology is especially worth flagging here. That ideology has offered a robust rationalization for self-interested behavior, which thinkers like Ayn Rand argued was not at odds with being moral—but rather the very foundation of morality.

Not coincidentally, sales of Ayn Rand's novels have been booming in the past decade or two. Conferences sponsored by the Ayn Rand Institute are booming with attendees. And one place where libertarianism is particularly strong is in the tech world, where many young entrepreneurs imagine themselves as masters of their own destinies with few debts or obligations to anyone else. What society may now define as rigid and suffocating had the advantage of providing clear incremental paths by which people grew into positions of power. Libertarianism also thrives in finance, where hedge funds have proliferated as more would-be masters of the universe have left the confines of major firms to strike out on their own.

In short, many of the sectors where entrepreneurial types thrive have greatly expanded in recent decades while also becoming most entranced with an ideology that legitimizes selfish and even rapacious behavior. The habitats for mean men are larger and more plentiful than ever before.

UNGOVERNED ENTREPRENEURS

The case of how, when, and why Dov Charney got dumped is a window into what many think is wrong with the governance of publicly owned corporations in the United States. Neither shareholders nor workers of American Apparel could feel much security in the knowledge that their board was looking out for them.

We have an expectation that boards of directors will stop CEOs from behaving badly. "It's a fantasy," says Nicola Sharpe, a University of Illinois law professor. She firmly believes most people—as well as regulating agencies, governing authorities, and legal scholars—all assume that shareholders and the general public can count on boards to rein in the bad actors. To that, Sharpe and others say, "Highly dubious."[4]

The reality of who actually governs the bad behavior in US businesses points to executive managers, not boards. Corporate governance specialists relentlessly make the point that a CEO's influence, if not complete control, resides in his ability to *select* the board of directors.

CEOs can have enormous control over the information that flows to board members, and they often dictate the actual board meeting agendas. Many critics of corporate governance, Nicola Sharpe among them, see other pervasive mechanisms that limit a board's independent authority. Regardless of who selects a board director (the CEO or the current board), all directors are subject to the CEO's control because they lack the time, knowledge, and information to make truly informed decisions. In the overwhelming majority of cases, they rely exclusively on the CEO to fill their knowledge and information gaps.

A truism around the world is that shareholders are the true principals of the corporation. In theory, directors and officers should "run the corporation in the interests of its shareholders," in this or similar language. But shareholders often get a raw deal from their agents—the directors—because their ownership position is intentionally removed from the day-to-day operations of the enterprise.

One of America's corporate governance problems, mentioned earlier, is the Royal CEO. When a leader is both chairperson of the company's board of directors as well as its chief executive officer, he (or, in minuscule cases, she) can dominate the board and be accountable to no one.

Critics argue that the arrangement creates a potential conflict, because the chairperson is responsible for leading a (supposed) independent board of directors, and the board's primary responsibility is to oversee fiduciary responsibility—to ensure the company is profitable—and to ensure a viable long-term strategy. In service to their goals, they hire, manage, and if necessary, fire the CEO. But if the CEO is also the chairperson of the board? Then the fox is guarding the henhouse. The result is often excessive CEO compensation and undeserved job security, in spite of structural measures taken to establish a sense of independence from the Royal CEO. An entrenched CEO can lead to empire building and a lack of sufficient red-teaming of ideas and strategies. This can extend to a look-the-other-way attitude if the CEO's behavior toward employees is toxic, and ultimately the destruction of shareholder value.

For other mean men, especially those good at not getting caught by the authorities, *we* are the real governing board—we the voters, the consumers, the fans. But what does a mean man have to do to lose *our* support?

"I've never met a better liar. And I've met a bunch." That's how film documentarian Alex Gibney reflected on the effect Lance Armstrong had on him.[5] But Gibney wasn't the only one taken in by Armstrong. For years, an entire nation was in thrall. While there had been skeptics all along, we now know the reality. Increasingly, news of Armstrong's use of performance-enhancing drugs, bullying to intimidate those in his path, and bald-faced lying to counter increasing accusations in the face of fresh evidence ultimately led to the confession Armstrong finally made to Oprah Winfrey. Not only did doping earn Armstrong his record Tour wins, Armstrong ended up being the mastermind of systematic drug-cheating in his sport, and you can't pull that off by being a nice guy.

But Armstrong was more than a strategist for illegal doping. He was more than a bold-faced liar. His meanness ruined innocent peoples' lives. Lance Armstrong called himself a bunch of things during his Oprah moment—"jerk," "humanitarian," and "not the most believable guy in the world." But the word that stuck was "bully." It's probably the most accurate for someone who steamrollered over teammates who wanted to stay clean, destroyed those who told the truth about his doping, and initiated litigation against so many others that—by his own admission—he could not recall their names. But conceding to being a bully is not admitting to an illegal act. Seemingly quite calculated in this confession, he was safe to label himself a "bully," not a defrauder or perjurer. If you're a kid, there may be slightly more penalties now for being marked a bully. But for a grown man like Armstrong, it doesn't come close to capturing the power he abused that resulted in devastated lives. It underrepresents his meanness.

Armstrong admitted to strong-arming the former massage therapist who attempted to out him in 2003, but his confession stopped exactly at the point where his behavior turned from unsavory character trait to legal action. Along the way he also threatened to use his clout to ruin the careers of cycling peers like Greg LeMond who he felt were suspicious of him. By 1999, after achieving a certain level of success, Lance distanced himself from several of the people who made that success possible through their investments. There was his mother whose third marriage was falling apart at the time; John Thomas Neal, an early mentor, who was fighting for his life and undergoing chemo; and John Korioth, his lifelong friend, cycling buddy, and cofounder of the Lance Armstrong Foundation, whom he kicked out of the foundation. After severely fracturing his hip, Floyd Landis returned to the US Postal Service Pro Cycling Team training camp in Solvang, California, to an unsympathetic Armstrong. For Armstrong the squad was a business; Landis would not be able to join the team for the 2003 Tour de France. He was just a cog in Armstrong's master plan—one that could be easily replaced. From horrific marriages and relationships to allegations he abused his foundation's power for personal gain, the list goes on and on.

Yet still Armstrong created a compelling myth—a vision—that not only can you recover from cancer, but you can come back even better than before. It was gripping enough to draw the world in, something Armstrong knew in spades. For him, the lie was a lucrative means to satisfying his entrepreneurial spirit. People bought bikes, clothes, and sunglasses because of the story. Companies made fortunes on his name. In the United States particularly, Lance's story was bigger than the sport itself. But in buying into the lies for decades, what did we, the American public, get out of it? Is it really accurate to say we were totally hoodwinked? Or did we prefer the lie?

Back in 2013, I asked my niece, a world-class triathlete, what she thought of the stories coming out about Armstrong and of the credible people stepping forward with evidence about the "real" Lance. She, like millions of others, had fully bought into his narrative. Leading up to this, I rarely saw her with fewer than two LIVESTRONG Foundation yellow rubber bracelets on her wrists. "I'm nauseous," she would tell me. "I just get sick thinking about it." Her suffering was the physical manifestation of cognitive dissonance. She just could not reconcile his extraordinary athletic accomplishments and the compelling old narrative with the truth, and she felt physically sick every time she tried to reframe the story in her head and put it all back together.

"He's very like Julian Assange," Gibney says. "Both are afflicted with this thing I'm obsessed by: noble-cause corruption. For a long time I used to perceive it as ironic if good people do bad things. Actually, I'm now convinced we're hard-wired for moral mediocrity. The more you see someone with a grand cause the more you can almost expect there'll be something about them at the other end of the spectrum."[6]

I'd hate to think that Gibney is correct, but what piece of Gibney's shared cynicism and our own belief that we're each more virtuous than we truly are plays into our role in propagating the culture of mean? We assume the outrageous politician will be tamed by a need to get reelected. That we can control the professional athletes by withholding ad buys and jersey sales. Mean men in the entertainment industry? They won't get *our* dollars. But in reality, does it work that way?

Conventional wisdom says that bad behavior will earn a politician a ticket home. Yet Michael Grimm threatens assault and gets reelected, and that's not really surprising. As with sitting CEOs, it takes a lot for an incumbent to get tossed out. In 2014, over 95 percent of representatives and senators in the US Congress running to keep their jobs did so, sent back by an American public that simultaneously gave them a 14 percent approval rating.[7] Six months before the election, Gallup reported only 22 percent of Americans thought the incumbents deserved reelection, an all-time low.[8] To many people, the fact that Trump won the 2016 election given his outrageous "meanness" was stunning. But isn't there a pattern in our ability to forgive and forget? Dov Charney is experiencing a resurrection in the business world, from disgraced CEO of American Apparel to promising new CEO of a made-in-LA line of T-shirts. In episodes of the Gimlet podcast series *StartUp* that focused on Charney, interviewee after interviewee dismissed his previous behavior, or said they were convinced he'd act better this time.[9] When asked if his behavior would change this time around, Charney himself told *Business Insider* this: "I'm sticking to my first principles. . . . I don't believe my behavior was bad. I don't think I was a bad person. I'm passionate."[10] For each of us, it's worth asking, what is our individual role in propping up the mean men in our society and an American culture of mean in general? Are we all loathe to give up our stake—in the politician we think is terrible but who fights for our share, in the athlete on whom we pinned hopes and a tantalizing comeback narrative—or have we come to believe that moral mediocrity is the best we can hope for?

WHEN MEAN IS NORMAL

Most of us shape our behavior by responding to cues in both our immediate environment and the broader culture. If you live in New York City, where people can be pretty pushy, there's a good chance you'll become assertive. If you live in a small Midwestern town where strangers greet one another on the street, you'll start to say hello. If you see lots of gay people on TV and in the marriage announcements of the newspaper, you're less likely to be homophobic.

Likewise, if it seems that mean is okay, you'll be more likely to be mean, especially if that predilection was already simmering below the surface. And what's happened in recent decades is many Americans have perceived society to be a ruder, meaner place, where maybe all we need are sharper elbows to take care of ourselves.

Any number of polls in recent years have found that Americans think authentic leadership is in decline. And Americans see the workplace in particular as a ruder, more competitive place. A 2011 survey found that 38 percent of respondents felt that the workplace was becoming ruder, with 65 percent of these people blaming top leadership at their office for setting this tone.[11] Other polls have found that Americans have grown less likely to like their jobs or see their employer as trustworthy and loyal to them.

Of course, one needn't go into the office to witness America's cultural descent; it can be seen on television every night on reality TV shows, which often feature backstabbing, conniving contestants. Change the channel and you'll find celebrity chef Gordon Ramsay reaming out nervous wannabes, or Real Housewives engaged in catfights, or the panel of investors on *Shark Tank* ridiculing silly start-up ideas, and so on.

We watch on these and other shows a level of public brutality that would have been unthinkable during the days of Norman Lear's merely sarcastic sitcoms. Even (the late) Tony Soprano, a TV character who will never be a candidate for canonization, contextualized his meanness, and he was psychologically troubled by it.

And then there is also the cheating and lax ethics of America today, as evidenced by an endless stream of scandals involving nearly every sector of US society: business, education, sports, law, medicine, and religion. Amid these news stories it's no wonder that a 2012 survey of high school students found that 57 percent agreed that "in the real world, successful people do what they have to do to win, even if others consider it cheating."[12]

A crasser, ruder, and less honest society brings everyone down. Nobody wants to be the nice guy in a shark pool. Nobody wants to be the chump who dots every "i" and crosses every "t" when other people are cheating like crazy. Mean men can, and do, point to the harsh world around them as an excuse for their actions. In turn, their meanness makes things even harsher in a self-reinforcing cycle. *Mean begets mean.*

But we've been on this path for a while now. The late professor and prominent psychiatrist Harold Greenwald was among the first to observe the behaviors related to psychopathy increasing in society overall. Both he and Nathan Ackerman—another psychiatrist and pioneer of family therapy—saw psychopathy as "a social disease that is contagious and virulent."[13] Even in the early sixties, Greenwald saw that "one of the growing problems today is that our entire milieu is becoming one in which psychopathy is the norm." He went on to say, "Sometimes it seems to me that we may be witnessing the birth of a new morality."[14]

Writing to other psychiatrists, Greenwald forewarned: "One important factor in treatment is the problem of countertransference—our own feelings about the psychopath." At a conference, a frank psychiatrist confided to Greenwald: "You know, if I were going to go crazy, and if I could choose the way I would go crazy, I would prefer to be a psychopath."[15] Similarly, those in professions such as psychology, psychiatry, and social work whom Greenwald had seen for training analysis have asked if he could help them become psychopaths. One such trainee recently said in a first interview, "What I would like is to be able to do whatever I choose and not feel bad about it. The hell with everybody else; just get mine— that's what I would like to do." Greenwald later commented, "I believe some aspect of psychopathy is in all of us, because this kind of behavior sounds quite attractive to most of us."[16] We see it in the forgiveness of wealthy corporations or well-positioned politicians who commit illegal or immoral acts, in the concurrent backlash against "political correctness," and in the nasty comments made by trolls on the Web.

All this is crucial context as we move forward to explore mean men in greater depth, looking at who they are, why they rise, and why they are allowed to get away with their behavior—or just get richer, rise in the polls, gather another twenty thousand fans on Twitter. Mean men don't operate in a vacuum. They operate in an economy that has empowered entrepreneurial individuals, in a business sector that values profit above all else, and a culture that has normalized mean.

CHAPTER SIX

CONTROL FREAKS

THE NEED TO ACHIEVE MAY be a dominant trait of entrepreneurs, but that need seldom operates alone. It goes hand in hand with other traits from the List of Ten, such as the desire for autonomy. In particular, the need to achieve is often coupled with a desire for control.

Not everyone who wants to be a high achiever is also a power monger. On the one hand, we have guys like Lance Armstrong, who early on in his Tour de France career bristled at the notion gaining traction in the sports media that legend Greg LeMond was "passing the torch" to him. "I'm not the next Greg LeMond," he would come to say during interviews. "I'm the first Lance Armstrong." The type of team member who felt he was the only one who counted, who didn't want to have to share his wins, and who even usurped control of the 2009 Tour de France team from the designated leader, Alberto Contador.

Among entrepreneurs, power—and the control that comes with it—is often seen as vital to great achievement. Great products and businesses can't be built alone, so working with others is unavoidable. But if an entrepreneurial leader has enough power, he can impose his vision without interference.

The need for power and control is very much a dual-edged sword. Like sports teams, companies require collaboration, too. Many start-ups fail because entrepreneurs simply can't get along with their cofounders, making all the compromises that shared management entails. And the need for power and control can underlie some very mean behavior, which we'll get to in a minute.

But first we need to acknowledge that the thirst for power can often be very constructive and is even a prerequisite for effective leadership. In a foundational article in *Harvard Business Review*, David McClelland and David Burnham reported on research they'd conducted on the need for power, achievement, and affiliation (a desire to be liked). They found that a majority of good managers had a high need for power, and the converse was true: poor managers weren't really that ambitious at all. In fact, effective managers had a higher need for power than a need to be liked.[1] That all makes sense, given that managing others can be stressful and exhausting, and if you don't really want the job, you won't be good at it. Likewise, if you go too easy on people because you want them to like you, that can spell trouble, too.

It's a fine line, though, between a need for power that leads to effective leadership, and a power-hungry obsession that leads to destructive aggrandizement—a line that McClelland and Burnham noted in research that's still relevant forty years later. They concluded that top corporate managers must possess a high need for power—that is, a concern for *influencing* people. But this need should be directed toward group benefit (making the company do and look better), not self-promotion. Moreover, the top manager's need for power ought to be greater than his or her need to be liked. Wielding power requires "emotional maturity" and the need for it must be "socialized" and tempered.

At times, we'll find an otherwise healthy control freak who ultimately finds the imperative to back off on that need. Take Bill Gates. His early years were marked by imperious, rude, and thoroughly controlling behavior both in meetings and in interpersonal exchanges. He didn't "get" the need to be more of a leader that others wanted to follow, particularly as the CEO of a firm in an industry that was both nascent and undergoing constant disruption. I was discussing mean men with the senior editor of a leading business magazine who agreed with my observations about Gates. But her first follow-up question spoke to me of influence I hadn't considered: "Have you spoken to Melinda Gates?" Since Melinda isn't in my social circle, I just looked at her, a bit dumbfounded. "Bill was pretty mean when he met Melinda," she opined, "but I believe she is the force who tempered him and got him to reflect on the impact of his behavior. She saw there was—and could be—another side to him that could be developed, one that would benefit him. His evolution clearly helped the two of them. It clearly helped Microsoft before he left." And it could be that this tempering of his behavior helps the Gates Foundation to this day.

So what does this tell us about Gates? Though by all accounts he exhibited unappealing tendencies in his early years, unlike many of the subclinical psychopaths we've talked about, he was capable of change. Perhaps he needed wisdom and maturity (and a good influence) to help control himself rather than focusing his need for control on others. It would certainly explain his later turn to philanthropy and a somewhat gentler reputation in the media, at the foundation, and at Microsoft, one perhaps more doggedly intellectual than mean. Even the once-infamous "BillG reviews," where high-level employees would present new ideas, research, or product development strategy, are back at Microsoft, and while still littered with f-bombs, are also generally considered more Socratic in nature, meant to push and ask the hard questions rather than to humiliate. In a *New York Times* article on Gates's return to the company as a product and technology adviser to CEO Satya Nadella, a former Microsoft researcher thought Gates had gained perspective in his time away, looking at the world through a different lens: "I expect that any tunnel vision that he may have had prior to leaving full-time status is now completely replaced with a new appreciation for how others view the world and what is really important to them."[2] However, earlier I said that it was likely that true mean men who operate in the red zone probably will always demonstrate this behavior. It got Pincus in trouble. Had he gained perspective when he reassumed his position? Control is a legitimate and serious yearning for entrepreneurs who must raise money for their companies, because they often end up sharing power with venture capitalists who may have their own agenda and vision. Mature entrepreneurs can often handle these relationships, and the tension inherent in their strong need for control, with finesse. Less mature founders can become paranoid.

Between August and September 2012, six high-level executives left Zynga, including its chief operating officer, its chief creative officers, its VP of marketing, and its top technologist.[3] In June 2013, Zynga laid off over five hundred employees, a reported one-fifth of its workforce, and shuttered its New York and LA offices. A month later, Pincus finally relinquished the CEO post, becoming the chairman and chief products officer, only to return a couple of years later.

Many wondered, could Pincus pull a Gates? Had he matured to the point where he could reflect on his past behaviors and the consequences they wrought? Did he trust a few close people enough to listen to alternative ways of leading? While the jury was out, the press reported the abrupt departure of Zynga's CFO. Current and former employees posted blistering reviews on Glassdoor about Zynga leadership. Wall Street remained dumbfounded by his return. Finally, with the promised economic turnaround nowhere in sight, Pincus was replaced yet again as chief executive in early 2016.

CONTROL GONE BAD

The best leaders are those who are able to trust in their teams and cede power to others. That skill is especially important in any kind of large, complicated venture. A pop star may be able to get away with being a control freak, micromanaging his small empire; not so for an entrepreneur who finds himself running a company with hundreds or thousands of employees or for other types of entrepreneurial leaders, like a politician who must find his way in Congress or an athlete on a pro sports team.

Consider Seattle Seahawks quarterback Russell Wilson, a humble member of the already elite group of NFL quarterbacks who signed one of the most lucrative contracts of the league in 2015 and ended that regular season with the highest quarterback ranking in the NFL. Taking time each week to visit pediatric cancer patients, the young man beat the favored Broncos handily in the Super Bowl just one year after he entered the pros. The next year, after a late play-off win over the Packers that would send his team back to the Super Bowl (to an infamous defeat), Wilson gave a famously tearful postgame interview in which he praised God and his team, in that order. Though he's the one charged with calling the plays and he has plenty of drive, ambition, and confidence, he also has trust in others to play their positions while he plays his.

Sports fans know that in that play-off game in 2014, Wilson was faltering. In fact, everyone including Wilson knew that if the rest of the team hadn't carried the offense until he got his mojo back in the final minutes,

Green Bay would have gone to the Super Bowl instead. Hobbled by a slew of injuries in the 2016 season, Wilson never missed a practice or a game, once again counting on his team to get the wins. There are a number of talented performers or athletes with strong abilities and plenty of drive but no need to control every aspect of the game. They know that with the support of the team, they are stronger. These are the CEOs who solicit ideas from every level. The politicians willing to cross the aisle so long as the legislation makes it through.

The paradox of entrepreneurs, one that can be fatal for new ventures, is that they have the vision and drive to build something new, but their same core personality traits make it difficult for them to ever let go. Sometimes investors are only able to pry an entrepreneur's hands off the steering wheel after they've already driven their venture into a ditch. According to Noam Wasserman's book, *The Founder's Dilemmas*, a full four out of five founders who step down as CEO do so because they are pushed out forcibly by investors.[4] In that sense, Mark Pincus's exit from Zynga was quite typical. And like many entrepreneurs, he went kicking and screaming.

In his classic research on the need for power, McClelland outlined traits that perfectly describe Pincus and are in sync with the List of Ten. Those with a high need for power bristle at the thought of being controlled by others and are most satisfied when they are the ones in control, setting the direction. These individuals, said McClelland, tend to be highly argumentative and assertive in group settings. They don't suffer fools gladly and are quick to think fools of others. They are risk-takers, because big risks can lead to big rewards—and more power. And, said McClelland, they are more likely to pile up bling and show off their wealth. (Pincus bought an $8 million house in 2009 and then traded it in a few years later for a $16 million mansion in Pacific Heights even as Zynga's stock was cratering.)[5]

The need for control is closely tied to another key characteristic of entrepreneurs found on the List of Ten: self-confidence. The linkage here is obvious enough. If you think you're the smartest guy in the room, as many entrepreneurs do, it can seem to follow that you'll have the best ideas and make the best decisions on matters both large and small. Better if you call the shots, in your infinite wisdom, than leave things to underlings who may produce a mediocre result. Recall Pincus's reported comment to a subordinate: "When you come to the conversation understanding that I'm always right you'll have a better outcome." Or President-Elect Trump's given rationale on why he eschews intelligence briefings as expressed to Chris Wallace in a FOX News interview: "I'm, like, a smart person. . . . I don't need to be told, Chris, the same thing every day, every morning."[6]

Self-confidence is a necessary trait for an entrepreneur, given the steep odds that a venture will fail. While ordinary people tend to think that they'll lose if the odds are stacked against them, highly self-confident people can convince themselves that they'll always be part of the 1 percent, not lost in the statistic mass of losers. With some research showing that less than one in five first-time entrepreneurs will succeed, this brash belief in oneself is a prerequisite for anyone starting a new venture.[7]

But self-confidence can easily go too far and become hubris. A number of researchers have documented the prevalence of hubristic thinking among entrepreneurs, showing how and why they suffer from a dangerous level of overconfidence. All this, the data suggest, is a recipe for "venture failure."[8] The very same self-confidence that enables founders to move forward at the start may doom them in the end.

Because the need for control is such an intrinsic part of the entrepreneurial personality, it can trump other important goals—even the need to achieve. Some entrepreneurs would prefer a smaller, less profitable venture that is the perfect embodiment of their vision, and which they fully control, over a larger enterprise where they ceded power to others. This is not an imagined trade-off: Noam Wasserman's research found that 52 percent of founding CEOs were gone by the time their companies were big enough to raise a third round of investment funds.[9] Given the choice of staying and minimizing the firm's growth prospects or leaving to cede control to a more skilled and experienced executive, a great many founders will go for being "king." The desire for control and autonomy is more important to them at a deep psychological level than a thirst for wealth or seeing their initial vision come into closer view.

My research into "founder's dilemma," the illogical dynamics of nonprofit founders often doing whatever it takes to stay in control of the organizations they created after they have formally "retired," is a glaring case in point. Rather than hand the reins over to a successor (in theory) chosen and approved by the board, they will put themselves on the board, write themselves long-term consulting contracts, move sideways to a newly created position, or cling to control in even more creative ways, like staying in the corner office and relegating the new CEO to a smaller, less well-appointed space down the hall.

The founder of a nonprofit that became the leading social services organization in a southeastern US city wanted to avoid founder's dilemma but could not find ways to let go and to give his successor free rein. After discussing the highly probable consequences of his lingering desire to keep his hands in it after relinquishing the executive director title, he still decided to appoint himself as a paid one-year "coach" for his replacement and strategic consultant to the board. Though strongly advised against this, and encouraged to seek board positions at other organizations to align himself to similar causes where he could give his successor complete breathing room from the founder, he demurred. He just could not walk away.

His reaction is not uncommon. Often founders will find creative and symbolic ways to assure that the new CEO feels like Medvedev to their Putin. And when the new CEO finally begins to tinker with the nonprofit's vision or cultivates new donors, the founder may put his metaphorical foot out just enough to sabotage his successor's success. In many cases from my research, the successor eventually leaves out of frustration.

Still other mean men are ready to leave their place at the top, but not unless their successor shares precisely their vision, ideas, or politics. A man who's built an entire career on the narrative of control, former New York mayor Rudolph W. Giuliani, compares himself to a boxer who never takes an unanswered punch.[10] Giuliani was a street-fighting mayor in a city known for political brawling. But more than any politician, historians, journalists, and his predecessors say, his toughness resembled ruthlessness. Anger and meanness became defining aspects of his mayoralty (and were solidified as his brand when he became one of Trump's key surrogates). While no one could say definitively that this accounted for the fact that he never made it into the senatorial and presidential primaries, two offices he publicly aspired to, it sure didn't help.

As the command-and-control mayor, he took on companies, council members, and comptrollers alike. Yet his storyboard of these events never seemed to square with reality: "It wasn't my sensitivities I was worried about, but the tone of civility I strived to establish throughout the city," he would write in his book *Leadership*.[11]

In 1999, he explored a run for the US Senate. But to get that seat, he found, he would have to vacate his office early. By city charter, the public advocate would take his place should he leave, a condition the mayor was unable to accept. At the time, the public advocate's position was held by liberal politician Mark Green, a man referred to by Giuliani as both "idiotic" and "inane."[12]

What to do? Change the rules, of course—and Giuliani formed a Charter Revision Commission to do just that. But Giuliani's intent seemed not to be on righting a wrong he felt would affect other would-be candidates who deserved to hold office if they sought a higher post. Instead, it was control of who sat in the mayor's seat that Giuliani sought to retain. If not him, then certainly not Green. If not for Green, he confessed to the *New York Times Magazine*, he might not have picked this particular fight. His reasoning did not sit well with his predecessors, with Ed Koch lobbing the first cannonball. "You ought to be ashamed of yourself, Mr. Mayor," he publicly announced.[13] That wasn't enough to dissuade Giuliani, and nor was the advice given him by Frederick A. O. Schwarz Jr., former chairman of a previous Charter Revision Commission, that "targeting a particular person" would "smack of personal politics and predilections." Once again, the mayor was rebuked: "All this is not worthy of you, or our city," the widely respected Schwarz wrote.[14]

In all, did Giuliani's mean-man style garner the support and respect he needed to leverage his entrepreneurial flair for positions with greater power? Did his tight grip on control and his need for power get him what he wanted? Consider this: according to CNN, during his 2008 run for president, Giuliani "lost every caucus and primary he entered before dropping out with a grand total of only one delegate, a modern record for electoral futility."[15] In early 2015, Giuliani was roundly criticized for offering this observation of the sitting commander in chief: "I do not believe that the president loves America," Giuliani said at a private political dinner. "He doesn't love you. And he doesn't love me."[16] Perhaps it's more accurate to say in the end, America didn't love his brand of mean.

As chapter 10 of this book illustrates, controlling entrepreneurs and leaders who do hold on successfully to power pose profound risks to their organizations, not to mention the emotional health of the people around them. The risks can play out dramatically as an entrenched but incompetent CEO crashes and burns a company while tormenting his employees. Or the damage can unfold over a longer period, as a founder holds his company back from staying competitive and slowly drives it into the ground, inflicting emotional pain on others literally over decades. In the annals of history, the saga of Henry Ford is a great example of a founder, and mean man, ahead of his time, who did grave damage to his company and the people in it, including his son Edsel, in slow-motion fashion.

"AS LONG AS IT'S BLACK"

Henry Ford was a classic entrepreneur of a certain kind: he was a born tinkerer who loved to make things. Ford grew up on a farm, but the repetitive grind of farming under his father's control was not for him. A bright and innovative boy, Ford was considered a "queer duck" because of how he locked himself away in the barn with his projects. He was fired from his first real job after six days because he proved too clever about solving a problem that a number of other employees were working on all day.

Ford liked to do things his own way, and he clashed so much with the investors in the first company he started that he resigned. He became determined that he would one day have total control over his next car company. And no sooner had he found new investors and begun building Ford Motor, in the early 1900s, than he started shouting matches with his main investor. Ford soon bought him out, giving himself the control he wanted.

It would be a recurrent theme: Ford was driven by the need to achieve in the automobile industry, but in order to grow and manage one of America's first major companies, he would need the help of others—investors, partners, top executives, and his sons. But he never liked ceding any real control to others, and that would prove devastating for a company that could have dominated car manufacturing, but didn't.

Ford's fixation with control played out in various negative ways. For starters, he didn't take well to challenges to his very personal vision of what an automobile should be. The affordable black Model T, of course, was the iconic bestselling car that turned Ford Motor into a big company and opened car ownership to the American masses.

But Ford was irrationally possessive about the Model T and hostile to the mere mention of changes or improvements to the car. Once, when Ford returned from a trip to Europe, a top company executive and other Ford employees decided to surprise Henry with a new, streamlined version of the Model T. Upon hearing of this, Ford immediately headed for the Highland Park plant to see the new car.

When he saw the car at the plant, Ford asked a few innocuous questions like "How long has it been standing there?" Then he opened the driver's side door and ripped it off its hinges. He did the same to the passenger side door. Then he jumped on the hood and kicked in the windshield and, finally, jumped on the car's roof, stomping it down.[17] One employee who witnessed this outburst later said, "We got the message. As far as he was concerned, the Model T was God and we were to put away false images."[18]

But companies can't just freeze their top products in a block of ice, and by the mid-1920s, Ford was being crushed by competitors who were building snazzier and more up-to-date cars. It took years for his son Edsel to convince him to build the more modern, streamlined Model A. By then, though, Ford Motor had already lost its chance to dominate US car manufacturing.

Getting the Model A green-lighted by his father was one of the few victories that Edsel achieved at the company, even as he ascended to be its president. In practice, Henry never relinquished control, and while Edsel had big ideas for bringing Ford in line with the times, his impotence was well known. Once, for example, Edsel fired a top company executive who was hurting morale by bullying managers and workers alike. Henry quickly reinstated him. Ford Motor became the kind of company that talented auto executives and engineers left, further strengthening Ford's competition.

By the 1930s, as labor disputes flared, the plants at Ford Motor became akin to a police state, with workers under constant surveillance. Henry capitalized on threats by labor agitators to tighten his day-to-day grip on the company, even as Edsel nominally ran things, and he empowered thuggish lieutenants to do his bidding. Ford himself was known in the early days to walk around his plants and whack workers on the back who were chewing tobacco, which he disapproved of, so they would be forced to swallow their chew. And let's not forget Ford's Sociological Department and his enforcers of his "Rules for Living," a nearly Orwellian example of company control.

Even as Henry Ford tried to make his employees live by his rules, he maneuvered to ensure that no one—no investors, no board members, no high-level executives—could influence his choices. Eventually, he managed to push out all his investors through a series of battles, including legal challenges, that eventually give him total control of his company—more than any other major industrialist of the time. But Ford spent over $165 million to buy out those shareholders and live the entrepreneur's fantasy of full autonomy, money that could have been better spent investing in new products.

When competitors went public and used their new cash to bolster operations, Ford Motor remained private. Henry Ford, an anti-Semite, said he didn't want Jewish speculators to get their hands on his company, but the desire for control was surely the bigger reason for his resistance to going public. "Not over my dead body," he said. And, indeed, Ford Motor didn't go public until 1956, nine years after Ford's death and four decades after most of Ford's competitors had offered stock to the public.

Henry Ford's complete dominance of Ford Motor meant there were even fewer checks on his behavior that grew meaner, more controlling, and more self-aggrandizing as the years passed. Among other things, Ford insisted that he get credit for any technological or industrial advance that happened at the company. Regardless of who made the discoveries, only Ford's name was to appear on press releases. Which, of course, was the exact opposite of what smart leaders do when they intentionally build up the talented people who work for them.

Ford also moved to get rid of top executives who were not subservient enough to him, including William Knudsen, who had set up fourteen branch factories and was often considered one of the most talented and impressive executives at the company. Upon Knudsen's termination, Henry Ford said, "I let him go not because he wasn't good, but because he was too good for me."[19] Knudsen was hired by GM and built Chevrolet, which would soon become Ford's number one rival in the industry.

The Knudsen story underscores a key peril of letting controlling entrepreneurs dominate their firms. When these men drive away top talent (as Ford did), or create a climate that repels such talent to begin with (as Pincus did), they not only weaken their companies, they strengthen their competitors. In business, you don't only want the best people working for you; you *don't* want them working for the other guy, or worse, becoming a competitor themselves.

Henry Ford got more eccentric and difficult as he grew older. His persona gradually shifted from that of the great American entrepreneur to something of a crank. In the end, though, Ford would live longer than his son Edsel, who died an early death from stomach cancer after years of ulcers. Many believed it was his controlling father who drove him to the grave.

Henry Ford stands as a unique figure in American business history, known for his outsized flaws and extreme behavior. Yet so many of his actions fit a pattern we see with mean men born a century later and running companies in the here and now: the quest for total financial control of their companies, the desire to dominate product design, a difficulty working with executives who are true partners, the compulsions to manipulate others, the need to claim credit, the avoidance of taking personal responsibility when things go wrong because of their decisions, and the lack of desire to contain outbursts of rage.

The consequences of Ford's controlling, abusive personality are also familiar: Ford undermined his company's growth just as Mark Pincus hurt Zynga and Dov Charney brought big troubles to American Apparel. None of these companies would have existed or grown so large without the entrepreneurial drive of their founders. But all would stumble badly thanks to the dark side of the men who built them.

Henry Ford occupied the executive suite well before the rise of organizational psychology and management theory. But research over subsequent decades would confirm what is common sense: a controlling, abusive leadership style isn't deeply hurtful to people only. Mean men are also bad for the bottom line. A desperate need for control prevents collaboration and delegation, stifles creativity, and drives away the talented stars companies should want to hold on to.

Encouraging employees to be creative and conjure new ideas is hugely important for the success of companies, especially ones that make consumer products. It was important for car companies in the 1920s, amid fierce competition and fast-changing public tastes; it's even more important today. But creativity also matters for just about any organization, since finding new and better ways to do things improves efficiency and saves money, while developing new projects can open up promising avenues for expansion. But controlling leaders can squelch creativity throughout their organizations in ways that they may not even understand.

Researchers call it the "cascading effect" of abusive supervision. Employees are more likely to be creative when they have a high level of "intrinsic motivation," which is to say that they get rewards from what they're doing quite apart from their salary or a bonus. If you're really into your job, you're more apt to go the extra mile and think about ways to do it better and improve how well your organization performs. Great coaches use intrinsic motivation to coax the best performance out of their players. The most gifted politicians influence us by appealing to a sense of service or the betterment of country. If you're intrinsically motivated, you'll think about ways to challenge the status quo with novel ideas or approaches. In contrast, if you're only there for the extrinsic motivation of a paycheck and don't much like what you do, you're not going to go that extra mile. You're not going to turn over challenges at work while taking a jog in the morning and come to the office with an exciting idea for a breakthrough. You won't try to reach agreement on the budget package. You'll slump on the sidelines when the game's going south. Why try to improve a workplace you're not invested in?

The connection to mean comes because abusive supervision undermines employees' intrinsic motivation. If you're criticized at meetings, if your supervisor yells at you, if they claim credit for your accomplishments, or if they demean what you contribute, then—no surprise here—you're not going to enjoy your work as much. You're going to wonder whether you're really valued at your job. And you're going to feel a lower level of intrinsic motivation. You may keep the job for various reasons, but you're not going to go the extra mile. You're not going to think up some clever way to save the organization money or improve one of its products or services.

In fact, you may have a hard time even dragging yourself to work in the morning. Abused employees often become depressed, anxious, and emotionally exhausted. They end up just trying to survive and are alienated from their job—the very antithesis of the creative worker.

And it all starts at the top. People in organizations carefully observe the leaders and tend to model their behavior accordingly. If the person at the top is mean, that tends to flow downward—what researchers call a "trickle-down effect of abusive supervision across organizational hierarchy." If you find yourself yelled at and bullied and micromanaged, you're more likely to treat those below you in a similar fashion. On a larger scale, this trickle-down effect is at the heart of our culture of mean.

Several years ago, a senior strategist for a major consulting firm based in New York, one still led by its original founder, was seeking an executive coach. The strategist was apparently making rude outbursts to employees and voicing comments that were biting, hurtful, and sarcastic.

According to his direct reports, all of whom were interviewed, he had changed over the six months since he started at the consultancy. The wit and collegial banter slowly melted into meanness, and the meanness was increasing. As the meetings with his executive coach progressed over the first two months, the client looked up at the ceiling, eyebrows lifted as though he had an epiphany. "I guess shit really does roll downhill." "What do you mean?" his coach asked. He then described the firm's founder/CEO, a very mean man.

The "shit" doled out by the founder was, apparently, rolling down the organizational chain. The coach spoke to his client's wife, and she, too, was experiencing a profound change in her husband's temperament when he would arrive home after work. "He's angrier. He loses his patience more easily. He's becoming less of the smart, witty, easygoing guy I fell in love with." Mean men don't just crimp the creativity of those who report to them directly. They can inflict damage deep in the ranks of their organizations as executives model their behavior and spread terror downward, undermining the intrinsic motivation and creativity of a wide swath of people.

Research also confirms what Henry Ford learned the hard way: if your top people quit in a huff, they can do a lot of damage to your company. And that's not just because they go to work for a competitor, but also that they work with a special motivation—*revenge.*

A study in the journal *Human Resources Management* found that disgruntled employees performed better with their new employer, shared inside strategy from their prior employer who mistreated them, and worked harder to earn loyalty. The study mirrored what earlier studies learned about former professional athletes who leave a team disgruntled and join a new pro team: Athletes feel anger and pressure to prove loyalty to their new team organizations. They share knowledge of the former team's routines (which leads to superior performance against the former team).[20]

Heap on the abuse and you will incentivize exceptional performance—of your former employee for their new rival organization against *you.* Whether on sports teams or in more traditional work organizations, workers want to exact revenge for how they were treated. Regardless of the mean man in question, some things never change: When leaders are obsessed with control, they don't get the best from people. Oftentimes, they lose them altogether, with predictable results.

CHAPTER SEVEN

WHY WE TOLERATE THEM

THE BRILLIANT NOBEL WINNER JAMES Watson, one of the scientists who discovered the helical structure of DNA, held virtually all of his colleagues in disdain. Watson was convinced that the field of biological research "was infested by stamp collectors who lacked the wit to transform their subject into a modern science." At faculty meetings he radiated contempt. He shunned ordinary courtesy in favor of casual and brutal offhandedness.

Still, few called Watson out for his abusive behavior. And his students, many of whom would achieve their own prominence in biology, found his approach worked. As one put it, Watson "always introduced the right mixture of fear and paranoia so that we worked our asses off."[1]

Mean men set impossible standards and trample on people's feelings. Even when others meet those standards, they're given little credit. Yet, despite all their drawbacks, mean men are often magnets, not only for competent people but even at times for the best and brightest.

Why is that? Why are people drawn to and stick with them even as things get ugly?

The reasons people stay with mean men can defy logic, but the rate at which psychopathic entrepreneurs hold on to some people, in spite of the abuse they experience, is higher than one might expect. These people do not stay for the simple reason that they need the job. Some become so deeply invested in a company or organization that they simply don't want to leave, no matter how miserable they are. But other factors are usually in play: the very same leaders who can be controlling and abusive can also be very compelling figures. Mean men can be magnetic in the short run; for the longer haul, these men create subtle yet powerful ties that bind.

Much has been made of the charisma often associated with successful entrepreneurs, and much of this fuss is legitimate. Men with grandiose narcissistic personality traits often have a magnetic draw to go along with it. Their charisma enables them to assemble a group of followers who will embrace and march in unison to an appealing organizational vision, and keep marching even when things get ugly. Mean men on the psychopathic spectrum are invariably perceived as charismatic, since their complicated mixture of narcissism supports the kind of "big thinking" that makes it easier to conjure attractive visions.

Political intelligence is the way Stanford Business School professor Roderick Kramer explains how organizational bullies get what they want from people without the consequences one would expect—turnover or low motivation.[2] Typical organizational bullies, says Kramer, are consumed with humiliating others as a way to make themselves feel good. While mean men are not above bullying to get their way, Kramer claims the entrepreneur's savvy ability to communicate a compelling vision is his superpower.

Mean men with political intelligence still chafe at impediments, particularly those that are human. They are sure of themselves to a fault. And, as we have seen, they have a disdain for constraints imposed on them by others. They want control, and they default to "hard power" to get it. But the way they evocatively spin their version of the vision is something to behold.

THE HARD POWER OF CHARISMA

When leaders conceptualize a compelling vision, and then communicate it in a way that helps the listener identify closely with it, those listening are drawn not only to the vision but also to the person they assumed created it. It can be intoxicating on the receiving end. Vision-talented individuals don't have to be CEOs or Speaker of the House; the attraction often has little to do with organizational rank. It is an individual's ability to concoct stories and effectively communicate them that helps make them charismatic. Some of these visions are fabricated rhetorical bullshit; the mean man has no emotional commitment to actually work toward it. Or he may have stolen much of it from someone else. No matter. If the recipients are enraptured by the content and enthralled by the presentation, some will stay, thinking they are part of the next great thing.

Charismatics are able to create emotional reactions in others using more than just words. Using rhetorical style and expressive nonverbal communications, they enable you to visualize what they see; they can evoke your dreams or play on your darkest fears. Charismatics tend to be facile with language, making effective use of allegory, analogy, metaphor, and symbols to win people over. Nonverbally, they make sure to dress the part, maintain direct eye contact, stay conscious of their voice modulation, and even are mindful of how their bodies convey their emotions and intent.[3]

As a case in point, Steve Jobs was famous for his penetrating, unblinking stare. He would gaze into another person's eyes, ask them a question, and hold the stare while waiting for an answer. This wasn't an unconscious tic. No, Jobs *trained* himself to be able to stare without blinking for long periods. According to his biographer, Walter Isaacson, Jobs saw his intensity as an instrument of persuasion. And it worked. An early Apple employee said that Jobs reminded him "of Rasputin. He laser-beamed in on you and didn't blink. It didn't matter if he was serving purple Kool-Aid. You drank it."[4]

Beneath the tough exteriors and sharp edges are subtle insights into human motivation and organizational behavior. Psychologist Howard Gardner suggested the term "social intelligence" to explain how some leaders become adept at getting others to follow them; in the process, they extract a high level of sustained performance. Gardner defined social intelligence in terms of a leader's interpersonal skills, including an empathic understanding of another's emotional state and needs, and the ability to influence others on the basis of that understanding.[5] A number of contemporary researchers focusing on psychopathy have found that, while the psychopath may not be consciously attuned to his own feelings, he can "read" the affect of others with alarming accuracy. But his motive for this is not to become empathic or sympathetic. It's to *use* empathy and sympathy to get what he wants.

These are not leaders who have deep-seated values and beliefs that happen to resonate with others through the visions they create. They are highly attuned manipulators with an intuitive understanding that visions have their desired effect only to the extent that the message is attractive to others. When others imagine getting their own value-based needs met by following a vision, they will be drawn to it. Gardner's observations of how some leaders can accurately gauge others' emotional states and respond to them is pretty creepy, because social intelligence in no way implies the desire to be of help. The leader uses it to *influence*. Note, these leaders do not necessarily respond with empathic responses of understanding, but they *can* find the "emotional pulse" of the person they want to influence. Both politically intelligent and socially intelligent leaders are "good" judges of character and are able to influence others. But instead of having true empathy for others, mean men hold a particularly instrumental view of people; they are merely tools to get their needs met.

In keeping with the nature of charismatics, Jobs was famous for the visionary way he talked about computers and, later, music and phones. He spoke with great energy and dazzled listeners with his vision of what was possible, pushing them to think beyond what seemed feasible. Investors wanted to give him money; engineers and designers wanted to work with him. He was an object of near cultlike admiration.

But the reality of working with Steve Jobs was very different. Day-to-day, he was known for his tantrums, his put-downs, and his outrageous requests. He knew how to exploit those around him. Jony Ive, Jobs's longtime lieutenant at Apple, would say of Jobs before his death, "The normal rules of social engagement do not apply to him. Because of how very sensitive he is, he knows exactly how to efficiently and effectively hurt someone."[6]

Both socially and politically intelligent leaders excel at reading people, but the devil is in the details. Social intelligence can be used for good or for evil. Most of us want to work and interact with socially intelligent leaders who truly have our needs in mind and who realize those needs and emotional states are important for long-term relationships and success. However, rarely would the mean man have people's reciprocal self-interest in mind. Political self-interest is purely utilitarian. It's obvious when one confronts political intelligence because it's clear there will be only one winner. In comparison, mean men with social intelligence can make people *think* they're in the midst of a win-win exchange. Only after you've experienced social intelligence at work do you realize how one-sided the exchange actually was.

While socially intelligent leaders work to leverage people's strengths, politically intelligent leaders are always looking for the chink in the armor. Bill Moyers, once Lyndon Johnson's press secretary, commented that the president had "an animal sense of weakness in other men." A political scientist described Johnson as a great student of the details who observed and tucked away even trivial personal data and behavior to use against others as necessary.[7] (While real-life politicians of this ilk abound, to get the gist of a politically intelligent mean man, think Francis Underwood, the diabolical protagonist in *House of Cards*.)

Socially intelligent leaders pull the levers of empathy and "soft power" to build bridges for getting things done. But make no mistake: it is intimidation and hard power, used to exploit the anxieties and vulnerabilities of underlings, that is the raison d'être of mean men.

COMMANDING LOYALTY: TOOLS OF CONTROL

It's easy to imagine why otherwise normal and psychologically balanced people like you or me might initially be attracted to mean but charismatic men. More perplexing is why people remain after they show their true colors. The biggest reason is that mean men are so adept at manipulating and controlling others. But another factor is the psychological makeup of people who are willing to endure abuse. Let's explore both in turn, starting with a look at the dark arts of manipulation and control.

MEAN MEN HAVE A FLUENT ABILITY TO LIE PERSUASIVELY

Early in their collaboration, Steve Jobs lied to his then-close friend and Apple cofounder Steve Wozniak about payment for work they were doing for Atari. Jobs cheated Wozniak out of two thousand dollars without Woz ever realizing it—until he read about the incident in a book a decade later. And Wozniak would relate other, very similar experiences with Jobs. Yet he would hang in there with him for years, knowing he was being lied to and manipulated. Even in mid-2014, Wozniak's personal website led with a photo of Jobs talking to Woz, about a year before Jobs's death, with the headline: "Woz and Jobs: Old Friends." Jobs's ability to influence and hold people in sway was famously referred to as the "reality distortion field," the term Bud Tribble, an original member of Apple's Mac development team and then one of the cofounders of NeXT with Jobs after Jobs's firing from Apple, coined for Jobs's charismatic ability to sell the vision, irrespective of reality.

Deception is fundamental to how psychopaths relate to others. They are essentially hardwired to take advantage of people and exploit the cooperation of others. And guess what? If you lie, and do so well, it's easier to get your way with people. You just tell them what they need to hear in the way they need to hear it. In the TV show *Lie to Me*, a psychologist and his colleagues help law enforcement crack criminal cases by analyzing microexpressions and body language. The lead character, Dr. Cal Lightman, is based on a real person, the eminent researcher and consultant Paul Ekman. Ekman has spent most of his career studying how we communicate through nonverbal behavior.[8] But it has been his broad research on lying—what shows on the face and the rest of the body—that has attracted so much interest.[9]

Because a psychopath lacks key emotions, it makes it easier for him to lie in a more convincing fashion. He is so smooth that his targets don't perceive the simulated sincerity directed their way. Using Ekman's complex nonverbal coding system, some researchers have found that subclinical psychopaths are, in fact, more effective liars than those without the disorder.[10] Why? They seem to learn and practice deception in ways not obvious to others, ways that allow them to continue honing their "skill" relatively unnoticed.

How do mean men practice deceit and manipulation but manage to circumvent social scrutiny? Research suggests it is because they are able to hide clues to their lying, clues known as *leakage*. Virtually all (non-psychopathic) humans the world over exhibit consistent leakage in facial expressions, body movements, changes in tone of voice and rhythm of speech, and slips or verbal mistakes. All of these dimensions of leakage have the potential to signal to others our insincerity. While research has never found blatant behavioral clues specific to lying, there are multiple signals that a deceiver typically displays in the act of lying. Those with psychopathic traits are indeed more effective at deception than others;

they have less "leakage" than most. It is possible, even for those of us not trained like Paul Ekman to watch for microexpressions, to nonetheless perceive leakage on a subconscious level. When there's a certain tone of voice, a smile that seems inconsistent with the words of a message, or a lack of eye contact, for example, we may get a feeling in our gut that says, "I just don't trust this guy, even though I can't put my finger on it," or "It's like talking to a used-car salesman." We don't identify the leakage as much as the gestalt of it all and how it squares with our history of interacting with people who are genuine and trustworthy and those who are not. For us nonclinical observers, our gut is often spot-on. But psychopaths can fool us.

MEAN MEN LEAVE NO ROOM FOR DOUBT

Remember what film documentarian Alex Gibney said about Lance Armstrong? "I've never met a better liar. And I've met a bunch." (And he should know about Olympic-grade liars. His investigative journalism has covered the Roman Catholic Church, Jack Abramoff, Julian Assange, and the Enron guys.) "He's good, he's real good. The best."[11]

Armstrong was so good that he nearly took down Gibney's career and credibility. In 2008, Armstrong invited Gibney to film the inside story of his comeback in the Tour de France, wanting to create a record for history to bolt down his place as the greatest cyclist ever. Going to Gibney was a smart move, since he has emerged as the most renowned, fiercely forensic, independent documentary maker who finds the truth. "I went along for the ride," says Gibney of that summer. "I thought I was filming a tale of wholesome redemption."[12]

The reality of course is that Armstrong used illegal drugs on an industrial scale in all seven of his Tour wins. But Armstrong created a compelling myth—a vision—that not only could he recover from cancer, but he could come back better than he was. It was gripping enough to draw the world in. He became a master at smacking down the doubters, regardless of the evidence that surfaced. He pushed back so fiercely, and so artfully, that he squelched further challenges. "It was a work of genius," concluded Gibney when he finished the second version of his Armstrong documentary in 2015.[13]

"The lie was way bigger than it needed to be," says Gibney. "The fact is he could have gone through his career and kept his head down, just saying, 'I'd never been tested positive.' That would have been the truth—well not quite, but almost. Instead, he constructs this spectacular lie in line with this spectacular story he has of the cancer survivor coming back from near death to win the Tour."[14] In his way, Armstrong, a master story-teller, was a constructor of his own narrative. And it worked. Armstrong became the darling of corporate America, appearing in advertisements for Bridge Information Systems, American General Life Insurance, the US Postal Service, Nike, Bristol-Myers Squibb, and AIM Mutual Funds.

Researchers have looked closely at how those with psychopathic traits present themselves and their views to others. They tap into an assortment of verbal and nonverbal behaviors that reduce the listener's suspicions and also compel listeners to truly hear them. In terms of verbal techniques, psychopaths are adept at including poignant details in their narratives, thereby decreasing the listener's doubts about whether the psychopath is telling the truth. Psychopaths also display a tendency to speak at lower volumes than nonpsychopaths, the quieter voice working to draw a listener in and convince them of the speaker's sincerity.

Presentation was key to the emotional impact of one of the most influential leaders of the twentieth century. Rehearsing and studying his own movements and gestures with the fervor of a method actor helped him to become "an absolutely spellbinding public speaker," notes the historian Roger Moorhouse about one of the most powerful and notorious leaders of our age. "It's something he worked on very hard."[15] That leader's name? Adolf Hitler.

Mastery of the facts—or even the appearance of it—is an effective tactic for keeping a reality distortion field alive. It often doesn't matter all that much whether the "facts" are correct at all. Even a misleading or inaccurate data point, when framed with absolute confidence and dropped into a conversation with perfect timing, can leave little room for argument or doubt. It is only later, when there is more time to check the accuracy of a statement, that people realize they've been duped. But by then, it is too late. When it comes to making an impression or anchoring an argument, the mean man has already seized the advantage.

MEAN MEN LACK FEAR AND REMORSE

Ordinary people work hard to keep cool and mind their behavior, in part because they're worried about what others think. And when they do throw temper tantrums or act abusively, they tend to feel bad afterward. Mean men often lack both inhibition and remorse, which can make them relatively fearless, with low levels of anxiety. They lack shame, contrition, and the ability to learn from negative experiences. And because they don't fear social reprisal, it's more likely that they'll continue their anti-social acts.

All this is even more applicable when a mean man sits atop a business organization that he built from scratch, or when he is an athlete at the top of his game . . . and the world. The narrative Lance Armstrong constructed so well wove a magical web around the lies that he piled one on top of the other. In response to a 1999 *Le Monde* article reporting that Armstrong tested positive for the banned substance corticosteroid in the first round of the Tour de France, Armstrong (in collaboration with his team members) concocted a plan involving medical fraud (having a doctor backdate a prescription) and lying to journalists and the International Cycling Union to say that he had corticosteroid in his system due to a medication prescribed to him for saddle soreness. When confronted, Armstrong categorically denied that the US Postal Service team had ever used Actovegin for performance-enhancing purposes, and he made extra efforts to show his lack of knowledge regarding the substance referencing it as "Activ-o-something" on his website in December 2000. He threatened skipping the 2001 Tour de France if the investigation continued. He also consistently denied ever using erythropoietin (EPO), a hormone normally produced by the kidney that promotes the formation of red blood cells by the bone marrow. In its synthetic form it is normally used with cancer patients, in treating anemia, and for other conditions. But in this case, its sole purpose is to enhance performance. Armstrong even went so far as to lash out against those in the press who expressed suspicion of him and threatened to use his clout to ruin the careers of cycling peers like Greg LeMond who he felt were also suspicious of him.

In addition to playing indignant, Armstrong's disingenuous theatrics reached a high point with his self-righteous attacks against "all those other cyclists" that were bringing down the sport with doping. After winning the Tour de Suisse, he referred to several riders by name, indicating, "These guys must be thrown out of the sport without a backward glance. . . . They don't respect the sport, the champions of the past, or the fans."[16] All the while, Armstrong did everything possible to evade drug testers. Even when he "confessed," most people came away from the first session of Oprah's interview appalled by Armstrong's lack of contrition. The word "sociopath" was used—inaccurately—by more than one media observer to describe what many viewed as a personality disorder.

As the Armstrong case illustrates, it's also easier to perfect the dark arts of deception and manipulation in the absence of pushback. Added to that, the fearlessness displayed by many mean men, Armstrong included, can be like an aphrodisiac to those who wish a larger dose of that within themselves. More willing to overlook potential faults in their leaders, they are drawn to this power.

MEAN MEN SATISFY "FANTASY NEEDS" OF GROUPS

"Apple is Steve Jobs with ten thousand lives," noted Guy Kawasaki, once Apple's chief evangelist. "Few corporations are such close mirror images of their founders."[17] But where some see the control freak, others see a desire to develop a seamless, end-to-end user experience and, now, an entire "ecosystem" of product design. To some he was a pathologic perfectionist; to others he embodied the pursuit of excellence. And instead of screaming, hurling humiliating abuse on employees, Jobs's behavior was conflated with a "passion" to make a dent in the universe. His personality traits summed up his business philosophy.

At Apple, the corporate culture always trickled down from Jobs. Just as Jobs was exceedingly demanding of the people who reported to him, Apple's middle managers demanded the same high level of performance from their staff. The result, internally, was a reign of terror. With Jobs in the wheelhouse, everyone was in constant fear of losing their jobs. At NeXT, Jobs's computer firm between his stints at Apple (that happened to be one of his flops), employees and colleagues experienced the trademark "hero/shithead dichotomy" Isaacson and others noted where "you were either one or the other, sometimes on the same day."[18]

Internally, Jobs was in fact considered one of the great intimidators, a category of fearsome business leaders who "inspire" people through fear and may cross the line of "bully." Often characterized as stern father figures, these mean men motivate through fear as well as a desire to be pleased. Great intimidators tend to be clustered in industries with high risks and high rewards—Hollywood, technology, and finance.

And like other great intimidators, Jobs was forceful. He pushed and cajoled. He could be brutal to ruthless. He put the fear of God into people to get things done. Mean men have other ways to keep their followers, too. And one is playing to the varying unconscious needs of the others within their groups.

The influential British psychoanalyst Wilfred Bion believed that no matter how emotionally healthy or how diverse the people are within a group, they behave in distinct ways when they come together in that group. He saw individuals operating on the basis of shared—but unspoken—basic assumptions and needs when they are in a group setting. These basic-assumption groups tend to fall into three related categories that Bion labeled the *dependency* group, the *pairing* group, and the *fight-flight* group. Individuals in each of these groups succumb to a complex dynamic ripe for one person, particularly the one to whom control and manipulation are second nature, to influence others' beliefs, needs, and goals. As offensive as the perceived leader may be, the group members' needs can create an attraction to a leader who may resolve their anxieties. Here's how it works:

The *dependency group* turns to what appears to be an omnipotent leader for the presumed security he offers. Behaving as if they do not have independent minds of their own, individuals in a small organization (a start-up or a political campaign) may blindly seek direction and follow orders unquestioningly. Regardless of their otherwise reasonable levels of confidence, sense of independence, and clear thinking, these qualities deteriorate inside a group with this corruptive leadership. Their leader's real or imagined power drives their newfound need for security and moves them to idealize the leader. The group trudges through a collective period of denial, irrationally waiting for the leader to provide some insight that will resolve their concerns. What is most interesting is that he never needs to deliver on the group's fantasy that he will solve all their problems. They may eventually experience anger and disappointment with him if he doesn't, but it won't stop their collective dependency on this leader. It's difficult to unwind the underlying assumptions and needs that made individuals so susceptible in the first place. By the principles of Bion's theory, not only will the leader (our mean man) create these anxieties, but also those under him will become dependent on him to resolve the same anxieties he is feeding them. We see this beyond the organizational world in wider social systems. Dependency was a key lever of influence that Rudy Giuliani pulled as he engaged in fearmongering, stirring up anxieties of many New Yorkers with a narrative around how totally out of control some (particularly minority) elements of the population were behaving. It didn't matter that crime was dropping precipitously before he came into city hall—he spoke as though it were only getting worse. When dissident voices surfaced, he quashed them, ensuring that his scary imperative remained intact. *You have to trust me and my policies to get us through this Armageddon*, seemed to be his message, influencing so many New Yorkers to feel dependent on him to lead them through to the other side.

President Trump used the same tactics during the 2016 election.[19] Data from the FBI, Census, and American Community Survey, as well as other studies, show that not only does the United States have net-neutral Mexican immigration, immigration does not "wreak havoc on our population" as Trump claimed.[20] Studies gathered by the American Immigration Council show that as immigration rises, crime rates drop. These studies also prove that immigrants are statistically less likely to land in jail and also less likely than US-born citizens to engage in criminal behavior.[21] Regardless, Trump built momentum in his campaign by vowing to defend America's borders with "a big, beautiful wall" to keep out the "rapists" and "criminals" Mexico was sending our way. At an event in Phoenix, Trump pointed to Mexico's crafty leaders, alleging, "They're killing us at the border and they're killing us on trade."[22] The rhetoric seems to have been effective. Not only did Trump win the electoral vote, but the number of registered voters who said immigration matters affected their vote rose from 41 percent in 2012 to 70 percent in 2016.[23]

In a *pairing* group, individuals act as if the goal of the group is to bring forth a messiah, someone who will save them. We see this in relatively young companies that seem to be sucking in their last gasp of life. As competitors move faster at seizing market opportunities, revenues decline and investors panic. Typically, the founder is no longer at the helm, but senior executives and the board feel pressure to either bring on someone with characteristic entrepreneurial stripes, hoping the firm can get its mojo back, or they even woo back the original founding entrepreneur, which is how Jobs got a second bite at the apple. Pairing differs from dependency in that the group does all it can to elevate the omnipotent leader even further or works to bestow power on someone they see as their savior. Bion's dependency dynamic gets triggered when someone with mean characteristics is already in place and makes his power obvious. With pairing, the mean man seeks further power and influence and gets it by conveying to the group how he represents the solution to a big problem. He rises by virtue of his dexterity to influence others.

Finally, dynamics of a group *fight-flight* mode are influenced by a perceived outside threat, such as another organization poised to destroy a company through any competitive advantage. If facing a period of severe political, economic, or technological instability or any other type of (perceived) imminent threat, individuals are prone to seek solace from certain personalities. They will be particularly receptive to the reassuring rhetoric of a leader who displays supreme confidence in his ability to ward off the disaster looming on the horizon. No surprise, therefore, that mean men can—and do—create this perception among groups of employees. Supremely confident rhetoric is one of their superpowers.

When Dov Charney was at the helm, the employees of American Apparel seemed victim to Charney creating a fight-flight environment. Over the years, his enthusiastic rallying cry for immigrant rights, rants about other casual clothing retailers who seek the cheapest offshore manufacturing locations, and general blustering to employees about how the firm was under constant threat from the media, politicians, and Wall Street all served to galvanize employee attraction to the leader.

A former senior manager of Charney's, whom I spoke with in depth on many occasions, could hardly explain the irrationality of how long she stayed with American Apparel—and him. "He was disgusting. I avoided interacting with him in any way I could. His mercurial, loud, in-your-face behavior was intolerable." Yet, "I loved the company and the people. I felt for years—from working at the store level all the way to senior management at headquarters—we were on an important mission. We were making a statement about how America could once again be fair to manufacturing employees, and immigrants in particular. Dov made me feel we were part of some movement, with so many outside the company wishing we would fail."

The fight-flight leader is appealing because of his espoused aggres-siveness and tenacity (it's a role that overlaps well with the List of Ten and psychopathic characteristics). The pairing leader becomes the sav-ior, while the dependency leader is experienced more as superhuman, a figure to whom his followers can genuflect, even as they are treated horribly.

In each of these groups, the leader's power emerges from the needs of individuals, based on assumptions and behaviors that are more often than not operating at collectively unconscious levels. The leader's adept-ness at playing into the group dynamics is second-nature to a mean man, and a dynamic I've seen replayed over and over in my forty years of work-ing with managerial and executive teams, especially in firms driven by entrepreneurs. In these settings particularly, all three basic-assumption groups emerge. When the entrepreneur holds forth in the group with his bold, emphatic pronouncements that sound to an outsider (me) like utter bullshit, it's the familiar "script" of the subclinical psychopath in action.

MEAN MEN CAN SPOT THE GIVERS—AND KNOW HOW TO KEEP TAKING FROM THEM

Normally, organizations are right to nurture "giving" behavior. Many organizations work at developing a cultural norm where employees natu-rally want to help and collaborate with colleagues, to act in others' inter-ests. Politicians work to encourage civic participation and sacrifice in the name of the greater good. In most cases, this spirit of generosity works; in firms where all feel a reciprocal desire to go out of their way to help others it has been found to increase innovation and quality. But heavily control-oriented leaders destroy the good that can come from those who have a propensity to give and abuse it for self-gain. In very real terms, they destroy the social capital of their organization and prevent it from achieving what others—those with piles of social capital—accomplish.

Selflessness can be punishing, as Wharton professor Adam Grant found in a 2013 study.[24] Givers who exhibited the characteristic of timid-ity, the opposite of those assertive mean men, couldn't muster a "no" in response to those who asked for their help or labor. Employees who are uncomfortable advocating for themselves also find it difficult to set limits on their availability to help, how they help, and who they help.

Beyond the obvious inability to say no, this group succumbs to the takers by falling into the *empathy* trap. Empathy, or the ability to "feel with" someone and truly understand and get inside another's experience, is an admirable trait and noted in recent psychology and management research. Those who can convey empathy, the theory goes, can have powerful positive effects on others because people who feel empathy are willing to put others' needs ahead of their own. That's how much we desire empathy, to have our feelings understood. In effect, there's reciprocity for those who exude empathy; we appreciate what they give us and want to help them. But crave empathy too much and one becomes susceptible to manipulation, according to sociologist Daniel Batson.[25]

Mean men are masters not only at recognizing timidity, but also at playing empathetic employees, voters, fans, and spouses. By the time the giver is thoroughly depleted from trying to meet the taker's needs, it's often too late for reshaping the relationship. The dynamic has been set. Many years ago I taught in the MBA program at the University of Massachusetts in Amherst. I commuted regularly to Chicago to see my wife, who was in medical school there. I was finishing my doctorate in Massachusetts, doing consulting work for some clients in New York, and working like a dog. I loved those years but had my weary moments. I was also a more private person then and didn't reveal very much that was personal, let alone emotional, to those around me.

I taught one section of students who were enrolled in an executive program and came to class for full-day sessions every few weeks. They were older, with full lives also, and I enjoyed being with them. Except one. Craig was a guy who never got assignments in on time, could not work collaboratively in student teams, and seemed the perennial dealmaker when I counseled him about his performance. One day he came for an appointment and managed somehow to draw out of me my personal situation at the moment. I revealed my difficulty, and he had a very "feeling" response.

Even as I allowed his empathy to waft over me, and for once permitted myself to feel legitimately tired, I realized this was coming at a price. Craig used this knowledge over the next few weeks to keep his empathy train on the track (and it seemed genuine in the moment). I also became aware that I wanted to "give back," his empathy a small gift he had given to me. But in short order I saw the deal-making attempts pick up: Could he have an extension on the next important assignment? Could I do a reassessment of the grade on his last paper? While I would not now characterize Craig as one of our mean men, he certainly used one of their influence strategies. Empathic behavior was his way in to leverage the "pull" his newfound power was earning him. This was precisely that trap that sociologist Robert Cialdini found in his research on influence and persuasion used particularly by highly skilled salespeople.[26] The secret was in taking advantage of the implicit human desire to respond reciprocally when someone does something for us, however subtle and small it may be. Lucky for me I awoke to the ruse and caught myself in time, reinforcing the boundaries and expectations. But how often are mean men successful in keeping the manipulation coming?

MEAN MEN MOTIVATE DECEPTIVELY

Mean men are great at getting people to "rally round the flag." They mobilize their employees by presenting projects that are simultaneously rash and spectacular. Their schemes may be supported not by careful planning or factual arguments but by the ways they generate excitement and bring attention to the guy at the helm (usually themselves). As we will see in chapter 8, research on highly narcissistic CEOs (a complex component of psychopathy) has found, for example, that they are far more likely to engage in risky acquisitions, many of which turn out badly and drive down shareholder value. They favor strategic sensationalism over more sensible and profitable strategies, like incrementally improving products. And they are brilliant at playing down the risks and playing up the benefits—so much so that even individuals who have doubts will protest only faintly, if at all. But it can have the impact of rallying employees with hope that the future will be different, exciting, and seemingly bigger than life.

Much acclaim has come from the concept of emotional intelligence (EQ) since Daniel Goleman published his bestselling book *Emotional Intelligence*. EQ is about one's capacity to understand emotions. It's a way to measure how effectively a person recognizes emotions in him- or herself and in others, and manages these emotional states to improve interpersonal interactions and relationships. In comparison, one's intelligence quotient (IQ) is a number that indicates a person's capacity to learn, solve problems for logic, understand, and apply information and skills in a meaningful way. There are plenty of people with rather high IQs who nonetheless may be very difficult to have on a team or as a member of a group because of their relatively low EQ. In business organizational circles as well as in modern parenting, EQ is a popular concept. If we can teach children to manage emotions, it's believed, we'll have more cooperation and less bullying. If we can develop emotional intelligence among our organizational leaders, it's argued, there will be more caring workplaces.[27]

As with giving and empathy, mean men are able to take a good thing and twist it, using it to their own advantage. Jochen Menges's research at the University of Cambridge found that improving your emotional control and skills in reading people makes you a better manipulator. Not only can you more easily disguise your true feelings, you can more easily convince others to work in your—not their own—best interests.

Menges found, for example, that when leaders gave emotion-laden talks or speeches, the emotion was what the audience remembered, rather than the content (though the audience would swear the opposite). Menges and his colleagues call this the *awestruck effect*; it might as well be called the dumbstruck effect.[28]

My colleague at the Austen Riggs Center in 2009, Vamik Volkan, emeritus professor of psychiatry at the University of Virginia, spent much of his career researching world-class psychopaths—despots who rule countries, leaving trails of terror and death. Reflecting on Hitler, he mentioned how the Führer's political persuasiveness came from his ability to express emotions with strategic precision. His emotional affect during speeches became amplified, and followers in his audiences were so influenced that they would "stop thinking critically and just emote."[29]

Even in the case of pedestrian subclinical psychopaths, research projects by Stéphane Côté at the University of Toronto and Martin Kilduff at University College London have concluded that those who are masters of others' emotions can rob us of our capacities to reason when their motives are thoroughly self-serving. Mean men have a type of emotional intelligence that enables them to disguise one set of emotions while expressing another solely for personal gain.[30]

MEAN MEN HAVE AN ABILITY TO SPOT CHINKS IN PEOPLE'S ARMOR

The first hallmark of a social predator is the ability to recognize vulnerability in others. It provides him with an opportunity to select and successfully manipulate those traits he considers an invitation for victimization: gullibility, communication difficulties, problems with establishing and maintaining boundaries, low self-confidence, and a strong eagerness to please others.

Mean men are uncanny at detecting points of vulnerability, and this is incredibly useful for controlling people and keeping them loyal. While flawed in understanding and showing genuine emotions, mean men are skilled at *seeing* emotions in others and at assessing people's level of assertiveness and their insecurities. Our emotions offer powerful clues to our intentions, our motivations, and—crucially—our fears and weaknesses.[31] Those who are skilled at reading these clues have powerful advantages in social and professional relationships. For mean men, it is a window into exploiting the anxieties and vulnerabilities they detect.

MEN MEAN FAKE CONCERN

Another reason these men may be so successful at drawing people into their webs is their skill at pretending to care about others, and at just the right time. It's not real caring, of course, but it sure seems that way. *Simulated consideration*, the clinical term that describes this phenomenon, to the layperson boils down to manipulation and exploitation.[32]

Supported by several empirical studies, the theory offers a newer framework of leadership pathology known as the Dark Triad of personalities, the combination of psychopathy, Machiavellianism, and narcissism.[33] When their overlapping characteristics present themselves in an organizational leader, the more common psychopathic attributes abound: high impulsivity, callousness, interpersonal manipulation, exploitation, stimulation seeking, superficial charm, and remorselessness. Psychopathy takes center stage in all three disorders.

While he may initially be outgoing and charming, these temperament traits are what another will eventually find the most compelling, attractive examples of his disorder. The public's lack of awareness about the misuse of power and dominance is a reason that he is able to fool others—often trained professionals. Since most of us do not have a reason to be on high alert to the intrapsychic problems of a dominant mean man, he simply "looks" caring and charismatic.

He is master of what we may call the ice-breaking technique. He becomes aware of some issues in your life (such as my student did with me), or perhaps perceives another's natural human kindness, both of which he sees as weakness to be exploited. He will be sure to present himself as in love with his family, friends, dogs, and children. But his simulated consideration may go deeper and become far more pernicious, depending on the level of psychopathy involved. Dovetailing with what we've learned so far, his simulated consideration will extend beyond appearing to be the nice guy others want him to be. Instead, understanding another's soft spots and interests will become a focus as a means for further exploitation of that person. Though seemingly filled with love, compassion, empathy, remorse, or conscience, in reality he is predatory, deceptive, and Machiavellian.

CHAPTER EIGHT

CRUELTY'S COST

THE MAN WHO "BROUGHT SILICON to Silicon Valley" was a brilliant physicist named William Shockley.[1] Unlike that rebel Bill Gates, there is no evidence that Shockley was ever a juvenile delinquent, but he did have a violent temper as a child and struggled with rage and depression through much of his life. Along the way, though, he helped to invent the transistor, paving the way for the semiconductor and the computer chip, and the rise of the computing age. He also won the Nobel Prize in 1956.

Shockley could have died a very rich and celebrated man. Instead, his last years were spent in modest circumstances, alienated from his family and former colleagues. The title of an authoritative biography of Shockley says it all: *Broken Genius*. William Shockley's story is a familiar one, only he climbed higher and fell harder.

After getting a PhD in physics from MIT, Shockley started his career at Bell Labs, where he worked with John Bardeen and Walter Brattain, the two scientists who were principally responsible for developing the transistor. But all three would share the Nobel Prize together for this invention.

The collaborative environment of Bell Labs, one of the top research facilities of its time, proved to be a poor fit for Shockley. Brattain eventually refused to work with Shockley, and Bardeen quit Bell Labs altogether to avoid working with Shockley again.

During his time at Bell, according to *Broken Genius*, Shockley developed a reputation as a "credit hog" and being insensitive and uncaring, "literally running a dozen men out of the labs when he decided they did not meet his exacting standards."[2] Because of his lack of people skills, his career stagnated at Bell while his colleagues were promoted to higher positions with higher pay.

Though his colleagues readily admitted that he was a gifted scientist, John Moll, a physicist who did not work on Shockley's team at Bell, reported that Shockley would worm his way into getting credit for work he did not do. Moll said, "Every once in a while we'd come up with a patentable device or process. We'd always have a meeting with the patent attorneys, he'd always be at the meeting, and he'd always claim that anything I could think of was already in his notebook."[3]

Many people who start their own businesses or who work in an entrepreneurial role will explain that they just can't stand working for somebody else. The truth, though, is that they often can't stand working *with* anyone else, at least as full equals. So it is that William Shockley inevitably left Bell Labs to start his own venture, becoming the founding director of Shockley Semiconductor Laboratory. His company was backed by Beckman Instruments, Inc., a company in Mountain View, California, run by Arnold Beckman. Although Beckman housed and supported Shockley's operation, it was Shockley who called the shots with his team and their research.

It didn't take long for his past behavior to become problematic again. Shockley's lack of social and managerial skills and his increasingly paranoid behavior reached critical mass just one year after Shockley Semiconductor was founded, when the employees considered to be the eight most talented scientists at the company, including whiz kids Gordon Moore and Robert Noyce, quit. Shockley from that point forward referred to those scientists as the "traitorous eight."

Events leading up to the departure of the "traitorous eight" included an incident in which a secretary cut herself on a piece of metal stuck in a door. Locked in a haze of paranoia, Shockley became convinced that someone had placed the piece of metal there on purpose. He then demanded that his employees take lie-detector tests in an attempt to discover the culprit. (It was later determined that the dangerous metal was the result of the glass head of a thumbtack breaking off, leaving the metal pin in place.)

Shockley Semiconductors was eventually sold to Clevite Transistor and then later to International Telephone & Telegraph Company. William Shockley never made a profit from his company, taking a teaching job at Stanford instead. At Stanford, he alienated both colleagues and students. In the end, he was estranged even from family members.

As for Robert Noyce and Gordon Moore, part of the "traitorous eight," they went on to found Fairchild Semiconductor and then a little company called Intel, eventually becoming celebrated billionaires.

NO, MEAN DOESN'T "WORK"

Ruthless and abusive leaders are often defended on the grounds that they produce results. Yes, a few eggs get broken, but the omelet comes out great. Writing about Larry Ellison, a business reporter had admitted, "By all accounts, he is a bad listener and a big talker, whose brash, take-no-prisoners approach tends to alienate employees and customers alike. Yet, in the past 35 years, the jet-flying, sailboat-racing renegade has built Oracle into one of the most important tech firms on the planet, with annual revenues of $27 billion."[4]

This is the standard rap about authoritarian leaders. Profile after profile of Steve Jobs or Donald Trump note their tough personalities and then breezily move on to the good news: a growth in profits or a staggering net worth.

The story of William Shockley is an extreme example of how mean can backfire and destroy a company. But there are plenty of other stories of mean men who undermined the companies they led, too. The truth is that *mean doesn't work*. In fact, evidence shows the opposite: mean and controlling leaders create unrelenting inauthentic leadership in the workplace and in their groups and, more broadly, subvert our idea of the acceptable price of success. It undermines morale, diminishes the chance to build strong teams, drives away talent, stymies innovation, and exposes organizations to excessive risk. Let's look more closely at these different kinds of fallout.

MEAN HURTS THE BRAND AND DRIVES AWAY CUSTOMERS

If you knew the founder of a company was a jerk, would you buy its product? Maybe not.

Georgetown University professor Christine L. Porath and University of Southern California professors Deborah J. MacInnis and Valerie S. Folkes set up an experiment where half the study subjects watched a "bank teller" being dressed down publicly by a supervisor for making a mistake. Of all those who witnessed the bank "encounter," only one-fifth said they'd want to do business with the bank at some point in the future, and almost two-thirds reported anticipatory anxiety in interacting with the bank employees. The company had a much better impression on those who hadn't seen the dressing down; 80 percent of that group would consider doing future business with the company.[5]

What's more, when various scenarios were tested, they found that potentially mitigating circumstances—such as the mistake being possibly illegal or even selfish (taking a handicapped spot)—didn't matter to those who viewed or heard the exchange. The participants reacted negatively to the employee's mistreatment regardless.

Also, research finds that when employees are treated badly it can negatively affect how they deal with customers and clients. For example, a poll of eight hundred managers and employees in seventeen industries found that 25 percent of workers who have been on the receiving end of inauthentic leadership admitted to taking their frustration out on customers.[6]

MEAN UNDERMINES MORALE

When Steve Jobs died in 2011, he was most known as the brilliant innovator who brought us iTunes and the iPhone—and helped propel Apple past its former rival, Microsoft, to become one of the most valuable companies on the planet. And when details surfaced about what a jerk he was, people shrugged: *Sure, but look at the results he got in building Apple.*

Yes, Steve Jobs famously brought Apple back from the grave. But he also helped put it in that grave.

When you're dealing with a company leader like Jobs, you know instinctively that the mean, egotistical, and erratic behavior is damaging.

And now there's a growing body of empirical research that shows just how this unfolds in other firms. For instance, a 2012 study in the *Journal of Applied Psychology* has documented the negative effects of the Machiavellian head games that narcissistic CEOs play and the broader negative effects of narcissism in the executive suite.[7]

The full range of ways that meanness can undermine morale is striking. The aforementioned poll of eight hundred managers and employees in seventeen industries showed that mean management had the following effect on employees:

- 48 percent intentionally decreased their work effort.
- 47 percent intentionally decreased the time spent at work.
- 38 percent intentionally decreased the quality of their work.
- 80 percent lost work time worrying about the incident.
- 63 percent lost work time avoiding the offender.
- 66 percent said that their performance declined.
- 78 percent said that their commitment to the organization declined.
- 12 percent said that they left their job because of the uncivil treatment.[8]

MEAN SABOTAGES TEAM WORK

Effective teams are all-important to successful organizations, but mean leaders tend to sabotage team work in a variety of ways.

This can happen when they are directly leading a team, as Jobs was at various times before he was pushed out from Apple. His negative impact on teams—which are particularly critical in tech companies—was a main reason Apple's high command sought to limit his power in the company. In 1978, well before the Mac was developed, Jobs headed up the team developing Lisa, which was designed to be an inexpensive personal computer with a graphical interface. Jobs was forced out as head of the Lisa team after two years when he was also stripped of his post as vice president of research and development. Why? Because he not only didn't know how to manage a team, he actively weakened the Lisa team with his difficult and abusive behavior.

Mean men can also sabotage team work by pitting teams within an organization against each other, turning a healthy competition into a toxic internal feud. Again, Steve Jobs's early days at Apple furnish a great example: When Jobs was forced off the Lisa team, he joined the team to develop the Mac, which was just getting going. And he promptly used this position—along with his wider clout in the company as a top shareholder and board chair—to try to undermine the Lisa project. Friction emerged between the two teams as they jockeyed for company resources, and with Jobs raiding the Lisa team for people and ideas. Jobs also refused to make the Mac compatible with the Lisa. The Lisa would be a massive failure for Apple for many reasons, but Jobs's antagonism to the project after he was forced from its leadership didn't help matters.

Internal divisions can be extremely damaging to companies, and these divisions are more likely to emerge under a Machiavellian leader who takes a dog-eat-dog view of the world.

Well before Zynga crashed and burned, the *New York Times* head-lined an article in November 2011 "Zynga's Tough Culture Risks Talent Drain."[9] The story said that Zynga's competitive culture had helped it become successful, but that it "could become a serious liability, warn[ed] several former senior employees who agreed to speak on the condition of anonymity because of fear of reprisals."[10]

The situation at Zynga was that the different teams, working on different games, were pitted against one another. As the *Times* explained, "Led by the hard-charging Mr. Pincus, the company operates like a federation of city-states, with autonomous teams for each game, like FarmVille and CityVille. At times, it can be a messy and ruthless war. Employees log long hours, managers relentlessly track progress, and the weak links are demoted or let go."[11]

Governor Chris Christie of New Jersey rose to fame as a brazenly incautious politician who made mean his brand. He was the "straight talker," defined by his blistering rants, searing insults, and perennial public feuds, a style that chafes at some and draws admiration from others. "Harmless theatrics," he once said. In a press conference, Christie responded to those who consider him too harsh. "Politics ain't bean bag . . . Everybody knows that. . . . I don't hide my emotions from people. I am not a focus-group tested, blow-dried candidate or governor. . . . I am who I am. But I am not a bully."[12] Writing in the *Washington Post*, Ezra Klein disagreed. "There's a lot about Christie that's deeply appealing.

But there's one big thing that's not: He's someone who uses his office to intimidate people and punish or humiliate perceived enemies." While Klein admits Christie's ruthlessness helped get him to power, he also posits that "it might be why he falls, too."[13]

Perhaps this is part of why Christie flamed out in the 2016 presidential election race, a contest he spent much of 2014 and 2015 grooming himself for—the nomination once considered his to lose. What happened in the intervening time was Bridgegate, the New Jersey lane-closing scandal rooted in a ruthless act of political retribution, which promises to be a visible narrative of how belligerence, something voters often find endearing, can instantly twist perceptions 180 degrees. In early May 2015, three of Christie's most loyal and trusted lieutenants were indicted. Brigid Harrison, a professor at Montclair State University, opined that that was probably the death knell for Christie's national aspirations. "Even if he is not directly connected to the indictments," she noted, "he is guilty of creating a political culture in which corruption was allowed to flourish."[14] In 2016, both Bridget Anne Kelly and Bill Baroni, Christie's former chief of staff and a Port Authority official respectively, were found guilty of nine counts of conspiracy and fraud. By March 2017, Kelly was sentenced to eighteen months in prison, Baroni getting a full two years.[15]

There's backlash, too, for Christie throwing his trusting staff under a bus. "Exoneration of the man is not exoneration of his leadership style," commented the *New York Times*.[16] The alleged target of Christie's ire for Bridgegate, Fort Lee mayor Mark Sokolich, had this to say: "It is now proven this was retribution aimed at me. There was a complete disregard for thousands of others put in harm's way. This can never happen again. This trial shed a very bright light on a sad set of circumstances in NJ. If reform does not come from this, we should all be ashamed."[17] Christie and his staff are infamous for punishing those who have crossed him. But when times get rough and you need friends, that kind of behavior makes others run. Early on he was the envy of the Republican Party for leveraging his brashness to fill his campaign coffers. But his once-clear path to the presidential nomination got buried in the underbrush. His favorability ratings plummeted. Voters openly taunt him about Bridgegate. Longtime allies defected to rival campaigns. In the end, it was widely believed that the Bridgegate convictions caused even mean man Donald Trump to distance himself from Christie. Once thought to be a lock for Trump's chief of staff or attorney general, Christie was replaced as chairman of the president-elect's transition team by Mike Pence soon after the convictions were handed down.[18]

American voters have historically shown considerable forgiveness for personal scandals (and one need look no further than Bill Clinton). But the public sees Bridgegate not merely as Chris Christie's scandal, but as a singular case of public betrayal, an event notable for its meanness and indifference to the thousands of people who were affected by it. And by all appearances, it took Christie down.

Christie is a particularly prescient example of the popular mean man who has earned a pass by excoriating Democrats and Republicans alike, perhaps the man who made the candidate Donald Trump possible. Because anyone he disagrees with is a potential target, his meanness is propped up by the idea that he is an independent thinker, beholden to no one. His popularity has come as a result of the thinking that "does not play well with others" translates into "leader."

The "self-made man" ideal of America came into being in the early 1820s, roughly at the same time that Frenchman Alexis de Tocqueville took his jaunt around the country studying democracy in action. He observed a chronic restlessness, which he saw as the pivotal psychological characteristic of the American self-made man. In *Democracy in America*, de Tocqueville is struck by how individualism began as the first "language" through which Americans tended to think about their lives, how they valued independence and self-reliance above all else.

These qualities are expected to earn success in a competitive society, but they are also values as virtues in themselves. American individualism demands personal effort and stimulates great energy to achieve. But it provides little encouragement for nurturance. This narrow view adopts a sink-or-swim approach to moral development as well as to economic or political success. It admires toughness and strength and sneers at softness and vulnerability. Win, win, win.

During times of economic prosperity, Americans have seen individualism as a self-sufficient moral and political guide. In times of social adversity, they are tempted to say that it is up to individuals to look after their own interests. But in good times, too, I would argue there is something missing in the individualist set of values in that individualism doesn't enable people to see a basic reality of their lives: interdependence with others.

The consequences of radical individualism have potentially important relevancy to mean men. If a mean man represents this type of alienating individualism, then what is endangered by mean might be commitment, community, and citizenship. Said another way, the cost of cruelty, aside from the diminished personal identities of those forced to interact with it, is the depletion of social capital, those bonds of interdependence that unite us and lift us up as a whole.

Robert Putnam's *Bowling Alone*, noted earlier as perhaps the most widely disseminated case on the need for, and diminishment of, social capital in America, explains social capital by making the simple and profound argument that "relationships matter."[19] While it may seem blatantly obvious that "social networks are a valuable asset," the benefit of building community and knitting together our lives with common purpose cannot be overstated.

But here's the rub: social capital alone can't explain everything it's been hailed to achieve. Researchers over the past decade have posited that trust is a precondition to cooperation in social and political environments. If trust is present, they have argued, people won't exploit each other or cheat in their relationship, and then they can truly benefit from their cooperation. There's chicken-and-egg confusion concerning the concept of social capital and its relationship to trust: Is trust an integral element of social capital, as the leading scholars of the concept have claimed? Or does social capital beget the building of trust?

As an organizational consultant, I would argue that it might not matter. You've gotta have both. But meanness and trust mix like oil and water. As Putnam points out, this essential concept of social reciprocity was best summed up by one of America's wisest thinkers, Yogi Berra: "If you don't go to somebody's funeral, they won't come to yours."[20]

In my own work, I've seen how abusive dynamics in the workplace can undermine teams in ways you might not expect. One surprising finding from the research, for example, is that witnesses to inauthentic leadership were less generous in helping others overall, regardless of whether the beneficiary had any connection at all to the person who was uncivil in the first place. Only a quarter of the subjects who'd witnessed inauthentic leadership volunteered to help, whereas 51 percent of those who hadn't witnessed it did.[21]

This returns us to Putnam. Important not only to the vibrancy and success of cities and towns, social capital accounts for successful organizations, too. In any workplace—from start-ups to campaigns, from basketball courts to the Tour de France—wherever social capital is jeopardized—through mistrust, conflicting values, or an inability to come to mutual understanding—cooperative action derails. Ultimately, nobody wants to get behind the guy who socially tears us apart.

MEAN DRIVES AWAY TALENT

Zynga may have faced serious business challenges, but Mark Pincus's management style and decisions hastened the company's decline. Zynga's toxic culture, which flowed from the very top, put the company at a disadvantage in the fierce competition for top tech talent in the San Francisco Bay Area. Why work for a guy like Mark Pincus, or one of his slave-driving underlings, when you could work for somebody like Mark Zuckerberg, who has routinely been rated among the most-liked CEOs in the tech field? Why work at Zynga, and be called in on the weekends, when you can work at a place like Google, which not only tolerates, but encourages, engineers to pursue their passions on the company's dime?

A fast-food restaurant, retail store, or other commoditized service business *may* be able to get away with an authoritarian workplace, with mean leadership, because there's an oversupply of low-skilled workers who need the job and have fewer options. But it's a different story where skilled workers are essential and when interviewees now can take a look at the culture of their prospective employers.

One way the Zynga culture became a liability is how quickly word spread that it wasn't a great place to work. The Internet and social media have made it easier than ever to get and share information about a company's internal culture or the jerky behavior of its CEO. Think of how the callous missteps of Tim Armstrong, the head of AOL, have gone viral, like when he fired Abel Lenz, the creative director at AOL Patch, on a conference call in 2013 with a thousand Patch employees listening in. Why was Lenz fired? Because Lenz took Armstrong's picture with his phone during the call. The firing was an instant Internet sensation, and the story surely gave second thoughts to anyone considering a high-level job at AOL, as did Armstrong's later comments about the kids of certain employees incurring health-care costs for the company. Who wants to work at a place where heads can roll so quickly for minor transgressions?

Even more powerful, though, are Internet sites like Glassdoor that allow employees to describe the culture of companies and dish dirt anonymously. The "Top 10 Worst Companies to Work For" makes the Internet rounds every December like clockwork. Compare that kind of assessment with how Google cofounder and Google parent-company Alphabet's CEO Larry Page is seen, with 95 percent of Google's employees who used Glassdoor approving of Page as of this writing. Zuckerberg's approval rating is even higher at 97 percent. And one reviewer wrote about Facebook: "Fantastic place to work. . . . Incredibly smart people. Hierarchy agnostic. Ideas bubble up. Best ideas win. . . . Fantastic benefits."[22] It's not uncommon for talented techies looking for new work to get multiple job offers. Why take the job in the company known for its abusive leadership and unsupportive work culture?

Toxic workplaces don't just repel talent; they hemorrhage it, too, and this can be even more damaging to a company's bottom line. Researchers have confirmed what is intuitively obvious. A 2000 study, for example, found that subordinates who perceive their supervisors as more abusive are more likely to quit their jobs. Much additional research backs up the HR adage that "employees leave their bosses, not their jobs." For those who stay and perceive their supervisors as abusive, there is lower psychological engagement in their work.

If a top engineer or executive walks away at a crucial moment, a company can face big problems in terms of developing products and following through on initiatives. That's all the more likely to happen in industries where the competition for talent is intense and headhunters are constantly trying to get sought-after workers to jump ship for the promise of higher pay or a better work environment.

Even more damaging, as we've seen, is when companies lose talent to their direct competitors—like when Henry Ford drove off William Knudsen, who was known as Ford's most talented executive. Knudsen hopped over to GM and revived its Chevrolet division, which became a leader in building inexpensive cars and one of Ford's top competitors for the lower-end market.

Ford Motor would survive its steady exodus of talent over the years and eventually be revived by Henry Ford II, who—as one of his first acts upon taking over the company in 1945—quickly fired Harry Bennett, the main henchman his grandfather used to control the company. William Shockley's venture didn't fare nearly as well thanks to his abusive leadership, which led eight of his most talented top staff to leave the company en masse in 1957, as discussed in chapter 8. Shockley Semiconductor never recovered from that exodus. Even though Shockley was the man who "brought Silicon to Silicon Valley," it was his alienated ex-employees who reaped fame and fortune from his innovations.

MEAN SCARES AWAY INVESTORS AND PARTNERS

It's not just employees who may steer clear of companies run by mean men who foster toxic cultures. It's also investors, partners, and other players—the kind of powerful allies companies need in order to grow or enable a lucrative exit.

Why? Because these players understand that organizational culture matters in terms of future growth and profitability. It matters for all the reasons we've been discussing: culture affects employee morale, which affects creativity and productivity. If a company has a reputation for being a snake pit, potential investors or acquirers may decide to stay away. Who wants to deal with problems like that in a hands-on way?

Paul Graham cofounded and now runs Y Combinator, the first of a new type of digital start-up incubator. They've funded over a thousand start-ups including Dropbox, Airbnb, Stripe, and Reddit, and he firmly believes you can be nice and succeed. Graham has been known to proselytize the themes in Bob Sutton's *No Asshole Rules*, and he chooses to not invest in personalities with our mean-men profiles. Investors and founders forge intimate and intricate business relationships, and Graham would rather be choosy from the start.

"The reason we tried not to invest in jerks initially was sheer self-indulgence," Graham has asserted. "We were going to have to spend a lot of time with whoever we funded, and we didn't want to have to spend time with people we couldn't stand. Later we realized it had been a clever move to filter out jerks, because it made the alumni network really tight. We've funded over 630 startups now, and when founders of different startups meet there is an automatic level of trust and willingness to help one another. Much more than alumni of the same college for example."[23]

"It's certainly possible to build a multi-billion dollar startup without being a jerk," Graham has observed. "We've funded several, and the founders are all good people. In fact, based on what I've seen so far, the good people have the advantage over jerks. Probably because to get really big, a company has to have a sense of mission, and the good people are more likely to have an authentic one, rather than just being motivated by money or power."[24]

MEAN BLOCKS INNOVATION

Nearly all companies, organizations, and groups need to innovate in order to grow and succeed over time. But that can be hard to do with a mean man at the helm. Such leaders can undermine or block innovation in different ways.

First, their need for control can make it hard for those below them in the organization to take leadership and be creative. Mean men don't build up and empower those below them; they tear them down and leave them feeling frustrated and impotent.

The drive for control can block innovation even more directly, as when a leader stops new projects that threaten their vision for the company or their status within it. Recall how Henry Ford physically smashed the prototype of a new car that his people had developed when he was away from the company, overseas. It's hard to think of a better example than Ford Motor of a company that was badly hurt by its failure to innovate. By Henry Ford tyrannically insisting that the company only produce the no-frills black Model T, the company fell behind as consumer tastes evolved, with people clambering for luxurious styling and add-ons—desires that other carmakers profitably satisfied as Ford remained stuck in time.

One dramatic case in point from the government sector is the incumbency of Rudy Giuliani as mayor of New York. His two terms represented a noteworthy drop in the rate of innovation across city agencies compared to other mayoral governments, even if one looks only at the four mayors who served as "bookends" to Giuliani: Ed Koch and David Dinkins before, Mike Bloomberg and Bill de Blasio after.

As we have seen, innovation requires risk-taking at many levels of an organization, including those in the public sector. Risk is always haunted by the shadow of failure, yet it's the consequences of failure that give us a window to any organization's culture. For example, if the mandate is to *innovate!*, then one can learn a lot by looking at the leaders' reactions to the innovative solutions or missteps that follow. If the efforts didn't succeed, look closely. Does punishment follow failure (punishment for trying)? Or does failure from reasonable risk lead to expectations to *learn* from the failure so one can innovate in newly informed ways as a result of this learning?

Unfortunately, the culture shift across New York City agencies was fast and fierce once Giuliani took office. Commissioners were lectured on how the mayor would take credit for success, but failures would be laid at their doorstep. Add to that, there better not be any mistakes or failures in the first place, regardless of how meaningful and reasoned the actions to fix a civic problem may be perceived. Few would dispute, and many would admit in the media and academic venues, that the culture inside this administration was characterized by fear.[25] The independent Citizens Budget Commission was not kind in their assessment of Giuliani's management of New York, and in turn and true to character, he tried to exact revenge on them. Rather than innovate, Giuliani was perfectly positioned to exploit many myths that he was the great innovator effecting change.[26]

In reality, both the crack and AIDS epidemics were waning to the point that quality of life was noticeably improving. A lucky recipient of favorable social-health trends, Giuliani nonetheless happily took full credit for making New York "safe" again. Beyond the demographic shifts that contributed to a drop in crime even before he took office, the legislation and mechanics for overhauling Times Square had been set in place by his predecessor. David Dinkins, pilloried by Giuliani during his campaign as being "soft on crime," raised property and income tax rates to hire six thousand community police officers and fund a "Safe Streets, Safe City" initiative focused on improving community-police relations. Giuliani would soon undo the community approach working with police commissioner William Bratton and turning to CompStat, a system used to track crime, to focus resources.[27]

With the culture of fear and top-down obsessive control as a tailwind, commissioners went about things business as usual. Better to make do than try to innovate and potentially make a mistake trying. And if someone in an agency did create a new approach to housing for the poor, reducing traffic congestion, opening up bike lanes, or keeping the streets clean, then it was a sure bet the only one who got credit was Rudy. He also claimed he cut spending (it rose), said he hired four times the amount of police officers he did (3,600 rather than 12,000), and took credit for leg-islative tax cuts.[28]

In terms of full disclosure, I will also say that my organizational change and leadership development consulting engagements with the New York City government started with Abe Beame's mayoralty in the mid-1970s. Back then, the city was verging on bankruptcy, and we saw the infamous New York *Daily News* headline summarizing the willingness of the federal government to infuse the Big Apple with federal funds: "Ford to City: Drop Dead."[29] These consulting engagements have continued all the way through to the city's current mayor, de Blasio. But there was one notable exception. During the Giuliani administration, all change management was handled by top-down edicts from the mayor's office, the fear factor almost palpable across the complexity of the city's varied agencies.

But one commissioner was willing to take that risk. He had left a fast-track, highly paid position in the private sector to make a difference in his city. He hired me for an ambitious project that would realign his large agency's culture and breathe life into new approaches to address-ing essential services for lower-income families. It was a massive change initiative for a sclerotic bureaucracy. I was taken aback when the client said during my second long meeting with him, "We have to do whatever it takes to keep this change project hidden from city hall." Digesting those words while sitting in his office, I looked out the window and gazed at the building mere blocks away where Giuliani sat, and I thought, *We're screwed.*

It's just politics, you may say. Every leader has his own agenda, and low-income services was not then a priority issue for city hall. But more than just different politics, this was mean-man leadership, where every city employee quaked with fear and people did what they were told. The ones trying to think outside the box had to expend all that extra mental and physical energy just to keep their ideas and initiatives quiet, energy they could have used in service to the city. In the absence of safety, inno-vation doesn't happen. Compare this with start-up culture where throw-ing off the strictures of corporate America—even relatively benign ones like offices with doors or face-to-face meetings or long pants—is thought to free the mind and create space to come up with the next big thing.

Whether it's innovation or creativity, research has found that abusive supervision undermines employee creativity for commonsense reasons. When your boss is mean, you're less excited about coming to work and you start to dislike your job. You become less likely to go the extra mile, to think up a clever way to improve a product or streamline a process. Why bother if your suggestions will just be ignored or even ridiculed? Or if your boss is going to hog the credit? Or if trying to do that new clever thing will just get you hassled by a boss, or a city mayor, who has to control everything?

In a 2007 study led by Christine L. Porath and Amir Erez, participants who suffered rude treatment were 30 percent less creative and brainstormed 25 percent fewer ideas; the ideas they did come up with were on the whole less creative than those envisioned by others in the study. Asked to come up with a list of uses for a brick, the participants who were treated poorly suggested the most obvious, such as "build a house" or "build a wall," while the suggestions from others required a more dramatic shift of perception, such as selling the brick or seeing it as "abstract art."[30]

WHAT IS THE OPPOSITE OF MEAN?

Whether in business, politics, or sports, you can recognize "civil" leaders by the fact that they engage in important behaviors with predictable outcomes. This is what civil leaders do:

- Spend more time on values than they do on mission. By explicitly stating their values and getting others to sign on, they make it easier for themselves and their group to ensure everything they do aligns—on the field, in the halls of Congress, or in the boardroom.
- Reward collaboration, not just competition. By forging connections and building trust in their teams, they build a culture that leverages the individual gifts of the group.
- Encourage people to "fail forward." Entrepreneurial leadership is about innovation, and innovation isn't possible without some degree of risk and the inevitable failure that comes from trying new strategies. Civil leaders create a safe space

to learn from failure and use those lessons going forward.

- Share power. By giving their constituents greater autonomy and supporting their individual growth, leaders reap the collective rewards.
- Give recognition. Civil leaders are quick to reward and highlight innovation, excellence, and demonstrated commitment.
- Support and celebrate the community. It's not just results that matter, but the environment that engenders them.

The result of these "civil" leadership behaviors? Motivation levels increase, team performance improves, and loyalty and commitment are fostered. These leaders are experienced as having a high degree of personal credibility and are more effective in meeting role-related demands.

MEAN ENCOURAGES EXCESSIVE RISK

You don't become an entrepreneur unless you're comfortable with risk. And any number of great companies would not exist if their founders hadn't gone far out on a limb. But an appetite for risk is yet another entrepreneurial character trait that can badly backfire, and that's especially true in the case of these narcissistic men who think they're the smartest guy in the room and who won't defer to the judgments of others.

This isn't just a speculative point; it's a key research finding by Penn State business scholars Donald Hambrick and Arijit Chatterjee. They have spent the last six years delving into the downside of CEOs with complex narcissistic personalities—what Hambrick and Chatterjee describe as "malignant narcissism" (which has since been equated with psychopathy).[31] Along the way, they published a cited paper titled "It's All About Me: Narcissistic Chief Executive Officers and Their Effects on Company Performance."[32]

These leading management researchers became interested in this area after they realized that others hadn't looked very closely at self-absorbed CEOs—perhaps thinking, as they explained later, "that executive narcissism is not of much theoretical or practical significance. Our study shows that narcissism in the executive suite can have major consequences for organizations."[33]

To conduct their research, Hambrick and Chatterjee came up with an interesting methodology. They selected 105 companies in the technology software and hardware industries from 1992 to 2004. Then they analyzed annual reports to see how far and wide the CEO's photo was plastered over this document. They also considered how front and center the CEOs put themselves in their respective company's media strategy and how often they used pronouns like "I" and "me" in press interviews. They then looked at the CEO's compensation as compared with the next highest paid individual in the firm. Last, they compared observed levels of CEO narcissism with the decisions those CEOs made and the performance of their companies. "In contrast to the idea that strategic decisions are arrived at by cold rational calculations," they were instead "interested in the human element of strategy, focusing on the strategists themselves."[34]

What they found was that malignant narcissist CEOs tend to choose options that have the greatest potential for attention and applause, rather than the greatest potential for long-term sustained growth and meeting the needs of various stakeholder groups. They favor "strategic dynamism" and grandiosity, as opposed to "strategic incrementalism" and stability. This leads them to make more acquisitions and larger acquisitions, deals that represent quantum actions that are big attention-getters. They tend not to focus on incremental improvements of product quality, lining up new distributors, or reducing costs—actions that tend not to attract much acclaim.

While they didn't garner much applause, grandiosity and narcissism might explain the sixteen-day federal government shutdown of 2013, when entrenched feelings around the Patient Protection and Affordable Care Act (Obamacare) brought the House and Senate to loggerheads. It earned headlines for grandstanders from both parties, but the more intransigent Republican leadership saw how such a dramatic action would attract attention. While Democrats pointed to Republicans, Republicans pointed to Texas Tea Party freshman Ted Cruz, who reportedly got dressed down by angry members of his own party accusing him of urging the shutdown without an exit strategy. For his part, after the crisis was over, Cruz said on *Face the Nation*, "I think it was a mistake that President Obama and the Democrats shut the government down this fall."[35] With politicians trading blame for a high-risk gamble that went nowhere, many Americans felt Congress had played fast and loose with their jobs, their money, and their credit. According to Standard & Poor's, the shutdown cost the US economy roughly $24 billion, evoked the ire of foreign investors, and increased US borrowing costs. Though Hambrick and Chatterjee studied the world of business, one could see how increasing "strategic dynamism," in fact, may explain much of the public brawling witnessed in Washington, particularly since 2010.

While Hambrick and Chatterjee found that, in general, narcissistic CEOs "generate more extreme and irregular performance than non-narcissists," their research did not find that they ultimately generated "better or worse performance." But other research has posited a closer link between a need for acclaim and decisions that hurt the bottom line. For example, a 1997 study in *Administrative Science Quarterly* sought to explain why CEOs overpaid for companies they acquired. The study found that CEO hubris is closely associated with the size of the premium paid, with the result of diminishing shareholder wealth.[36]

Risky behavior can threaten firms in other, more extreme ways, too, through actions that put companies in the crosshairs of government regulators or produce bad press and hurt the brand. Research in the United Kingdom over the past decade has established a correlation between firms accused of environmental degradation, corruption, fraud, or financial misrepresentation with strong indicators that these firms were directed by men who exhibited psychopathic-related behaviors. Mean men, in other words, are more likely to break laws and expose firms to legal liabilities.

This research helps explain the trouble that Apple found itself in in early 2014, as revelations surfaced that the company—under Jobs's leadership—conspired with other Silicon Valley firms to forge an agreement that they wouldn't poach one another's employees, a move that helped keep wages down and was in violation of antitrust laws. Jobs was said to be the driving force in this effort. Herbert Hovenkamp, a professor at University of Iowa College of Law and an expert in antitrust law, said that Jobs "was a walking antitrust violation. . . . I'm simply astounded by the risks he seemed willing to take."[37] Apple and other tech companies paid $324 million in April 2014 to settle a class-action suit brought because of its anticompetitive practices.[38]

Beyond the antipoaching pact, Jobs was behind an effort to fix the prices of e-books for its own gain. A federal judge later ruled that "Apple played a central role in facilitating and executing that conspiracy." Hovenkamp said about Jobs's behavior in both cases that he "was so casual about it, so bold. Didn't he have lawyers advising him? You see this kind of behavior sometimes in small, private or family-run companies, but almost never in large public companies like Apple."[39]

Steve Jobs also took enormous risks in backdating stock options at both Apple and Pixar to increase their value. As James Stewart wrote in the *New York Times* about that case, "Mr. Jobs himself received options on 7.5 million shares, which were backdated to immediately bolster their value by over $20 million. Apple admitted that the minutes of the October board meeting where the grant was supposedly approved were fabricated, that no such meeting had occurred and that the options were actually granted in December."[40] While other executives went to prison for backdating options, Jobs was never charged.

The research correlating risk-taking with narcissism also offers insights when thinking about Dov Charney, who greatly damaged American Apparel through his risky personal behavior. The lawsuits against Charney, and the bad press they generated, made some investors wary of American Apparel, fearing that new scandals could emerge.

But it was Charney's use of undocumented workers and false statements to regulators that actually produced the biggest liabilities for American Apparel. In September 2009, American Apparel dismissed over 1,500 employees in Los Angeles after a government investigation revealed discrepancies in the company's employment records, such as the use of false Social Security numbers.[41] (Wages and labor laws were not subjects of the investigation. American Apparel reportedly paid its employees between $10 and $18 per hour and offers health and life insurance benefits.)[42]

A California class-action complaint against Charney stated that he claimed in an SEC filing that his company adhered to all employment and immigration regulations and that all American Apparel's factory workers were documented. Court documents refute the accuracy of this statement. American Apparel also didn't clearly disclose to investors that it had previously paid a fine to the Immigration and Customs Enforcement agency (ICE), and in fact it had made false statements in SEC filings about that matter.[43] Payment of the fine to ICE was not a catastrophic event, but omitting to disclose it to shareholders, and perpetuating a story line that implied that American Apparel was the model savior to immigrants, turned into the catastrophic snowball rolling down the hill.

This revelation—that Charney and the company's CFO failed to disclose material information affecting financial performance—proved to be very damaging to the company, leading to a decline in the company's stock price to the point that it was delisted from the American Stock Exchange. As of this writing, American Apparel's stock, which had once reached a high of sixteen dollars, is trading at fifty cents per share.

Even when risky or abusive behavior doesn't hurt a company's stock or its brand, it can inflict other costs. Human resources professionals know the havoc just one incident of alleged misconduct can wreak. Additionally, according to a study conducted by Accountemps and reported in *Fortune*, surveyed managers and executives spent the equivalent of *seven weeks a year* cleaning up after uncivil leadership.[44]

Self-confidence, such a prevalent characteristic of mean men and for entrepreneurs in general, can easily edge into hubris. Researchers have documented the prevalence of hubristic thinking among entrepreneurs, showing how and why they suffer from a dangerous level of overconfidence. One study developed "a hubris theory of entrepreneurship," arguing that founders tended to be overconfident in multiple ways, overestimating their knowledge, making unduly optimistic predictions about the future, and having an inflated view of their own personal abilities. That's a deadly combination for anyone starting anything. But it gets worse. According to the study, overconfidence was most closely indexed with "highly complex, dynamic tasks related to the new venture."[45] One stark example is Donald Trump accepting the Republican nomination in the 2016 election. In the face of war and destruction, poverty and violence, a nation poised on the brink, he had high hopes for his own performance: "I am your voice. I alone can fix it."[46]

The summary of a decade of research on the effects of CEO hubris and, more specifically, its undesirable outcomes was published in a 2012 issue of the *Journal of Business Ethics*. The results were unambiguous: "The finding that hubristic tendencies in a CEO entail negative or non-optimal outcomes for the organization is highly relevant to interested parties in the business community, such as investors, lenders, regulatory authorities and competitors. The effects captured are economically negative and significant."[47]

All this, the authors suggested, was a recipe for "venture failure." The very same self-confidence that enables founders to initially surge may doom them in the end.

CHAPTER NINE

GETTING AWAY WITH MEAN

IF MEAN MEN CAN INFLICT so much damage on organizations, why are they able to stick around? How can high-level leaders behave so badly and get away with it?

In some cases, of course, they don't get away with it, and plenty of difficult founding CEOs get drummed out of their own companies by investors who understand the value of authenticity in leaders.

But often mean men escape any accountability for their behavior and are able to reign unchallenged in positions of power. Why is that?

The answer tends to vary, depending on the situation, and a combination of factors are at play. A key factor, as we've seen, is that mean men can be enormously charismatic. They draw others to them with the force of their vision and the allure of their creativity. Subordinates and wives may suffer enormous emotional pain, but they hang in there because of the upsides of being around such a strong life force.

Beyond that, though, more practical factors are at play that deserve exploration before we move on to consider constructive ways to deal with mean men.

ABSOLUTE POWER

Entrepreneurs who manage to build companies without giving up much equity can come to wield absolute power over their realms, seemingly unaccountable to anyone. We've seen that with some of the men we've met so far in this book: Dov Charney always believed that being the dominant stakeholder in American Apparel—no matter how outrageous his behavior, or how damaging to the company it would become—meant he couldn't be forced out by shareholders. Henry Ford bought out his investors as soon as he could, in large part to satisfy his large appetite for total control. Only after his advertising firm was bought out did Peter Arnell have a boss and independent directors who had a say in how he ran the place. And Mark Pincus carefully orchestrated things so it would be very difficult for investors in Zynga to remove him as CEO.

The Google guys and Mark Zuckerberg of Facebook—while not identified as mean men—have crafted elaborate, separate-tier founder classes of stock in their respective companies that creates a founder-controlled governance structure. Their decision to stay running these businesses is entirely up to them. Virtually impenetrable governance structures eliminate the possibility of stockholders or their boards firing them.

Business leaders with majority ownership of their organizations are hardly new, but they've become more common in recent decades thanks to changes in the economy. Capital is easier to come by for entrepreneurs, and the falling costs of technology have made starting certain kinds of companies a lot easier. So while most young people interested in business used to go work for large corporations, starting their own thing is now a more viable option. That's especially true in the creative and information sectors, where scrappy entrepreneurs who operate with a lean model can build profitable companies that they fully control.

The success of Harvey Weinstein is a case in point. Weinstein was born in Queens, New York. His father was a diamond cutter, and his mother was a stay-at-home mom. After high school, he attended the State University of New York at Buffalo where he and friend Corky Burger formed Harvey & Corky Productions to promote rock concerts. The company did well, and Weinstein dropped out of college to pursue his career as a concert promoter full time. In 1979, Weinstein sold his stake in the company so he could pursue his film interests with his brother, Bob.

The company they formed, Miramax, started out operating with a very small budget. Their first major success, *The Secret Policeman's Other Ball*, was very profitable because they acquired two concert films inexpensively overseas and edited them into one film suitable for a US audience. The Weinstein brothers built up their business slowly through the 1980s with foreign and artistic films before scoring a major success with *The Thin Blue Line* and then releasing the major breakout film *Sex, Lies, and Videotape*. By the late 1980s, they controlled a large and profitable film company—all without sacrificing any significant equity to outsiders.

But while Miramax enjoyed enormous success, it was also a hellish place to work, by many accounts. *Vanity Fair* published a revelatory depiction of the Weinstein brothers and the culture the brothers created within Miramax. Ex-employees described the company culture as "very fierce" and "all about aggression." Myrna Chagnard, known as a ballbuster in her time, couldn't hack it, telling *Vanity Fair*, "I almost had a nervous breakdown. . . . I couldn't take the stress anymore, of having Bob say, 'You're fired!' I would get my stuff and go down to my car, and then he would call me back. I started to lose weight. I was moody, depressed—it almost destroyed me. I went on workmen's comp and stayed out for three or four months. I was a basket case." A former publicist said that "working there was like having your feet held to the fire. Everyone had terrible stories, everyone was petrified of them. My first experience with Harvey was when he was flying out for a premiere. He would usually arrive the day of the screening, and he called from the plane and said, 'When my plane lands, if I don't have 25 tickets in my hand, you're fired!'"[1]

Former employee Jeff Rose, once a favored employee at Miramax, said he fell from Harvey's good graces when he was with Harvey at Cannes: "We were in a staff meeting at seven a.m., and he said something about some deal. I disagreed, and instead of saying, 'Hey, you know what? We're going to do it my way because I'm the boss,' he took a table set for breakfast and just tossed it on me."[2] After that, Rose was off the short list of favored employees at Miramax. Within the next six months, Rose, too, lost weight, became more worn down, and finally quit. "He pushed me to the edge—I definitely looked over—and I left."[3]

Employees were genuinely afraid of both brothers; some were more afraid of Bob than Harvey, and for others it was the reverse. Alison Brantley, former head of acquisitions, said that when Harvey became angry, "he would kind of puff up, like the barometric pressure had changed, so you'd think he was going to explode. Sometimes he would explode. His face got really red, and his whole expression would go to stone. It wasn't like he was going to throw chairs. It was more you thought he was going to go right for you, strangle you."[4]

Mark Lipsky said, "When Harvey [lashes out], he wants to hurt people. He has moments of dementia where he really loses it—he gets so into whatever it is, he's not thinking straight. There isn't a woman in that office that wasn't made to cry. Could be anything, even a marketing concept. Once I saw him so flummoxed, and so bent out of shape about something, that he was screaming at a woman, just berating her beyond belief, and he was calling her some man's name—he didn't even know who he was talking to. . . . When he turns on you, it's with venom. And it is personal."[5]

Weinstein was aware that his behavior was problematic, and he once blamed his ill temper on a poor diet and poorly regulated blood sugar. At one point, he agreed to see an anger management specialist. But at no point did he put his leadership at risk through his excessively abusive behavior. Because Harvey and Bob had total control of Miramax, they could get on with being as mean as they wanted.

COMPLICIT OVERSEERS

After Miramax was acquired by Disney in 1993 for $60 million, Harvey and Bob finally had bosses with the power to curb their excesses. Only that never happened; Disney let the Weinstein brothers run Miramax as they saw fit, as long as it kept generating hits and profits.

In 2000, Harvey drew negative attention when he put a reporter for the *New York Observer* in a headlock and dragged him out on the street as the paparazzi snapped pictures. When Harvey released the reporter from the headlock, he yelled, "You know what? It's good that I'm the fucking sheriff of this fucking lawless piece-of-shit town."[6]

Normally, there would have been repercussions if a top executive of a major public company did something like that. But not in this case. In addition to churning out hits like *The English Patient*, which won an Academy Award for best picture in 1996, Miramax made a reported $145 million profit for Disney in 2000. Top Disney executives may have considered the Weinstein brothers "pigs," as one observer put it, but they made plenty of money and so they were left alone—even if Harvey did assault reporters in public, or allegedly scream at the then-chairman of the Democratic Party, Terry McAuliffe, "You motherfucker! I'll rip your balls off!"[7]

This is not uncommon: top executives and boards see their main jobs as generating growth and profits, and such values as basic authentic leadership are often viewed as secondary. That's a mistaken and narrow view, given the costs and risks associated with having mean men in leadership positions, as discussed in chapter 8. Moreover, as we'll see in chapter 10, there are major upsides when companies are run by collaborative leaders with high emotional intelligence.

Still, these realities are not yet conventional wisdom, and the view of many board members is that "style" is less important than "results." As long as the results are seemingly strong, bad personal behavior may be either forgiven or overlooked.

Like the Weinstein brothers, Peter Arnell eventually sold his private fiefdom to a larger company, Omnicom, in 2001. After the acquisition, he, too, still enjoyed wide latitude to run things as he saw fit, and there is no indication that Omnicom pushed him to change a personal behavior style that could be highly abusive. Arnell's relationship with Omnicom soured only when he made missteps that hurt the bottom line, such as the infamous redesign of Tropicana's packaging that led to a precipitous drop in the product's sales. It was okay with Omnicom for Arnell to be an abusive person who made the firm money. It was not okay to be someone who hurt the firm's business.

When Dov Charney was finally forced out by American Apparel in June 2014, after a long string of scandals and a falling stock price, what was remarkable is that he had survived so long. Charney was ousted after the company's board hired a law firm to investigate his misuse of company funds for personal expenses and how he dealt with a former employee who accused him of sexual harassment. The investigation found that "Charney had known about but failed to stop a blog created by an American Apparel employee that displayed naked photographs of former saleswoman, Irene Morales, who had sued him."[8]

Of course, that sort of behavior should hardly have been surprising after years of revelations. So why did it take American Apparel as long as it did to finally fire Charney? Perhaps the biggest reason was that Charney owns 27 percent of the company and, as both chairman and CEO, was able to stack his board with directors who tolerated his risky behavior. In an April 2014 proxy statement, amid ongoing calls from shareholders for better management of American Apparel, the company suggested that the board really did engage in meaningful oversight. It said that one of the directors, Allan Mayer, was a "lead independent director" whose role created "a balance of power between the Chief Executive Officer and the independent directors," allowing Mayer and his team to "provide objective and thoughtful oversight of management."[9]

But Mayer, a PR professional by trade, didn't play that role until the very end. When Mayer was asked after Charney's firing why that step hadn't been taken sooner, he said: "A board can't make decisions on the basis of rumors and stories in newspapers."[10] We'll revisit and dig into the lessons from the Charney termination in chapter 11, "Surviving Mean."

Board deference to CEOs is a common problem, even when that executive isn't a huge company shareholder. As a 2004 study noted, "a CEO-centric model of corporate governance is predominant in the U.S. as boards, subordinate officers, gatekeepers, judges, and shareholders largely defer to the chief executive, even in the Sarbanes-Oxley era."[11] That study was published after the Enron scandal, but before the even more egregious risk-taking by top executives brought the U.S. economy to the brink of collapse. In the wake of the 2008 financial crisis, "dysfunctional deference" to CEOs was again cited as a reason why dangerous behavior went unchecked.

Even more deference is paid to company leaders who were entrepreneurial founders, not just because they are major shareholders, but also because they have outsized talents and can become cultlike figures. In the case of American Apparel, the result was disaster.

MURKY STANDARDS FOR CONDUCT

How mean is *too* mean when it comes to an organizational leader? While management consultants and apostles of executive EQ may be able to give a clear answer to that question, the proper boundaries of authentic leadership for leaders remain largely uncodified. And this in turn can make it difficult to mount an intervention in the face of abusive leadership.

In contrast, a range of behaviors by leaders are unequivocally out of bounds, and the list of those behaviors has grown in recent decades as a result of changing norms and litigation. Sexual harassment and alcoholism, along with racism and homophobia, may have been no big deal in the *Mad Men* era, but they are risky kinds of behavior today—and often clearly prohibited by organizational codes of conduct and local legislation. Likewise, there tend to be clear rules around conflicts of interest and disclosure of sensitive proprietary information.

The destructive attributes of mean men can be as damaging to organizations as any of the behaviors mentioned above, but they can be harder to identify and document. Moreover, the business world has been slow to codify standards of conduct in this area. As we'll see in chapter 10, some leading-edge companies do explicitly bar abusive supervision, regardless of level, and more are moving in this direction as evidence mounts of the negative effects of mean. But this remains far from the universal norm. Lawsuits brought in response to workplace bullying may accelerate the pace of change here, just as litigation in other areas has led to new codes of conduct. Even as that happens, though, the persistent problem remains that concretizing the behaviors discussed in this book is difficult: How controlling is too controlling? How much undermining of subordinates is too much? How many put-downs or outbursts does it take to cross the line?

We'll discuss how to tackle this problem more in the final chapter, but the point here is that the murkiness of standards in this area stands as yet one more reason that leaders can get away with meanness: as a practical matter, mean can be hard to call out. Confronting a leader about his style and personality can be uncomfortable enough for a board member, investor, or other stakeholder, but it's even trickier in the absence of concrete company standards that can be invoked. Companies with strong cultures of behavioral expectations, feedback, and evaluation have found ways to ensure that such hard conversations can happen, as we'll see later, but many companies don't have that kind of organizational culture—especially those that have been built and shaped by mean men.

The challenge here is not just having a board of directors with the wherewithal to intervene and processes for delivering tough feedback. It's also crucial that overseers recognize the linkage between an executive's personal behavior and the ability of an organization to truly thrive. Making that connection can be difficult given that hard metrics are elusive on this score. On the other hand, plenty of metrics exist to measure when a company is moving in the right direction—and if those metrics are strong, it can be tempting to ignore disturbing information about a leader's abusive behavior and hard to stage an intervention.

When Steve Jobs became de facto CEO of Apple in July 1997, the company's stock was trading at around fifteen dollars a share. When he resigned from Apple in August 2011, shortly before his death, the stock was trading at nearly four hundred dollars a share. Given those results, it's no wonder that Apple's board didn't pressure Jobs to change his ways.

Dov Charney also enjoyed wide latitude when times were good for American Apparel. But the day before Dov Charney was fired, American Apparel's stock was trading for sixty-five cents a share, and the board had been under intense pressure for months to show it was serious about turning the company around. If the stock hadn't fallen so low, Charney might still hold the CEO position today.

Apple's success under Jobs is often cited as evidence that the abusive and just plain weird behavior of a genius CEO should not be held against him if that person is getting results. But as we now know, Apple barely dodged some serious bullets caused by Jobs's risky behavior. In a different regulatory climate, the company could have faced a major scandal and government fines for either its antitrust practices or its backdating of stock options. If American Apparel's board had moved faster, that company might not have ended up in such the bad shape it was in by the time Charney was finally ousted.

Earnings, profits, and stock price are not the only factors to consider in looking at a company's health. Organizational culture matters, too, and so does the example set by the leader guiding that culture.

MEAN UNDER THE RADAR

The outbursts of men like Steve Jobs and Harvey Weinstein were (and are) legendary, as was the sleaziness of Dov Charney, and it would have been hard for the boards of Apple, Disney, or American Apparel to not have some awareness of how these three men behaved. But it's quite possible these overseers didn't know the full extent of the abusive or controlling behavior. In more subtle cases, those in the position to check mean behavior—whether board members, investors, or partners—may know very little about how bad things are inside an organization.

That might be true for different reasons. For starters, abusive behavior in work relationships often goes unreported, just as it does in personal relationships. Those subjected to abuse may blame themselves, make excuses for the behavior, or fear retaliation if they call it out. Or the actual behavior may be borderline in a way that makes it difficult to say unequivocally that it was bad and why. That can be especially so in the case of leaders like Steve Jobs who inflict emotional pain or play power games in very sophisticated ways. It's one thing to know that a leader is engaged in behavior that is harsh and controlling in a way that undermines people and is destructive to morale. It's quite another to articulate a detailed and useful complaint about such behavior.

And, anyway, who do you complain to if the CEO is the perpetrator? Even high-level executives at a company may not feel comfortable approaching board directors and investors to complain about a CEO. And many companies, especially newer ones, may have no mechanisms in place for staff evaluation of the CEO. In short, there simply may not be easy ways for those with the power to take action against an abusive leader to get the information they need in order to take that action.

In New York State, Attorney General Eric Schneiderman pushed for legislation that firmly protects the rights of whistle-blowers for exposing misdeeds by executives. While the law did pass and took effect in July 2014, it only applies to nonprofits.

The board of American Apparel took the highly unusual step of hiring a law firm to investigate its CEO, at which point it accumulated enough information to remove Charney from the CEO role. In other cases, which we'll talk about later, boards or investors have brought in management consultants to gather intelligence about what's really happening in a company. But these sorts of steps require that there is suspicion of destructive behavior in the first place.

A FREE PASS FROM THE MEDIA

In theory, the media can be a powerful force for exposing mean men and creating a drumbeat for action. The media certainly plays that role when it comes to leaders who make bad business decisions and preside over failing companies, or leaders who enjoy excessive compensation and perks (like Steve Ballmer at Microsoft).[12] Business news is filled with articles skewering young entrepreneurs who overreached or CEOs who didn't see the next big thing.

Rarely, though, does the media go after business leaders for their abusive or controlling behavior, and worse, it often overlooks or downplays such behavior in press coverage. Walter Isaacson did serious damage to Steve Jobs's reputation by revealing just what a terrible person he was in many ways. But Isaacson's book came out after Jobs was dead. And while plenty of other book authors had chronicled Jobs's personal flaws over the years, the mainstream business press seldom amplified those reports or drew on them to present a more balanced—and less flattering—portrayal of Jobs's leadership at Apple. In 2009, for example, *Fortune* named Jobs "CEO of the Decade" and wrote an overview about the years since he'd returned to Apple.[13] But beyond noting in passing that Jobs was a "tyrannical perfectionist," the fawning article had nothing to say about Jobs's treatment of people, nor the talented people who could no longer stomach his abuse and went to other tech firms. The article noted the stock-option backdating scandal only in passing, quoting Jobs as saying that it was "completely out of character for Apple."[14] Overall, Jobs emerged from the article as a towering hero of modern-day business.

To be sure, some business leaders do attract negative coverage for their bad behavior, which hit a zenith with gossipy online publications like the now-extinct *Gawker* and *Valleywag*. But reporting on such bad behavior is often mitigated by lavish praise and the rationalization that the geniuses are often flawed and, well, that's just the price of genius. The coverage of Harvey Weinstein is a case in point. Incidents like his assault on a reporter and his threats to the chair of the DNC were too high-profile to ignore, but articles that recounted these instances tended to nonetheless be positive overall. As a long *New York* profile gushed, "all the legendary bad behavior cannot obscure an objective fact: Harvey Weinstein is a cultural good."[15]

Why does the media tend to overlook or apologize for abusive behavior? First, like board directors and investors, business reporters are keenly focused on the bottom-line results of leadership, and the overriding interest in assessing a leader often boils down to whether he is succeeding or failing at generating value. Tech reporters specifically tend to be interested in innovation and what's new. Personality traits get attention to the degree that they feed into a bigger narrative. Like too many directors and investors, many business reporters don't understand that leadership style and organizational culture can be central indicators of a company's health and chances of success.

Second, and related, many of the reporters may buy into the assumption that good leaders often need to be tough to get results. Because business is ultracompetitive and the stakes are high, mean can be seen as an asset. So why criticize an entrepreneur who is just doing what is necessary to survive?

Third, getting sources to talk about abusive behavior may be extremely difficult, especially if they are still in high positions at a company. Walter Isaacson was able to get Apple's chief designer, Jony Ive, to talk about the grief of working for Steve Jobs. But Isaacson was an unusually high-powered writer, and he was working with Jobs's support. It's unlikely that Ives would share similar information with other reporters.

Fourth, and perhaps most important, journalists are extremely concerned about maintaining access to sources and to organizations as a whole. During the 2016 election, Trump pulled the press credentials from the *Washington Post*, BuzzFeed, Politico, the *Des Moines Register*, and the *New Hampshire Union Leader*, all based on their coverage he didn't cotton to. He went on to call the media in general "disgusting," "phony," "crooked," and "dishonest."[16] In February 2016, Trump went so far as to say if elected he would "open up our libel laws so when they write purposely negative and horrible and false articles, we can sue them and win lots of money. . . . We're going to open up those libel laws. So when The New York Times writes a hit piece which is a total disgrace or when The Washington Post, which is there for other reasons, writes a hit piece, we can sue them and win money instead of having no chance of winning because they're totally protected."[17] Digging up damaging information about a leader's personal style and behavior can put a journalist's access at risk.

In short, whether an entrepreneur is a major jerk may seem like a side story that's unrelated to the bigger focus of the reporting, but it's also a story that's hard to source and which may carry career risks. And so very often the media doesn't play the watchdog role it could when it comes to mean men.

THE IRONY OF ACCOUNTABILITY: IT'S ABOUT THE MONEY, NOT THE MEANNESS

Perhaps the best evidence of how much latitude mean men are given for their toxic personalities lies in the stories of how these men finally fall. They are rarely brought down for being mean; nearly always it's their failure to keep hitting home runs in business. Which is to say that in today's era of bottom-line triumphalism, it's fine to be a royal jerk who makes a lot of money for shareholders, investors, and owners. It's not okay to be a royal jerk who fails at that essential task.

Consider Peter Arnell. Heaping abuse on employees for years was not something that bothered Omnicom, the company that owned Arnell's firm, so much that it took action against the marketing guru. But disastrous and embarrassing advertising missteps—well, that was a different story.

The "Tropicana Controversy," as it became known by the advertising community, ensnared Peter Arnell in the biggest trap he ever set for himself. Arnell's company secured a brand redesign contract from PepsiCo focused on revising Pepsi's iconic logo and also freshening up Tropicana, part of PepsiCo's house of brands. While there were mixed opinions on the new soda logo, Tropicana's new look, to put it lightly, fell flat. Customers ranted along with bloggers, one of whom called Arnell "the Bernie Madoff of brands."[18] Call it Arnell's New Coke. In February 2009, weeks after the new design's launch, Tropicana announced it would scrap the new design and revert to the old packaging, eating millions in the process.

Meanwhile, a leaked twenty-seven-page pitch memo Arnell wrote for PepsiCo titled "Breathtaking" was so full of pretentious babble that many thought it must be a joke. Page 21 diagrams how the Pepsi logo's "symmetrical energy fields are in balance," modeling Earth's magnetic fields, while page 26 details the "establishment of a gravitational pull" from the Pepsi can sitting on the shelf to the consumer trolling the aisle, allowing for a "shift from a 'transactional' experience to an 'invitational' expression." Not a hoax—pure Peter.[19]

In the small world of advertising and design, Arnell's stumble became cause for celebration, though he seemingly didn't care about the hit on his reputation. Arnell himself went on to describe his logo rework in a *Newsweek* feature story as "bullshit," adding, "So what the hell—I got paid a lot of money."[20]

CHAPTER TEN

THE POWER OF AUTHENTIC LEADERSHIP

"By the standards of the rest of the world, we overtrust. So far it has worked very well for us. Some would see it as a weakness."[1] That reflection came from Charlie Munger, vice chairman of Berkshire Hathaway and Warren Buffett's business partner and best friend.

Munger was ruminating on the state of corporate life while at Berkshire Hathaway's annual meeting in the spring of 2014. Governance at the firm Buffet and Munger built seems to blast through the expectations of how a diverse amalgamation of companies should be run, and, by all accounts, they seem to run it more like a gargantuan entrepreneurial venture than a lumbering conglomerate. Both men are allergic to distrustful corporate cultures, but how do you use "trust" to manage the fifth largest company in the United States, with $162 billion in revenue and three hundred thousand employees worldwide? How do you manage this hodgepodge of dozens of businesses without a risk-managing general counsel overseeing it all? How can you avoid a finger-wagging centralized human resources department telling every operating unit what to do or not do?

In other words, how do they dispense with all the control mechanisms that would keep a mean man from feeling utterly omnipotent? To some this may seem like corporate negligence or, at the least, corporate naïveté.

But to behavioral scientists—and insightful, psychologically healthy leaders—"trust" is perhaps the most powerful force to earn within organizations, and usually its potential remains unlocked and misused. Buffett and Munger get it: their active management philosophy is based on trusting their managers and giving them lots of autonomy. Over the years, they've shown how this creates more value than if they stacked headquarters in Omaha with heavy control-oriented functions keeping close tabs. Does it work perfectly all the time? No, but neither does any organizational process. Yet they gladly take the risk, and acknowledge that "300,000 people are not all going to behave properly all the time."[2]

At a 2007 meeting, Munger said, "A lot of people think if you just had more process and more compliance—checks and double-checks and so forth—you could create a better result in the world. Well, Berkshire has had practically no process. We had hardly any internal auditing until they forced it on us. We just try to operate in a seamless web of deserved trust and be careful whom we trust."[3]

The belief that an entrepreneur—or any CEO—can accomplish more by developing a culture of trust over one that uses multiple layers of control, including the "hard" control discussed in earlier chapters, may seem unrealistic in today's age of complex, fast-growing start-ups. But two management professors at the University of Zurich have shown that when a firm focuses on layering on control, or in technical management-speak, adding more monitoring and sanctioning for governing, the appearance of new problems only gets worse.[4]

Control-heavy leadership not only doesn't solve the challenge of getting people to behave in a particular way, but it has the paradoxical effect of encouraging them to take advantage of the firm they are supposed to care about. Researchers Margit Osterloh and Bruno Frey call this phenomenon *governance for crooks*.[5] Organizations that avoid this situation place heavy emphasis on baking trust into their culture, and where it's achieved people act in more ethical, civil, and productive ways.

In firms run by mean men, trust is doled out like small crumbs, yet vacuumed away just as easily. They cannot build genuine sustainable trust because they cannot let go of control. They see the act of trusting others simply as an act of diminishing their personal dominance. Though these entrepreneurs will probably not surround themselves with a large group of literal crooks, the absence of trust creates its own self-fulfilling prophecy. Where people do not *feel* trusted, they will actually require a closer level of supervision. Intrinsic sources of motivation evaporate, and they become more focused on what they want to get from the organization, rather than what's right for the organization.

In this chapter we'll look at the converse of meanness—authentic leadership. In particular, we'll focus on what it takes for an organization and its leaders to make authentic leadership a priority, and the rewards of what comes back when they do. The power of authentic leadership is a quantifiable one. Many entrepreneurially driven firms measure it. They are convinced of the tangible benefits that accrue when maintaining authenticity and building trust become the modus operandi for interaction, innovation, and collaboration.

THE PRIZE FOR AUTHENTIC LEADERSHIP

Though I have been thoroughly intrigued by leadership and organizational dynamics for my entire career, sober studies on these topics rarely make it to the top of my popular reading list. Except one.

For the past twenty-five years, one annual survey has identified the one hundred best places to work in the United States. It takes more than winning a popularity contest to make it on the list each year, and annual results become a playbook for learning the most cutting-edge practices for building trust and employee engagement. It doesn't take a research genius to see that qualifying companies, many launched years earlier by entrepreneurs, achieve more than simply being acknowledged as special employers. Firms that make it to the top one hundred each year show consistently impressive financial outcomes, typically far better than their industry counterparts. And the way they are led offers a stark contrast to the firms created and run by the mean men discussed in this book.

The results of this study, produced by Great Place to Work, have been licensed to *Fortune* magazine for the past two decades, and the annual special issue they appear in is always highly anticipated.

Those on the *Fortune* 100 Best Companies to Work For list grow at a faster clip than firms overall, with turnover significantly lower in side-by-side comparisons with other firms in each industry category. In my own research, tracking financial performance of the 100 Best that were publicly owned and listed on stock exchanges, I found stock price rising faster than market indices overall. Other researchers, delving into more complex metrics of financial success, have uncovered results in the same direction. (The 100 Best also includes privately owned companies, non-profit hospitals, and law and consulting firms.)

Is there some vague warm fuzziness about these places that elevates them to this list? Do they simply overwhelm employees with the tangible benefits like child care, free snacks, a gym, and other stuff we see at the Googles, Genentechs, and Intuits (who happen to score within the top ten)? Hardly. If you spent a week in any of these firms, you would experience a combination of reasons but none more important than the way they carefully, and in many cases obsessively, manage their cultures and demand that people act with authentic leadership toward one another.

Sure, creating a great place to work has tangible rewards, but creating these environments takes determination and explicit strategies. Everyone, bottom to top, is held accountable for behaving in ways that exemplify the desired culture. Employee development is more than a tagline but a top strategic priority, since people are given significant responsibilities that require their readiness. Absent the micromanagement we too often see with other firms, people here are provided with enough elbow room to innovate, take risks, and even fail when a good idea goes south.

How do highly effective entrepreneurs shape the essential organizational characteristics that enable these firms to become rockets for growth? What results do we see from organizations as a consequence of being led by such leaders?

The question of what makes a fine leader has been debated for millennia and researched by scholars in business and organizational management for at least a half century. What's gotten less attention, though, is the more specific question of what leadership characteristics are required of entrepreneurs who want to create scalable and sustainable organizations. It obviously goes above and beyond having a great idea, raising money, and building something new. Many—if not most—entrepreneurs cannot successfully make this transition to being an authentic leader. But those talented and insightful ones who do tend to share a couple of core traits.

OUTLAWING MEANNESS

Spend a week in Ann Arbor, Michigan, and you'll inevitably find yourself at one of the Zingerman's Community of Businesses. Paul Saginaw and Ari Weinzweig founded it as a traditional Jewish deli, but these entrepreneurs realized early on that growth was dependent on figuring out how to assure each employee thrived at work. They figured it out; Zingerman's grew.

Their brand is known nationally, and the "community of businesses" includes imported gourmet foods, a bakery (Zingerman's Bakehouse), dairy products (Zingerman's Creamery), and a second restaurant (Zingerman's Roadhouse). Acknowledging the value of their brand, they created Zingerman's Mail Order, Zingerman's Coffee Company, ZingTrain, and Zingerman's Catering and Events, among others. By 2012, the firms' revenues rolled up to nearly $60 million.[6]

Wayne Baker, a management professor and head of the University of Michigan's Management Department, has written a few cases about Zingerman's and its approach to achieving sustainable growth. Baker and others firmly believe their growth—and the promise of its sustainability—is thoroughly dependent on the principles that Saginaw and Weinzweig hold about managing people.[7]

They share enormous amounts of information with every employee. Practicing "open book management," teams within each firm see exactly how their division does on a weekly basis. This flies in the face of control-oriented leaders, who believe that withholding information is the front line for controlling people. Zingerman's holds back no information that has any relevance to deeply understanding the businesses and their performance.[8]

They provide decision-making discretion. Employees are encouraged to share ideas, and they have a flexible hierarchy that allows employees to learn and grow continuously.

They are explicit in their intolerance of anything approaching meanness. Leaders are expected to treat employees in the same way they expect customers to be treated. Zingerman's has built a civil environment where leaders set the tone and serve as role models. Managers are taught how to deal with employee issues so that conflict is resolved.

Another key to the company's success is that each unit has a managing partner who owns part of that business. "They make the push to go for greatness," Weinzweig says, and they operate as one business with "semiautonomous units."[9] Zingerman's was so successful they created ZingTrain as a company meant to spread the word to other businesses, offering seminars such as "Fun, Flavorful Finance: Why Our Dishwashers Know Our Net Operating Profit."[10]

USING EMOTIONAL INTELLIGENCE FOR A GOOD PURPOSE

Emotional intelligence (EQ) can be a double-edged sword. At its core, EQ advocates a need for us to recognize, understand, and manage emotions. But as we saw in chapter 7, mean men will use what seems like EQ for diabolical goals. After two decades promoting EQ as a universal panacea, investigators in the United States and United Kingdom are now acknowledging how too many studies that once glorified EQ's organizational benefits are now being vilified for their shoddy research designs.

All is not bleak about EQ, however, and a very positive yet nuanced view of its value is emerging. One critic of the pervasive promotion of emotional intelligence is Wharton professor Adam Grant, but even he has found it to be consequential for moments critical to start-ups: When a new or altered strategy was warranted, it's the emotionally intelligent employees who offered ideas and to greater effect.[11] When colleagues were treated unjustly, those with higher EQ not only felt the righteous indignation to speak up but were also able to keep their anger in check and reason with colleagues. They were more effective in managing up, mollifying more senior leaders through infectious enthusiasm. The great entrepreneurs keep an eye out for hiring talent with a high EQ, and they don't abuse their own EQ to manipulate others.

One of the best studies on the connection between emotional intelligence and entrepreneurial success is a 2012 dissertation by management professor Erin McLaughlin, who surveyed over six hundred entrepreneurial leaders at different companies across the United States. She carefully uses her data to analyze the leader's EQ, along with their company's successes, and identifies linkages between the two. Her findings are summarized this way:

*The overall measure of emotional intelligence showed a signifi-
cant, positive correlation with financial entrepreneurial success,
performance relative to competitors, and personal entrepreneurial success. . . . With a greater ability to identify, understand,
and manage the emotional responses of themselves, and others,
entrepreneurs will obtain a competitive advantage that sets their
business performance apart from their competitors.*[12]

That's certainly a finding that we can see in action by looking at the founders of successful new companies who are still in leadership positions. Sergey Brin and Larry Page of Google are prime examples. The two founded Google while still in their twenties and were mature enough to see early on that they needed a seasoned CEO to help lead the company and to cede some measure of control to that person. But they wanted a CEO who would also value and nurture the culture they had started to create at Google, a culture that valued people's individual creativity and was supportive of their personal goals.

Eventually, though, Eric Schmidt, their first choice, stepped aside, and Page remained as CEO of Google until Sundar Pichai was appointed in August 2015. I'm often cynical about companies who shout to the world what great employers they are. But Google's ability to grow highly multifaceted product and service offerings on a global scale, with an organizational structure of mind-numbing complexity, while remaining a place where employees feel valued and empowered is, well, awesome.

Facebook presents a similar story. Mark Zuckerberg was very young when he cofounded it but was able to recognize where he needed to grow and the help that he required. He's reportedly worked hard to develop his emotional intelligence (for good purpose), both with executive coaching and help from Facebook's chief operating officer Sheryl Sandberg, who is known for combining high IQ with her (civilly practiced) high EQ. While stories proliferate about "Zuck" stealing the idea behind Facebook and pushing out his partner—enough to justify a movie, *The Social Network*—he has built a firm that some of the world's best young minds want to be a part of.

Zuckerberg's position atop Facebook is secure given his stock holdings and the structure of Facebook's board. With a team of seasoned, and well-balanced, executives offsetting his still relative inexperience, he is ranked as one of the most well-liked CEOs in Silicon Valley.

WHAT MAKES FOR AUTHENTICALLY LED ENTREPRENEURIAL FIRMS?

THEY VALUE THE IDEAS OF OTHERS, GIVE CREDIT, AND SAY "THANKS"

Smart and evolved CEOs know they don't have all the answers. They also know employees must be empowered to solve problems and work creatively. Beyond that, they're keenly aware to value and recognize the ideas of others and to bestow recognition when it's due.

Research has found time and again that creativity flourishes best in less hierarchical environments where ideas are valued no matter where they come from—even if that's way down the chain of command. But such environments can exist only if the leader at the top is willing to share with others power and control—and also the spotlight.

Marcus Ryu, the CEO of the software company Guidewire, which we'll look at more closely in a moment, has said that his goal is to create a collaborative organization that supports getting to the right answer, no matter where it originates from in the company.[13]

Of course, all this stands in stark contrast to how Steve Jobs did things at Apple, where he tended to presume that his ideas were the best ideas and that his instincts were almost surely right. Jobs was also accused by many people of absconding with others' ideas and calling them his own.

Great entrepreneurial leaders and the managers who work for them get personal in ways that seem obvious to most of us; they go out of their way to thank people in person or with a handwritten note, for example, or give rewards tailored to someone's specific interests and likes. And that doesn't go just for people directly reporting to them or on their team—great leaders know and recognize efforts across the organization.

In giving recognition, they are also specific in their praise and give it immediately—they don't wait for an annual review. It's not just the show-boats who are singled out, either; great leaders take the time to recognize everyone's contribution, from the admin to the warehouse worker.

THEY CREATE STRONG TEAMS AT THE TOP

Whole Foods Market is led by a seven-person "e-team" with long-standing relationships and who exhibit a level of trust never found in the firms mentioned earlier in this book. As examples, co-CEO and cofounder John Mackey and executive vice president Jim Sud (an early investor) began their friendship forty-seven years ago. CFO Glenda Flanagan joined the company when Whole Foods had six stores. (They have 360 as of this writing.) Though they work in different regions of the United States, those in the leadership group try to spend leisure time together, usually by taking trips together to far-flung places in the world.[14]

As a result, the team realizes better communication and a shared commitment to tackling problems and issues with an eye toward a common goal.[15]

Mackey's views resonate with one leg of research I conducted for my last book, *Guiding Growth: How Vision Keeps Companies on Course*. Data uncovered significant benefits for cohesive executive groups—more than I was actually expecting—and illustrated the power of the senior-most group when they keep their interactions civil. They actually encourage divergent thinking, elicit and manage conflict well, and seek out opportunities to collaborate. When a big challenge hits the firm, they are ready to analyze it from multiple perspectives and seek diverse solutions—all without turf or ego battles.

But none of this is possible without founding entrepreneurs who are able to cede real control to others and truly share power.

WHAT AUTHENTIC LEADERSHIP PRODUCES

Companies run by emotionally intelligent entrepreneurial leaders who trust others and foster strong teams are great places to work, and it's no surprise they annually end up on the 100 Best Companies to Work For list or are killing it on Glassdoor. Of the 515 employees who have reviewed Guidewire on Glassdoor, 97 percent approve of CEO Marcus Ryu, and 88 percent would recommend the company to a friend—ratings that are exceptionally high.[16]

Why does the behavior of the founder and CEO have such a large impact, even in large companies? Because positive values flow downward from the executive suite just as abusive and controlling tendencies do. The investor David Cohen likes to tell entrepreneurs that "your character, values and style will set the tone for the entire organization."[17]

In turn, that tone influences things far beyond the pleasantness of the work environment. It can also improve the bottom line—because a positive and empowering organizational culture has a number of proven benefits.

THEY'RE A MAGNET FOR TALENT

In 2010, the *Boston Business Journal* named HubSpot—the Internet marketing company—as the best midsize company to work for in Boston.[18] The award was gratifying for Brian Halligan, the entrepreneur who had cofounded HubSpot in 2006 and serves as its CEO, because he'd worked very hard to create a positive organizational culture—which he saw as one key to attracting top talent in Boston, where competition is fierce for skilled tech workers. Halligan created that culture in a few ways, including putting a great deal of trust in employees and being extremely transparent about his decision making.

So, for example, Halligan decided there'd be no vacation policy at HubSpot: people could just take time off when they needed it. And Halligan would regularly write wiki articles about what the company was doing, what was on his mind, and what challenges he saw. "The articles are widely commented on and some of our best initiatives get spurred by these discussion threads," he wrote in the *Huffington Post* in 2010.[19] He also created a HubSpot Fellows Program, enabling staff to take courses to improve their skills and also, said Halligan, "to attract employees who like to learn."[20]

Halligan has described the organizational ethos of HubSpot as a "post-modern culture."[21] By which he means that talented people have aspirations that are different from those of their parents and grandparents. Instead of focusing on their pension, they're focused on finding purpose. Instead of hoping for a good boss who treats them well, they want to be in a collaborative setting. Instead of wanting to keep traditional work hours, they want to follow their own rhythms to be most productive.

Most organizations haven't changed to accommodate these new needs. But the ones who do have a competitive advantage in attracting talent. And, of course, better people means better performance and a better bottom line.

It's well known that Google has often been listed at or near the top of *Fortune*'s 100 Best Companies to Work For (and came in number one in 2017).[22] But as significantly, Google also regularly tops Universum's "World's Most Attractive Employers," which surveys thousands of American college and graduate students about where they would ideally like to work.[23]

Prospective talented employees are more likely than ever to evaluate potential work environments, using an increasing number of new online tools like Glassdoor. The higher up the food chain a job seeker is, the savvier they'll be about avoiding toxic bosses and trying to land in a strong, trusting organization.

A growing body of research shows that building strong teams is a key to scaling new ventures and how this, in turn, requires leaders who can place trust in others and also inspire trust. Just as abusive behavior can "cascade" downward, as we've seen, so, too, can "authentic" leadership at the very top shape trust and civility.

If abusive leaders were not so toxic, I would be humored by the frequency with which I find them thinking they have teams, and using the word "team" ad nauseam. What they actually have are groups of people who follow directions. True teams require that members feel empowered to take initiative and make things happen. Controlling leaders are too infatuated with their own vision and, as we have seen, have a hard time ceding this kind of independence.

INNOVATION FLOURISHES

In 2016, the Silicon Valley software maker Guidewire was named the best place to work in the Bay Area for the fourth consecutive year by the *San Francisco Business Times* and the *Silicon Valley Business Journal*.[24] It's also widely regarded as a hugely innovative company filled with superbrilliant people. These are the sides of the same coin.

In contrast to many mature tech companies that have gone public, Guidewire is still run by one of its founders, CEO Marcus Ryu. And since 2001, Ryu has helped build an organizational culture that is premised on several core values. One of those values is rationality, which means—as Ryu has explained—that "decisions must always be accompanied by rational explanation and logic; role and authority are not adequate justifications in themselves." Guidewire is not a place where the "gut instincts" of a top leader are allowed to set the agenda. Rather, all views are valued, regardless of where somebody sits in the company's hierarchy. And one result of this approach, said Ryu, is that "important decisions at Guidewire are virtually always decided by *consensus* by all the relevant key parties."[25]

The emphasis on rationality is bolstered by another key value at Guidewire, which is "collegiality." While that phrase is tossed around at a great many companies, Guidewire has invested the notion with deep meaning—expressing, as Ryu has said, "the principle that Guidewire employees—from senior management to individual contributors—are a community of fundamentally equal professionals."[26] At Guidewire, hierarchy is minimized, along with organizational infrastructure. The only reason that Guidewire has managers at all, said Ryu, "is not to direct the behavior of subordinates but to ensure clarity of purpose and plan, and to create the conditions in which the right answer consistently wins within the team."[27] Like HubSpot, the company trusts its people to manage their time and whereabouts. And it doesn't tolerate "abusive behavior, regardless of seniority or performance."[28] In an interview with the *New York Times*, Ryu has said that the thing he most dislikes in an employee "is two-facedness, where they manage up in a very diplomatic and collegial fashion, but they're a tyrant down."[29]

Guidewire sounds almost like a commune, but it's no laid-back place. In fact, Ryu sees the organizational culture as crucial to its ability to innovate, operate with speed, and avoid screwups: "the devolution of power to individuals accelerates the pace of decision-making and provides self-correction against inevitable errors in management judgment. Were any individual in the company, including the CEO, to act in a dictatorial, dishonest, or irrational way, he would face strong and instinctive pushback from his peers."[30]

Guidewire's formula has been working: The firm, which designs software for insurance companies, has won numerous awards for its innovative products, and they have experienced exceptional growth. In some tough times as business cycles changed, they eventually went on to expand rapidly before going public in 2012. Since then, Guidewire's stock has more than doubled.

The link between organizational culture and innovation is nothing new; it has long been established by researchers. What sometimes gets less attention is the crucial role of evolved leaders in shaping this kind of creative culture.

EMPLOYEES STICK AROUND

Hiring and training new employees is expensive and time-consuming, and all the more so when it comes to senior staff. Which is why abusive leaders who drive away talent are hurting their organizations. But the flip side is also true: employees who work for evolved, supportive leaders are more likely to stick around, and the costs associated with turnover will be lower.

Keeping good people is especially crucial in the tech sector, where fierce competition for talent means that unhappy employees can easily jump ship and command bigger salaries. Worse, losing talent at a crucial moment can hobble a company's growth or prevent it from delivering on big contracts.

The link between organizational culture and retention has long been established by researchers, but making the connection itself is not that simple. For example, Google's famously popular organizational culture hasn't translated into employee loyalty. Quite the contrary: Google has one of the highest turnover rates among large companies, with the average tenure of employees being just 1.1 years. Yet the notion still holds true that employees are more likely to stay on in companies with highly evolved leadership, and here again, Guidewire is a great example. It has notably low turnover compared to other tech firms and a long-standing senior team.

CEO Ryu argues that the Guidewire's culture of "authenticity" is a big reason people stick around. Which is to say that when people are respected and empowered, they feel more fully themselves. Ryu has said that "authenticity binds like-minded professionals to undertake long-term collaborative work more effectively than economic incentives."[31]

Ryu is clearly a leader with high emotional intelligence, using it for purposes of building trust and not for devious manipulation. Same with many other entrepreneurial CEOs—like Brian Halligan of

HubSpot—who foster company cultures where people want to stay in their jobs. Researchers have specifically dug into the link between emotionally intelligent managers and employee retention, and confirmed empirically what intuition would suggest: Employees love working for such leaders. But, even more important—according to a 2012 study—employees are more engaged in their work when they report to emotionally intelligent leaders.[32]

IT'S ABOUT ENGAGEMENT AND TRUST

For today's smartest companies and organizations, the conversation has moved well beyond why abusive leaders shouldn't be tolerated—what should be a low bar—and on to a more ambitious challenge: to raise engagement.

Engagement not only begets better performance and increased profitability, it also embodies what the new generation of talented workers expects, and what most of us probably always wanted. A robust Gallup analysis of more than two hundred research studies found that companies who scored in the top 25 percent for employee engagement were 22 percent more profitable, had 10 percent higher customer ratings, reported 28 percent less employee theft, and had 48 percent fewer safety incidents than the companies in the bottom quartile.[33]

Trust is an even bigger deal. In its place, we see mean men using their manipulative, faux-charismatic charm to inspire passion from those who don't know him well. But the passion never lasts, or it pivots from passionate attraction to consuming repulsion.

Incivility, in any form, ultimately chips away at the bottom line, even if in some cases it bumps up short-term profit and stock price. Authentic leadership on the other hand, and particularly actions known as prosocial behaviors (think the opposite of antisocial), create workplaces that have greater loyalty, reduced absenteeism, increased reliability, and higher job performance. Recall our discussion earlier in the book about David McClelland's time-tested theory of the need for achievement and the need for power. We saw how entrepreneurs in general have a particularly high need for both (with the more effective entrepreneurs using "socialized" power toward good things, like building teams). The subset of entrepreneurs with particularly high levels of the List of Ten characteristics who emerge as mean men exhibit the same high need to achieve. Their need for power is used to *control* others, not to get people to work collaboratively.

Now here's the stunning observation from a group of UK researchers: When leaders act with authentic leadership, and infuse expectations for prosocial behaviors into their corporate cultures, employees become more high-achieving while losing their need for control. Authentic leadership and prosocial behaviors make us want to work harder while at the same time reducing our needs to micromanage.[34]

It all comes down to a matter of trust.

CHAPTER ELEVEN

SURVIVING MEAN
(OR, MEAN MARTIAL ARTS)

"ENTREPRENEURS"

PAST CHAPTERS FEATURED CHARACTERS WHO fit the conventional definition of "entrepreneur," like Dov Charney and Mark Pincus, business founders who grew ideas into large publicly owned corporations. But other types of characters match the more progressive, slightly expanded definition of the term, one that carefully extends beyond the parochial requirement of starting a new business to include a professional need for entrepreneurial aptitudes and traits.

I've presented illustrations of mean men from the worlds of politics, sports, entertainment, and nonprofits—in addition to those who launch and grow businesses. They have all been free agents, unmoored to the internal cultural forces of large organizations that tend to reject—or at least do their best to moderate—meanness. And in each of these fields, and more, we have seen what happens when one or more of the personality variables from the List of Ten moves into the hot zone.

One field particularly rife with entrepreneurs is the "business" of spirituality. Whether they are founding pastors of new churches, rabbis or imams with their own fiefdoms, or self-appointed gurus, they commonly express that same entrepreneurial fervor. Do I differentiate these men from Catholic priests? In a small way, yes. Priests are members of the world's longest-surviving bureaucracy, and as just noted, large bureaucracies tend to purge mean men before they rise to significant organizational prominence. But priests are obviously far from exempt from meanness and abusive behavior when they run amok with the power they hold over their parishioners. The potential for abuse, based on this perceived power differential, may be present, but it is not rooted in the entrepreneurial psyche. Entrepreneurial zeal, in this case, is at odds with the priorities of the organization's executive suite (the Vatican). In management-speak, we saw the extent of the Vatican's horribly broken performance-management system when the child sexual abuse scandals hit the papers and the courts.

I would venture to guess that we all know some story of a spiritual leader who personified the entrepreneurial characteristics discussed here and the personality profile that landed him in the hot zone, creating collateral damage among the most vulnerable: those who trusted him.

Take Mark Driscoll, the preacher who started a Bible study class in his rented Seattle home in 1996. Fast-forward to August 2014. His Mars Hill Church had grown meteorically to become the spiritual home for six thousand members, and thirteen thousand attendees, in fifteen locations in five states. He filled the Seattle Seahawks' stadium to preach, guested on prime-time national television, threw out the first pitch at Mariners' baseball games, and essentially saw the "franchising" potential of his brand. "Brand" is not my word; it's Driscoll's. He would refer to himself among other Mars Hill pastors as "The Brand," and he would make very clear that the draw of Mars Hill was him.[1] In fact, it's the kind of precision branding, matched with enterprise scaling, that any business entrepreneur would envy.

Driscoll knew his market: young families who showed up in jeans and flip-flops, disenchanted with more established versions of organized Christian movements. He grew and met his congregation on their terms. His charismatic rhetoric was edgy, his wardrobe that of the blue-jeaned hipster. For many years, thousands found his irreverent style charming. He was clearly outrageous, especially for those in his line of work, and for many years, his congregants were drawn to his at-times bizarre definition of what was godly or ungodly. Yoga, for example, was "demonic." His writing and sermons increasingly took on strong misogynistic overtones. He railed that mainstream Christianity characterized Jesus as "an effeminate-looking dude" and a "neutered and limp-wristed Sky Fairy of pop culture."[2] Driscoll declared that anointing a woman as an Episcopal bishop was akin to deciding to have "a fluffy baby bunny rabbit as their next bishop to lead God's men."[3] He joked on stage how wives who denied their husbands oral sex on demand were sinful. Why? Because, apparently, his read of the Song of Solomon fit his desired interpretation. If a follower rejected Driscoll's casual comments, it was like challenging God himself.[4]

But by the summer of 2014, a critical mass of Mars Hill Church congregants was calling for his resignation. They accused him not only of objectifying women but of being a bully. Dissent had been brewing for years, but he leveraged his magnetic style with a combativeness in order to decimate resistance. In response to those who questioned his vision he stated bluntly that they would be mowed down: "There is a pile of dead bodies behind the Mars Hill bus," he intoned at a meeting. "And by God's grace, it'll be a mountain by the time we're done."[5] His outward style charmed many, but behind the scenes, he was often vicious, abusive, and controlling.

Criticism began to mount, stemming from ex-members who said Driscoll was quick to shun those who questioned his authority. Fearful of his influence, many church members felt forced to complain indirectly or through third parties. Driscoll's strategy for defusing the discontent was to post a video in which he said he could not address some members' issues because the complaints were anonymous.

Individually, disaffected congregants felt powerless, and Driscoll did little to change that dynamic. What he did not understand, however, was the power of coalition that many members could create when joining together. In response to what many saw as outrageous behavior from "a man of God," a large crowd started to hold banners on the sidewalk during Sunday services, reading "WE ARE NOT ANONYMOUS."[6] And then others piled on, citing Driscoll's bullying and misogynistic ways in calling for his resignation. Judy Abolafya, of Renton, Washington, quit Mars Hill after fourteen years of membership. "It is not OK for him to be arrogant, abusive or prideful," she said. "He needs to step down."[7]

After eighteen years of stunning growth, an escalating string of newly empowered, openly complaining congregants resulted in driving other churchgoers away. Within months, attendance and giving had plummeted so fast that church elders announced it would have to close several Seattle branches and cut its staff 30 to 40 percent.

Driscoll had a knack, like many of his ilk, for deflecting blame. In 2013, Christian radio host Janet Mefferd accused him of plagiarizing fourteen pages of his new book from another preacher. She pushed Driscoll during an interview to be contrite. He offered a tempered apology but ended with an attack on Mefferd for raising her concerns in a public venue.[8]

According to reports on the incident, he responded by saying, "I think it's rude and I think the intent behind it is not very Christ-like. But I'll receive it and I'll try to receive it graciously and humbly. But I wouldn't allow you to pretend to take a generous, gracious moral-gospel high ground. I would not just give you a pass on that—out of love for you. Because I want you to grow as well."[9]

The accusations mounted, and by 2014, they reached a fever pitch. The former Mars Hill Church founder and pastor resigned in October 2014 amid allegations of emotional abusiveness, plagiarism, and misogyny. The church collapsed from a stampede of congregants to other houses of worship . . . and some lost faith altogether.

Driscoll's downfall is instructive in three respects. First, he was taken down not by the church's governing body but by those who—in small groups or individually—originally felt powerless. Second, they found their power in numbers and through their voice of public dissent, as well as through social and conventional media. Finally, his charisma and normally effective ability to "flip" the blame to deflect culpability became neutralized by those standing up in indignation.

Sure, there were Christian media heavyweights calling him out for plagiarizing others' work and his smarmy misogyny. But what brought him down was his arrogance and abusiveness. Those current and former followers, who shouldered the risk of condemnation from others, stood together and exercised their power.

COPING STRATEGIES

Those of us affected by a mean man directly may have no choice but to cope with the situation. For all of us, on a personal level, we need approaches that at the very least blunt the impact of these characters. They try to dump their discomfort on us and seek to infect us with their temper and mood. They are often nonresponsive until they see weakness, and then suddenly they become energetic. For the mean man, there is one goal: to get the bad stuff unloaded from him and dumped onto us.

My organizational work has exposed me to mean men in direct and indirect ways. I have had clients who fit the profiles drawn here. As have others, I've struggled with navigating the bumpy terrain of having my buttons pushed, while simultaneously pondering my own impotence to effectively manage the person and context. So trying and pervasive have I found some of these experiences in my consulting role that twenty-five years ago I wrote an article titled "When Clients Make You Crazy."[10]

The clients who motivated that article were not mean, per se. Rather, they were relentlessly intimidating to the point that I was questioning my competence and confidence. I didn't want to be around them, yet I didn't want to cave into their intimidation on principle. I've fired clients for commitments they never followed through on, but I resisted when their behaviors would annoy me. In extreme situations, I began to question my credibility, even though feedback from others in client firms was positive. No matter: my buttons were pushed and I could not find the reset. While I was fully convinced of their blindness to the impact they had on others, they could not have cared less. I knew I had to understand this dynamic more fully if I was to ever manage it.

The personal soul-searching and deep dive into a body of psychological theory and research for the article mentioned above turned out to be a godsend. What I learned in developing the article, and subsequently expanding on practical applications for the theories and insights, led me to an ever-broadening repertoire of behavioral strategies and mental jujitsu techniques. I still did not like being around the type of men profiled here, but at least I was less intimidated in their presence and far more effective in dealing with them.

There's no guaranteed five-step solution to managing any mean man in any context, but that should come as no surprise. The people and situations vary widely. Becoming more facile with particular ways of responding, though, can go a long way toward finding sanity and peace of mind.

Recall the strategy undertaken by the senior manager for Dov Charney who survived by physically avoiding him and minimizing one-on-one communications whenever she could. Whenever Charney got a new idea, he'd corral any exec he found to relate his brilliance. It didn't matter so much who it was; if one exec was missing from his or her workstation, he'd just find another. This manager strategically planned her workspace, and her workday, so as to always have allies around her when she thought Charney might be on the prowl. She even had colleagues call her if they knew he was looking for her.

While this may have worked as an interim tactic, it's no long-term solution. In many cases, when you have to maintain the relationship, it will take a new way of thinking about when and how his meanness has the most impact, and restructuring the situation in a manner you can influence. This manager wanted another year out of the job—the most she could stand under that leadership—so she found ways to avoid him without triggering further meanness.

As avoidance isn't the answer, let's explore some broad strategies that I and others *have* found effective. I should mention, however, that while these strategies may be fine-tuned to fit your situation, each situation will require new ways of responding, the development of new skills and approaches, and a need to stick with the methods until you feel more proficient and the approaches seem second nature.

1. BRING RATIONALITY TO YOUR EMOTIONAL STATE.

Detaching emotionally is the internal version of talking yourself down off a ledge and can be a good technique when you find yourself immersed in meanness and unable to immediately remove yourself. It requires viewing your situation from a fresh perspective so you can see your circumstances objectively, putting you in a better position to consider options. The emotional part of your brain requires balance with its rational part so it can cool down, calm down, and strategize. Detaching emotionally requires a rapid inventory of the situation:

1. *What's happening right now?* Take a quick inventory of the situation, and write down what you see, hear, and feel.
2. *What are the facts?* Assess your personal (and organizational) needs in the moment, and quickly summarize how you are being treated as a result of trying to get those needs met. What are you trying to accomplish? What do you need to get it done?
3. *What is he doing?* Add more detail on how he is acting and what you think may be triggering his toxic behavior. Don't try to psychoanalyze him; the best you can do is find the

"triggers" that set off this behavior.

4. *What am I doing?* As best as you can, determine the ways you respond to his behaviors now. List how are you reacting (behaviorally and emotionally) and how you have reacted to this same or similar behavior in the past. This is usually the toughest question of the five to answer.

5. *What are my options?* As easy as it may be to find a rational answer, it can be just as difficult to act on it.

When a situation causes emotional pain, our natural reaction is to blame the obvious offender and not do a gut check to see whether we have unintentionally contributed to our own reaction. Looking more rationally at our own role in—and vulnerabilities to—the situation can give us points of leverage for reducing the impact of mean behavior.

2. PROTECT YOURSELF BY GETTING INSIDE HIS HEAD.

When I feel myself getting emotionally wrangled into a client's or colleague's need for control and desire to manipulate, I redirect my thinking from how he's pushing my buttons to thinking through what might be pushing his. Nine years of research into mean men has given me, admittedly, a leg up for understanding what triggers their characteristic behaviors, but most of us can play the analysis game. It's simultaneously helpful in strategizing your responses and diffusing the fear, intimidation, and other feelings that are coincident to being abused or controlled. The need to control others, for example, is typically based on the fear of *losing* control if something unexpected were to happen. In the mean man's mind, acts of controlling and manipulating are efforts to prevent any unforeseen circumstance that might threaten his fragile internal self-control system. His exterior toughness belies the vulnerability.

But manipulation or control through verbal abuse *takes two*. It cannot work without the recipient reacting to his behavior, though it rarely feels like active participation on both sides. "He acts mean, and I respond to his meanness" is how we might size up the situation. Seizing opportunities to break the dynamic between a mean man and his target may require turning attention inward. You may need to look at the elements that have led you or someone else—usually unknowingly—to participate in this lopsided exchange.

Finding yourself on the receiving end of a mean man's behavior does not by itself provoke or cause these exchanges; the victim is not to be blamed. But over the years I have seen in many cases where someone unconsciously gives "permission" to a mean man; this "opening" for his controlling and manipulating behavior begins the dynamic. Though a difference in level of power may be palpable, those who find the courage to respond quickly to a threatening-sounding question, for example, with "I'm uncomfortable with the way you asked me this" show that "permission" is not given. If you've been in these situations, you may not realize in the moment that someone's demands are unreasonable. You may believe you are a good, respectful person, where being "good" means accepting another person's preferences almost without question—but to the mean man, saying nothing, when you are feeling something strongly in your gut, gives him his opening.

You also may be fully aware of the abusive behavior but feel internal pressure to prevent yourself from resisting it. That is, if you cannot "parse" the mean man's behavior and see how it is pushing your buttons in the moment, you may be unconsciously incapable of resisting. Absent this conscious awareness, it's difficult to respond accordingly in real time. With some, bad behavior sets off responses in you that feel almost programmed; your reactions feel automatic if not impulsive.

These are not relationships on equal footing. A power imbalance has been created because of the context. Unspoken rules inherent in organizational hierarchies tell us we are not equals; the roles of parent and child operate similarly. Some of us will succumb more easily to abuse of power imbalances, realizing that we have been manipulated or mistreated only after it has all happened—too long after.

If we were to investigate each of our personal vulnerabilities, we would find layers of personal history: the way we were treated, the self-image we carry inside, the ways we have been affected by impressions (e.g., people or situations) that remind us of something from our past. When events today remind us of something we've successfully kept buried, they can bring up reactions that overrule logic. They tap into a pure, raw emotion that has been stored away and simmering for some time.

We often see those around us who are particularly sensitive to actions by others. It's easy for us to spot a friend who is afraid of anger or tends to absorb blame. For the most part, we feel compassion for them if not empathy. We don't use that knowledge against them to get our own needs met.

Let's face it: we all have our buttons that get pushed. Some of us have more buttons than others; some of us have buttons that need barely a tap to engage. I have learned to (mostly) control my emotional reactions to these men by consciously thinking about the needs that drive them to act so inexcusably when I am the target of their actions. Often, I find myself thinking how pathetic their internal machinations must be in that moment, how their sense of helplessness and vulnerability (the opposite of how they are acting to me) is probably a theme in their daily lives. Trying to get inside their head always helps me get inside of mine; I have learned to better understand my own buttons and what happens when they get pushed. These facets of my personality, the flotsam and jetsam of life's experiences combined with what is hardwired, have created touch points within me. But if I thoroughly ignore my buttons, then I situate myself to become far more vulnerable if one is pushed. Even a somewhat intellectual awareness of their cause and effect tends to give me greater control in the midst of managing, say, a malignant narcissist.

What are the triggers these men see that show someone else's vulnerability to them? In addition to the dynamics I outlined in chapter 2, psychologists have identified five of the most persistent personality characteristics:

- Very high need for approval
- High level of self-doubt
- Low tolerance for conflict; strong desire to keep the peace
- Fear of anger
- Tendency to take responsibility for others' lives

In moderation, these are typically admirable traits. But they can also set us up for potential abuse.

A difficult but empowering exercise to fortify yourself against potential abuse is asking yourself the simple question "What am I doing?" It can help you find your own reactive patterns to the situations that highlight an imbalance of power, attempts to control, or a desire to manipulate.

For years after the engagement with Aaron was terminated, the consultant would get calls from Lisa, his former wife whom he left for another woman. Twenty years with Aaron had left her with "life's biggest enigma." She could not understand how he became such a master of manipulation, knowing how and when to pounce on her vulnerabilities. After about one year in which they didn't have contact, she emailed the consultant to set up a call. She had been working with a talented therapist, and with a commitment to herself to continue self-exploration, Lisa was starting to reap the rewards of her effort. She realized how her own personality characteristics were the ying to Aaron's yang (his ability to find and use Lisa's vulnerabilities). Her first epiphany was acknowledging how the transparency of her vulnerabilities made Aaron's life easier.

Lisa saw how each of the five personality characteristics noted above captured so much of her essence. It must have been effortless, she now believed, for Aaron to find the window to these elements of her soul. She now could understand how her openness during the period of their dating made her live bait for his fishing. Only after many years did she realize how her vulnerabilities had become an outlet for his acting out, his means to control her.

We tend to give in to meanness when pressure is placed on us, and a very quiet but controlling inner voice gives us clues in the form of these defensive responses:

A. I fear they will disapprove of me.
B. I fear their anger.
C. I fear they won't like me anymore.
D. They've been good to me, at times, in the past; I owe them.
E. I feel a duty to comply.
F. If I resist, I'll feel guilty.
G. If I don't comply, I'll feel greedy, selfish, or mean.
H. Saying no, or taking a strong contrary position, will make it so I'm no longer considered a good person.

Most of the time, it's about our fear (A through C), our sense of responsibility (D or E), or our guilt. And most of the time, regardless of the source of the voice, it's misplaced. Distancing yourself from fear requires knowing which values and judgments belong to you and which have been imposed by others. It requires the resolution to face disapproval while grasping tightly to your own values and beliefs.

Most of us haven't been taught how to deal with another person's anger, and most of us have a limited range of responses. It can be very effective to take a strong position and act strategically for yourself. The catch, of course, is that you must deliver on this new response to meanness, and that is difficult.

3. REVISE HISTORY.

Many people find one specific imagery technique to be helpful. When you find that you have given in on something because someone's behavior made you afraid, think of your mind as a video memory storage unit and recall the scene of a recent event. In this quiet and calm space, close your eyes and "replay" the words said by both you and the person intimidating you. Do your best to capture the subtle reactions and feelings of what you experienced throughout the episode. For example, could you feel your heart pounding? Can you recall the images racing through your mind? How did their meanness build to a crescendo? This replay is something you may already do unconsciously, trying to grasp what has happened.

But the second step to this technique is far less commonly employed. Replay the scene again, recall the other person's meanness rising, but then rewrite what happened.

See yourself saying confidently and competently something like "I'm not going to tolerate this. It's inappropriate, and I'm feeling pressured for something that I'm not responsible for." Now, repeat your revised script aloud several times. Monitor how each time you respond in this new way, you move from tentative to strong. You transition from a belief that you could never utter those words to one that you can, and you have a right to. Rewrite as many scenes as you like, and try it frequently.

When these characters want their way, they use power and fear as their approach. This technique helps us experience a leveling of the power differential when we are sharply aware that the differential is being used to scare us.

4. CAREFULLY CREATE—AND KEEP—BOUNDARIES.

Some experts believe that boundaries can work quite well for in-laws, plain vanilla narcissists, and others who are more annoying than abusive. Mean men, though, often see boundaries as a challenge to defeat.

Ed Catmull, president of Pixar and Walt Disney Animation Studios, worked for Steve Jobs for about twenty years until Pixar was sold to Disney. While he saw the effect Jobs could have on many people, Catmull found that creating clear boundaries was a way to reduce the interactions with Jobs that would drive others nuts. He created these boundaries by intentionally avoiding situations with Jobs that may have led to verbal conflicts. Boundaries do not have to be announced (and in many cases, should not be). When you let certain phone calls roll over to voice mail, it's a boundary. Not responding to emails immediately, or responding only at particular times of the day or evening because it seems to evoke less hostility, is another form of creating boundaries.

Fear is the best indicator for determining whether boundary setting is a smart strategy. If even the thought of feeling the impotence experienced from working with these men brings on a fear in your gut, it may signal that boundaries need to be an option.

To deal with less disordered personalities (mean men on the lower end of the red zone described earlier), following the guidelines for active listening can be effective. If you *actively* listen to the mean man, it can help you better understand how they are feeling (upset or problem-ridden, for example), and it can lead *them* to find potential solutions. Unfortunately, if they are higher up in the red zone, they will be oblivious to the specific feelings they may be experiencing and may react with annoyance, since they cannot access their specific feeling-reactions.

As much as I depend on active listening for my professional work and in my personal relationships, I find that it fails almost half of the time to work when dealing with subclinical psychopaths (the successful ones). In these cases, the answer often goes back to good boundaries. The neat "trick" about learning how to set and keep boundaries with mean men is to strive for opacity; to the extent that he never (or rarely) has insight into what you are doing, good boundaries may become a legitimate—even if partial—defense against the toxicity.

5. CREATE BOUNDARIES OF BOREDOM.

The personality structure of mean men requires they have considerable stimulation in their life, day after day. Simply put: they become bored more easily than the rest of us. Rather than the boredom most of us experience, it's more like the French term "ennui," which is an oppressive boredom, even lethargy. Mean men's recipe for staving off ennui is drama, but drama requires an audience and perhaps an additional actor or two. As the drama begins, they feel invigorated, alive. When they attempt to control and manipulate, they feel empowered because it invariably elicits others' emotions. Crazy as it may sound, they need to evoke emotion in others, regardless of what it is, so long as they see it as a result of their actions (the control thing, again).

Often, their need for power can be satisfied by gaining access to our emotions. He needs to know we are there to satisfy him in order to avoid his wrath. But he needs to create drama as a means for manipulating others' emotions. Often, he needs to evoke emotions in others to reaffirm his ability to control. The more his interpersonal reactions reflect this drama, the more it looks to an observer like an addiction. Therein lies a tactic worth considering: When the reward for drama stops coming, he can become agitated. He can become bored. If those around him show no emotion, he may decide it's not worth creating the drama if he doesn't achieve the effect on others he is seeking.

The strategy is to fade into the background, to—in effect—become boring to him. Thoroughly avoiding contact is rarely an option in the contexts we have discussed here, unless of course you have chosen to leave by terminating your employment or the relationship. Rather than avoiding contact, respond with boring, monotonous responses that minimize drama being injected into the exchange. Often, with time, a new person will be found to more adequately provide the drama he needs.

Mark Driscoll, the charismatic and abusive pastor, faced this and other tactics from his once-adoring congregants. Driscoll loved—some would say he was dependent on—the drama between his strong and confrontational rhetoric and the discomfort of his followers. Some left quietly in the early years, but eighteen months before he stepped down, some people found their "voice" to speak out individually, and others found power in numbers to rebuke his behavior. Essentially, his boundaries were tightened to the extent that he no longer could abuse anyone—their responses were boring. And as he took steps to set up a new church—behavior consistent with any entrepreneur who experiences failure—he found the consistent monotony of congregants' scripts having more power than his own.

6. REAFFIRM YOUR WORTH.

Working with someone dedicated to destroying your self-worth is depleting. Knowing your own worth armors you against attacks. In the heat of a dressing-down, use the moment as a cue to realize that what's being said is not necessarily a bald-faced lie but the mean man's interpretation of the facts—and that your view is probably far more reliable.

The mean man often confuses respect with fear, so deep is his need for adoration. When his behavior crosses moral or ethical lines, we might fear him, but he certainly doesn't earn our respect. Moreover, if his behavior begins to affect us in hurtful ways and we tolerate it, then we extend his lack of respect, and it compromises our own ability to respect ourselves.[11]

We feel so awful around these guys partly because they have made it difficult for us to maintain our own respect, so we must find ways to reaffirm our self-worth. Depending on the position we are in, we can confront the mean man directly, remain steadfast in our positions and perspectives, or enlist help to take him on.[12]

This chapter is titled "Surviving Mean," but we need to think more purposefully. The objective is neither to merely survive these characters nor to conquer them, though we'll get to how to conquer mean as a whole in the next chapter. This type of behavior is overwhelming, but trust me that there is hope. Understanding where mean men come from and how they tick enables our real objective: for each of us to work to overcome the power imbalances and recapture dignity and self-respect. Along the way, we reclaim collaboration and good will as forces for social and economic good.

CHAPTER TWELVE

THE BANALITY OF MEAN
(A CALL TO ACTION)

UNCIVIL. ABUSIVE. CONTROLLING. MANIPULATIVE. MEAN.

Of the many ways I have chosen to characterize the men profiled in this book, there is one descriptor that appears only in a direct quote from a victim of mean, and that word is "evil." It's a strong word. Truthfully, we could probably place most of these guys somewhere on the spectrum of evil, with some on the fringe and others landing dead center. Considering "evil" as the exercise of power to intentionally harm, to psychologically or physically hurt another, gives us a valid synonym for mean. But it also has religious overtones, and that bothers me inasmuch as it implies a moral framework. Rather than quibble with morality, this book defines meanness as represented by a range of behaviors most often motivated by psychiatric disorders rather than by immorality.

Many people reframe it in this way, outside of the black-and-white frame of morality. Social psychologist Roy Baumeister sees violent, abusive acts as a "breakdown of self-control."[1] In an interesting twist on how most of us think about evil as manifested in violence, he suggests that "you do not have to give people reasons to be violent, because they already have plenty of reasons. All you have to do is take away their reasons to restrain themselves."[2] It's intriguing reasoning because it begs the question, what circumstances exist in which any one of us has the potential to behave in deplorable ways? What causes that breakdown of self-control?

Since the behavior of mean men is tough to rationalize, when we hear their stories, we like to think of the behavior as evil, something that is not human, an aberration of human nature. This difficulty most of us have in wrapping our brains around the concept of evil and the behavior it elicits leads us to create narratives to attempt to understand or even rationalize evil actions. One is based in trauma and perversion; we might expect such behavior as a response to unbearable circumstances a person may have endured earlier in life. The other is based in psychopathy. Here we understand the behavior to be innate or more or less outside the control or influence of social relations. Hence, the doer of evil is therefore either bad or mad.

But there's a third way, to rationalize the perpetuation of behavior we may characterize as "evil"—a way that may be even more difficult to grasp. Evil people have followers, people who get drawn in by the perverse assumptions and beliefs of the mean man and then find themselves supporting him, or at the very least, passive observers who know on some level that what they are witnessing is just not right. Like the congregations around Driscoll, the employees of Arnell, the support team of Armstrong, the board around Charney, or the voters for Trump. At the extreme, taking the people who submit to dictators as an example, they are the people who "follow orders," who conform to some norm of nonresistance. "Following orders" is not limited to SS generals running concentration camps. It's actually a far more nuanced, complicated, and prevalent activity we see in many institutional or group contexts. Some of us follow along because we're caught up in the creative atmosphere, eager to bask in the glow of "genius." Others of us see a chance to regain a sense of power and self-worth by landing on the "winning" team.

For Frank, it was about believing that the culture of mean was able to coax from him his best work. Frank worked directly for Peter Arnell as a project consultant for many years. He emailed me in 2015 shortly after a blog post I wrote describing Arnell appeared. "It's all true!" he declared. "And in spades." After sending him more information I had amassed on Arnell, from legal transcripts to quotes in advertising-industry periodicals, and asking his personal reflections on the accuracy of it all, he agreed to speak on the phone. For almost two hours, he regaled me with ever more perverse and outrageous stories of Arnell abusing people. "Yet you seemed inclined to continue working with him through all of that," I observed to Frank. "Were you that dependent on him for your income that you had to keep him as a client?"

Frank said the creative projects Arnell brought in provided him with challenge and opportunities to hone his talent. "I saw how he treated his direct staff and found it despicable, but I figured they could leave if they wanted. Arnell was incredibly cruel to women and gays, constantly mocking people. But he was able to keep this atrocious behavior from his clients for so many years. And he enjoyed lying!" Long pause. "They stayed, I guess, the same way I stayed. We all wanted to be treated with more respect, appreciated for our contributions. But looking back, I guess this was the price to pay for being with a perfectionist who did get us all to produce extraordinary work . . . until the end came crashing down."

During that long call, it was as though Frank were describing two people: the monster Arnell and the aesthete Arnell. "Yeah, I guess my continued involvement may have perpetuated a guy like that, since I was responsible for executing many of his creative ideas, making them tangible." Like so many, Frank was following orders. Whether you consider Arnell mean or evil, some of Arnell's victims surely consider him the latter. In his years working with Arnell, Frank became swept up in the illusion that was Peter Arnell and helped sustained the illusion. Reflecting on our conversation after Frank and I hung up, it seemed to me that he was starting to regret it.

In her *Eichmann in Jerusalem: A Report on the Banality of Evil* in 1963, the philosopher Hannah Arendt tried to reconcile the actions of SS officer Adolph Eichmann, a primary architect of the Final Solution to the "Jewish problem" who orchestrated the deaths of millions, with Eichmann the person, who was eventually convicted and hung for his crimes.[3] Covering the trial in Jerusalem for a series of articles she would publish in the *New Yorker*, Arendt made a highly controversial argument that remains polarizing to this day. Neither Eichmann nor Nazi sympathizers, she claims, were motivated to commit their acts out of hatred and malevolence. Rather, they were the result of lack of thought, imagination, and connection to memory. Eichmann, she adamantly believed, was incapable of empathizing with his victims' suffering because he lacked the judgment needed to perceive it. If he had acted out of hatred, Arendt postulates, this would, ironically, have made him more human or at least someone with emotions most of us could identify with, apart from the form they took. Arendt concluded that the most inhuman element of Eichmann was his absence of hatred.

Arendt enraged scores of people by calling Eichmann "ordinary." She in turn was frustrated that her critics could not see that she was trying to capture a state of mind rather than a moral judgment. The state of mind she describes is one in which the depersonalization of the victim takes over and paves the way for licensed abuse, if not brutality. Even if the phrase itself has been complicated by controversy and diluted to the point of becoming cliché, the ideas it connotes are no less relevant. Her final assessment was that Eichmann's ability to do evil stemmed "from his inability to think from others' points of view or to have an internal dialogue with himself. Evil itself was banal, she said, in that it was 'thought-defying.'"[4]

In the realm of mean, I find Arendt's point hits home. We like to think of evil people as extraordinary, as unfathomable monsters. Yet the court psychiatrist observing Eichmann declared him a "completely normal man, more normal, at any rate, than I am after examining him." Evil, Arendt suggests, can take the form of extraordinary acts committed by otherwise unremarkable people. All the mental health professionals who examined Eichmann pronounced him "normal." And yet, this "normal" German bureaucrat was swept up in the tide of Nazism to become one of history's most perplexing criminals. How? According to Arendt it was his "inability to *think*, namely, to think from the standpoint of somebody else"[5] and because of this "was surrounded by the most reliable of all safeguards against the words and presence of others, and hence against reality as such."[6]

If as Americans, living as rugged individualists trying to get ahead, we do little to foster a commitment to the whole or develop the ability to think from the standpoint of another, these questions become both more personal and more universal. They extend beyond the mean man himself to the role we all play in perpetuating a *culture* of mean. If Nazi Germany proves too uncomfortable and extreme a comparison, let's return to Frank's situation. What would you or I do if faced with similar circumstances? Would we act for the greater good, maybe sticking our neck out, or would we mostly succumb to this more everyday "evil"?

The answer to that question that few wanted to hear was demonstrated by Philip Zimbardo, the Stanford psychologist who ran the now-infamous 1971 Stanford Prison Experiment. In his planned two-week study, meant to examine the effects of prison life and the role of authority, twenty-four well-adjusted middle-class male college students who answered an ad to participate in a study were divided into two groups by the flip of a coin. The first group, the "prisoners," were rounded up, publicly arrested in front of their neighbors, Mirandized, strip-searched, blindfolded, and then incarcerated in a makeshift "jail" created on campus. The second group, the "guards," were outfitted in matching uniforms and sunglasses, given billy clubs, and charged with overseeing their "prison" population. By the morning of the second day, the prisoners had staged a rebellion, barricading themselves inside their cells; the guards had assumed police-state tactics to bring them under control; and some of the participants were beginning to suffer mental breakdowns. By day six, Zimbardo shut down the study—it was clearly too damaging to the participants. Reflecting later on the emotions and dynamics the experiment evoked even in him, Zimbardo noted that he had to be convinced by his then-girlfriend's pleas to stop the experiment. (He followed her advice, and married her a year later.)[7]

Since that time, Zimbardo's career has focused predominately on seeking explanations for why ordinary people may find themselves in situations that result in them committing appalling acts. In his world, it's the barrel that can make all the apples go bad. Serving as an expert witness on behalf of one of the guards charged with torture and abuse at Abu Ghraib prison, Zimbardo said he believed strongly that the guard was neither innately evil nor sadistic. Rather, it was the context he found himself in, characterized by inexcusable mismanagement from above and dreadful working conditions that created an environment where evil could thrive. The CIA ran the prison; there was no one at the prison in an executive leadership role to establish a culture of civility. The guards were low-level, inexperienced military police slogging through twelve-hour shifts for forty straight days, with no oversight to guide or correct their actions under extreme stress. Before you dismiss the thought that you might have acted in similar ways given similar conditions, consider that more of us seem to be at least condoning the culture of mean if not outright propagating it than we'd like to think. In the end, maybe it's more than just the one person on trial who shoulders the responsibility.

Zimbardo concluded long before the Abu Ghraib case that in any situation similar to the one the soldiers found themselves in, it is critical that you are able to consider an issue from alternative angles, and particularly try to place yourself in the other person's shoes. This may not yield valid empathy, understanding precisely how the other person is feeling, but you will at least develop a more accurate view of what he sees. Only then can you make the right calls. And this brings us back to Hannah Arendt and her indictment of Eichmann in his inability to take into consideration an "enlarged mentality."[8] Absent this, for any of us, judgment can become thoroughly invalid, out of whack. We must be intentional in enlarging our mentality; we must train ourselves to see ourselves through the eyes of another.

Arendt's conviction was not anchored in "soft" notions about what unites people to each other. Her focus was on the commitment others make to seeing the world from another's point of view, rather than on morality or an imperative to do the right thing. This intention toward empathy was not about adopting another person's viewpoint. It was instead about avoiding the literal thoughtlessness she observed in a man who committed some of the most atrocious acts of the century. Arendt had a supporter in Richard Sonnenfeldt, the chief US translator at the Nuremberg trials. He, too, believed that Eichmann and his ilk seemed without remarkable intellect or insight, each distinguished only by being surrounded by flattery and ambition. "Dictators have no peers," he said at the time. "Only sycophants to do their bidding."[9]

And so we come full circle, to the thoughtless mean men surrounding themselves with yes-men and yes-women. Back to those men who cannot forge authentic connection but instead see people as impediments, objects, tools, cogs. Here it could not be plainer to see that the phenomenon we are talking about is anything but benign. Mean men are not annoying cubicle mates or self-aggrandizing local leaders vying for their fifteen minutes. They are the modern face of humankind's inhumanity to humankind. And here *we* are, all of us who surround the men who rise only when we let them. We are the ones who boost Trump's poll numbers for throwing out hateful epithets, who dismiss Jobs's abuse in the face of his genius, who refuse to see Armstrong's cheating tyranny for what it is as long as he pulls in another Tour win for the United States. One thing the Eichmann comparison points out is the fact that all of us have a part we play.

Increasingly, surveys and polls point to a potent lack of any active cultural rejection of mean men. They suggest instead that we are experiencing our own banality of meanness. Far from decrying a mean man's behavior, we're collectively making a passive shrug every time he shows his true colors. We're not denouncing his behavior—we're rationalizing it and creating reinforcing structures that only entrench his power. Which begs the question: If more of us did stand up, would it be possible to stem the tide?

TOO MUCH POWER CAN LEAD TO ABUSE

Nobody would question Barry Freundel's cred as an intellectual. He double-majored in chemistry and physics for his undergrad degree at New York's Yeshiva College and continued on to become a world-recognized Talmudic scholar and ordained rabbi with a PhD.

His rabbinical career and religious affiliation were rooted in a movement known as Modern Orthodox, a subset of Orthodox Judaism. Though Modern Orthodox attempts to synthesize Jewish values and the observance of Jewish law with the secular world, it maintains a strict set of rules, laws, and practices more closely aligned to traditional Orthodoxy.

Freundel first worked on the periphery of New York City, leading congregations in Great Neck and Yonkers, New York, and in southwestern Connecticut. Then, in 1989, he joined the big league—he was hired to lead one of Washington's most prestigious synagogues, attended by the DC elite including high-ranking government officials, well-connected lawyers, and other influential Beltway professionals. Since Freundel was no journeyman rabbi—remember, he's an intellectual—he also held adjunct faculty positions at American University, Georgetown, and the University of Maryland and was a visiting scholar at some of the top schools in the country.

Unlike priests in the Catholic Church, most rabbis operate like free agents, with negotiated terms for salary, housing, and other benefits that end up in term contracts. For some, the need for achievement leads them to ever-larger congregations or ones that may also be perceived as more prestigious. In addition, some choose to attach themselves to the movement's central governing organizations, furthering their influence in other ways.

Freundel rose in the ranks of the Rabbinical Council of America (RCA), an influential and the largest body of Modern Orthodox rabbis.

Most critically for the story that would unfold, he then became chairman of the committee overseeing religious conversions, a matter of international contention.

In February 2015, this intellectual paragon of virtue copped a plea deal for voyeurism, marking the beginning of Freundel's unveiling. The good rabbi wasn't "merely" some perv with a telescope; he was a mean man who had taken advantage of the faithful and the vulnerable in a quest for ever-greater power. In all, Rabbi Barry Freundel admitted guilt to peeping at fifty-two women while they went to the mikvah, the sacred ritual bath into which all female converts to Orthodox Judaism must wade. Using a small video camera embedded in a clock radio that sat on a shelf, he watched women undress and shower. Prosecutors say he spied on a hundred more women, but the statute of limitations had run out on those crimes. One of victims told the *Daily Beast* that the public got Freundel wrong in assuming this was just about sex. "People keep calling him a pervert and yes, he's a pervert, but he's also a power hungry sociopath,"[10] Bethany Mandel said. "It wasn't about porn. It was about power, and this was additional power no one knew he had."[11]

Were there signs? Did this really come out of nowhere? Interviewing several former congregants and professional colleagues, *Washington Post* reporter Michelle Boorstein details a long history of complaints ranging from a "brusque" style to a big ego to mishandling donations and funneling them to pet projects. As it turns out, the Rabbinical Council of America had fielded complaints going back two years before Freundel was arrested.[12] By all accounts he was gruff and hard to engage but, like many mean men, also a gifted thinker and orator. "That's why people put up with the things they didn't like," one congregant said, "because he was so outstanding."[13] Should his pattern of abuses have raised alarm bells in those who worked closely with Freundel? The rabbi's guilt has caused some of his most ardent former supporters to fall uncharacteristically silent. He projected such an air of authority that no one questioned the mikvah "practice dunks" he required of young women undergoing conversion, for which there is no religious precedent.[14] He also allegedly urged college students he taught at Towson University—including non-Jews and single women—to come try out the mikvah, flouting basic Orthodox norms around the sacred ritual bath.

Two new lawsuits in mid-2015 were filed to hold the RCA responsible in the scandal. They both allege that the Rabbinical Council of

America and Freundel's own synagogue were aware of inappropriate conduct by Freundel prior to the discovery that he was using a hidden camera. The lawsuits, seeking class-action status, charge that the RCA and Congregation Kesher Israel should have taken measures to remove him from his positions of responsibility based on his earlier behavior.

"The real issue with [Freundel] is, he was just bragging about the amount of power he had," said Steven J. Kelly, an attorney with the law firm Silverman, Thompson, Slutkin & White, who represented the plaintiffs in one of the two suits. "These women needed [his] stamp to get married in some cases . . . to do all sorts of things." The structure of decision making allowed him latitude to do as he pleased. One suit quotes an unnamed Kesher Israel staff member as saying that Freundel "treated the mikvah like a car wash. Every Sunday, six students at a time."[15] It also charges Freundel with leveraging his position within the organization's controversial conversion system to gain power over and sexually exploit those seeking to convert. The other lawsuit, filed by an anonymous plaintiff, describes scenarios and situations that should have put all parties "on notice" about Freundel's behavior.[16] Is Freundel an example of mean men so entrenched in a power structure as to seem untouchable, certainly by the ones being victimized but also to those who surrounded him?

Before the RCA was founded, rabbis handled faith conversions individually. It was the Geirus Policy and Standards (GPS) Committee that took that power away, granting authority to select rabbinical courts. Freundel operated in two distinct roles that elevated his influence in determining the process and legitimacy of conversions. In addition to leading the GPS Committee, he was also at the helm of a regional rabbinical court that held the power to approve conversions specifically in the Washington area. Kelly's lawsuit argued that Freundel leveraged this dual role to uniquely situate himself "to sexually and otherwise exploit converts, over whom he exercised great power and control."[17]

One plaintiff claimed the rabbi was wholly uninterested in talking about her spiritual development and desire to convert. Instead, he "made repeated references to [her] 'looks.'"[18] Others alleged that Freundel "bragged about his prominence within the RCA and touted his relationship with the Chief Rabbi in Israel," making a show of power that was clear: you've got to go through me to get what you want. The plaintiff, bothered by his concern with her appearance rather than her spirituality, told him she would go around him and find another rabbi to facilitate her conversion. "Fine," he allegedly responded, "but it won't be accepted in Israel."[19]

Rabbi Marc Angel expressed to the Jewish newspaper the *Forward* that Freundel's alleged abuses revealed the inherent flaws in the revised system. "This is a bad example of the fears we have had all along," Angel said. "If you concentrate too much power in few hands, then there is bound to be abuse."[20]

Freundel is, in many respects, no different from others featured in this book. His strong need for control, interminable ambition, propensity to take risks, desire for glorification, and confidence of being in complete control of his destiny (locus of control) qualifies him alongside the others we've met thus far. The fact that he is an ordained rabbi, albeit one in prison as of this writing, is another example that men like this cut across all sectors.

What is of significant consequence is how those with concerns and with the power to do something sat idly by. In Freundel's case, we cannot indiscriminately let these people off the hook. It's easy for other rabbis to engage in twenty-twenty hindsight of Freundel's power grab and his potential to abuse that power. But for anyone who actually knew what was going on to have done nothing about it before Freundel's final fall was completely irresponsible.

With each Steve Jobs, Dov Charney, Lance Armstrong, Peter Arnell, Mark Driscoll, Barry Freundel, or Rudy Giuliani, it's tough to explain why the loudest—and often only—voices calling them out are the voices of their victims. To a lesser extent, we hear the voice of coalitions, though still formed by less powerful individuals (e.g., congregants, advocates, or litigants). Rarely do we hear initially from more influential members of society, stakeholders who hold the powers of message amplification. Only when the fire gets too hot from a lawsuit, a cratering stock price, or a PR crisis that nobody can successfully spin do those in a strong position to take action actually do so.

Whether childhood trauma and conditioning or a hardwired lack of empathy or the crucible of American power are at the root of it, it's too easy to explain away meanness by bucketing it into "mad" or "bad." Even if the meanness emerges from madness or badness, it is our option, if not our responsibility, to hold up the mirror, show him the consequences, and, while we're at it, tell the world that there is a price we will not pay for genius and that there are lines we will not cross.

THE ROLE OF ACCOUNTABILITY

If civility is the inverse of meanness, and incivility perhaps a more sanitized way of speaking about mean, then a glimpse into Americans' experiences with (in)civility is sobering. One poll concludes that it "has reached crisis proportions" and that our "new normal" is rude. The 2013 annual report "Civility in America," a national survey of Americans conducted by PR companies Weber Shandwick and Powell Tate with KRC Research, was followed by another, more nuanced look at incivility, in 2014.[21] According to the earlier report, most Americans found incivility a growing problem, with more than half believing it will continue to grow unimpeded. Who's to blame? Up first, politics and politicians, followed by the media.[22]

"Civility," as Yale law school professor Stephen Carter defines it, "is the sum of the many sacrifices we are called to make for the sake of living together. When we pretend that we travel alone, we can also pretend that these sacrifices are unnecessary."[23] Carter and others believe humans have an instinct for self-seeking. He also believes this same selfish desire is immoral, and without forethought can signal trouble. Sacrifices we may make for others make social life easier, but they're also a signal of our respect for our fellow citizens. It marks them as full equals.

These studies point to a social contract—even a moral imperative—that people can recognize is being violated even while it is difficult for them to unravel the contributions or mean men and their destructive self-seeking behavior. The silent acceptance of mean pollutes the global society. But the adulation of mean men who blatantly treat people as worthless objects redefines social norms and writes a new social contract. Rules of civility, therefore, may act as rules of morality. Perhaps it's not a stretch to say that it is a moral imperative to treat our fellow citizens with respect and that it's morally unacceptable not to. But morality doesn't seem to be working. The emphasis on doing the right thing isn't enough.

Most Americans in the 2017 "Civility in America" survey are annoyed by a lack of common courtesy, like inconsiderate use of cell phones or by trolls spewing vitriol in online exchanges. But more than that, people reported dealing with rudeness and a marked lack of respect, especially at work and online, every day of their lives on a personal basis. Even children were not immune, with parents saying both in-person and cyberbullying were of issue. These findings are generally consistent with other research published in recent years showing a consistency in public perceptions and experiences of disrespectful speech and behavior.[24]

The report of a 2010 Allegheny College survey on Americans' views of civility in politics, for example, was revealingly titled "Nastiness, Name-Calling & Negativity."[25] A 2011 workplace survey conducted at Georgetown University found that almost half of employees reported that they experienced rude treatment from fellow employees at least once a week.[26] A Rasmussen survey found that some 76 percent of Americans felt that people "are becoming ruder and less civilized."[27] Much of the discussion generated by reports of increasing incivility focuses on its negative effects on democratic discourse or its direct costs to individuals.

Does this imply a multiplier effect of the hard-core mean men featured here? Not quite, but it does capture the latitude we give and the tolerance we seem to muster for others' behavior that moves from annoying to jerk, to asshole, and finally to abusive.

Various research initiatives have popped up to promote more thoughtful, less rancorous political engagement, while new "civility projects" and other initiatives aim to encourage people to "choose civility" by reducing stress in their life. How do they think this might come about? Typically, the belief behind these initiatives asserts that cultivating better manners and conducting affairs based on the Golden Rule will make our society more bearable, more civilized. All these efforts stress some form of "breaking the incivility cycle" by not responding in kind to uncivil treatment.

Here's the problem: data from the "Civility in America" project doesn't seem to indicate any "incivility cycle" among the general public. In other words, very few people acknowledge any uncivil *reaction* when confronted by the rude, mean, and inconsiderate actions of others. The one consistent reaction to rude or mean behavior? Avoidance. But avoidance constitutes a problem of its own. In unpleasant face-to-face situations, people tend to either leave, simply ignore the offender, or suffer while they are being pounded with uncivil behavior. Encountering online ugliness, they often respond by "defriending," quitting a site or online discussion, or dropping out of an online community. Who "wins" here?

Incivility at work has led people to quit their jobs, and disrespectful political remarks have led to the end of friendships. In response to children's experiences, parents have transferred their children to different schools. Although all of this is understandable, and at least in some cases unavoidable, most of these responses may be cumulatively fostering the incivility problem. Zygmunt Bauman and Leonidas Donskis argue in their book *Moral Blindness* that social fragmentation and atomization are two of the major factors contributing to our "loss of sensitivity."[28] These terms hold that all social values evolve entirely out of the interests and actions of the individuals of a particular society. If that's the case, then responding to incivility by limiting or cutting off relations—just walking away—is making matters worse. In the end, we must deal with one another and confront ourselves.

THE MILLENNIALS AND MEAN

The 2014 edition of "Civility in America" focused on Millennials, the massive subgroup of the population born between 1981 and 1996 that represents the largest share of America's workforce. With approximately 83 million Millennials in the United States, they outnumber Baby Boomers by 8 million. They do not yet outspend Baby Boomers, but their size and spending power suggests they have enormous potential to shape the future of the American economy as well as the tenor of our discourse.[29]

The culture in which they grew up dealt Millennials a blow. They are more likely than other generations to have experienced an uncivil encounter at school or online. Statistically, this generation can expect encounters of bad behavior *every twenty-four hours*. In fact, you could say incivility is defining Millennials' lives. Over one in four have quit a job because of it, and nearly 20 percent have moved to escape it.[30]

Yet while older generations have turned cynical and believe meanness to be an unstoppable force, Millennials are two to four times more likely to believe civility will improve in the near future. And we've seen some examples that indicate they're willing to be the change. The raucous calls to action against American Apparel's Dov Charney were all instigated by Millennials, even though it took the economic risk from the older white guys on American Apparel's board to finally give him the boot. In Mark Driscoll's case, young members of the congregation were the ones picketing in front of the megachurch and amplifying their voices through social media platforms.

A 2015 study of Millennials by Deloitte, the massive professional services firm, gives us a deeper look into the expectations Millennials hold about their work and about community.[31] They want affiliation with organizations that have a clear, positive purpose. For six in ten Millennials, a "sense of purpose" influenced their job hunt and their eventual choice of employer. Among the so-called superconnected Millennials, avid users of social media, a full 77 percent report their company's purpose was important. The power of social networking to elevate or dethrone people based on their behavior and beliefs is unmistakable.[32]

Remember from our early chapters that we equate "leadership" with imperious qualities? For Millennials, less so. Deloitte's study also peered into the changing characteristics of leadership and found that more than 30 percent of Millennials defined leaders as visionary, personable, inspirational, or strategic thinkers while less than 20 percent agreed that leaders were visible, well networked, or had technical skills.[33] Though we have seen that mean men can initially seem quite visionary and inspirational, their brand of vision rings hollow over time. As the workplace demographics shift and superconnected Millennials swell the now-cynical ranks, perhaps mean will face a new challenge.

EMPATHY AS THE GAME CHANGER

One of the most remarkable regular experiences I have living in New York is my subway ride on the infamous "A" train from the northern reaches of Manhattan down to Greenwich Village. Perhaps more than some subway lines it's a social-leveler, picking up and discharging passengers along the way from extraordinarily diverse neighborhoods. It's also a favorite for panhandlers. Going to and from work I've made the observation that, almost without exception, the people who give a dollar look like they have lesser means than those who don't. Not infrequently, the givers themselves look like they could use a few extra dollars in their pockets. It's rare that I see those who read as economically comfortable reach for something to give. They—like me—may rationalize that the social service agencies we donate to should be caring for these people and remediating their problems. It's a convenient rationalization. Am I without empathy?

Whether I give a dollar or not in this case does not indicate an overall lack of empathy (a point I'll get into below). While we think of empathy as the common glue of humanity, it is anything but banal. Empathy is not common to all people. It is not pervasive, ordinary, or unremarkable. Those of us capable of empathy assume that most people are similar in this way. But that's just not the case. Empathy is the ability to place ourselves in someone else's shoes and understand as best as we can how that person feels in the situation. If we are able to then express their feeling, that is known as the second tier of empathy. More common and distinct from empathy is the expression of sympathy—telling someone we're sorry for their loss, or feeling compassion for the poor. What makes empathic connection both rarer and harder to achieve is that to do it well we have to suspend judgment, confront our own biases, and truly listen. It requires honesty and openness, with ourselves and with the other, but yields incomparable understanding and increases trust between us. It's ironic how healthy and positive this often is for both people, yet how rare in actual practice. Perhaps as more research emerges on the positive, multidimensional impact of empathy, we as a society will focus on developing it as a critical social competency.

Why is empathy rare? Because it requires perspective-taking with another person, and this means staying out of judgment, not showering them with sympathy (which we think makes the other person feel better but often it's rooted in making our role easier). Empathy requires us to recognize an emotion in the other person and communicate that emotion back to them. Easy? Far from it. However, empathy is useful both in understanding where meanness comes from and in offering us a way to fight the place of meanness in our culture. Empathy, rarer in practice than we think but available to most, might hold the key.

Simon Baron-Cohen, a professor of developmental psychopathology at the University of Cambridge, offers a compelling explanation for understanding mean that has enabled me to consider how we can do a far better job managing it. His work on empathy has influenced me strongly since my research into this began. You see, Baron-Cohen and I both share a problem with the notion of "evil" per se, in large part due to the concept's moral and religious overtones. Rather than argue the word away, I'm with Baron-Cohen in suggesting a linguistic substitution—"empathy erosion"—that offers a useful visual metaphor for a common psychological response. Hate or envy, a desire for revenge, a need to protect, or a feeling of disgust can cause empathy to erode. Just as importantly, the erosion can stem from our beliefs. If we hold that some people deserve better treatment than others, that winning is the most important goal, or that we have a God-given right to get our needs for control met through others, then empathy erosion is already well under way.

One of the worst effects of empathy erosion is that it turns other people into objects. With empathy out of the way, we can more easily relate to people as things. Most of us do this from time to time. While I may watch someone in need on the subway and imagine what their life is like, I admit to "switching off" when walking past the rows of homeless people sleeping over subway grates in the middle of winter, just a few blocks from my Greenwich Village office in Manhattan. In these moments, my empathy erosion is palpable.

There are a lot of ways to define empathy, but I like Baron-Cohen's, which holds that empathy "is our ability to identify what someone else is thinking, and to respond to their thoughts or feelings with an appropriate emotion."[34] In order to do this, we are required to stop thinking only about ourselves and as ourselves, with single-mindedness. We must hold another's mind-view with our own at the same time—a tricky endeavor.

Empathy requires our brain to function in two stages: recognition and response. If I only recognize an event or another's emotions, then I haven't empathized. For example, when my consulting assistant shows clear difficulty completing a client report I need, and I ignore her obvious nonverbal signals, then I haven't empathized. If I read the frustration or anger or fear on her face and consider what she might be experiencing, then I'm getting closer to empathizing. But if I respond to this emotion ("Julie, you seem frustrated or confused by something," and my eyes convey genuine concern), then I'm empathizing with the required double-minded attention. It would be easy to see her obvious signs and think, *What the hell! I need to get that report to the client, and Julie's stuck on some stupid detail.* Though I may convince myself that my attention is on my client's needs, it is only my own needs I am concerned with. I care only about *my* immediate problem.

Baron-Cohen and others argue that empathy varies in the population and that if we measured everyone's level of empathy (which is now technically possible, but not reasonably practical), we'd end up with the classic bell-shaped curve. Our mean men reside on one tail of the curve, where empathy peters out, getting infinitely closer to zero. Devoid of empathy, they are cruel, abusive, and cold. They may be able to fake a certain type of empathy but not the kind the rest of us want and need. They are able to dehumanize others and, in their mind, turn them into objects. Psychopathy is in fact one of the three psychiatric disorders of that "zero negative" side of the curve, along with narcissism and borderline personality disorders.*

CONTROLLING THE EMPATHY PORTAL

Are we simply more tolerant of mean from the "leaders" in our culture, giving those zero negatives a pass? And, if so, what are the implications if empathy is tied so closely to this behavior? Does the erosion of empathy in general point us to a broader issue influencing our communities? And if a lack of empathy is so central to meanness, then how do we use this newer thinking about empathy in general?

Earlier in the book, we saw how even high-functioning, subclinical psychopaths get on the wrong learning track for life. When normal children hurt a sibling or get them in trouble, for example, they will be concerned by the pain they caused. But if the mean man starts life without this sensitivity, nothing is telling him to back off. All he may ever seem to learn is that hurting others brings benefits. What a great way to get toys or win games! He sees the upside of defeating others, and the result is a

---

* The individuals who find it very difficult to empathize but are not led to do awful things to others occupy the "zero positive" side of the curve. This is actually the heart of Baron-Cohen's research focus, these individuals diagnosed on the autism spectrum and with Asperger's syndrome with a disabling incapacity to empathize. Zero-positive empathy is also accompanied by remarkably precise minds that compel these individuals to uncover the pattern recognitions in daily life. Being zero positive requires them to create systems in their brain to organize much of their exterior world. While they may not be able to cognitively process the needs and feelings of others, they are different in that they *do* care about others.

very different learning curve that matures into a skill for manipulating and intimidating people as objects.

But there is no hard line separating those who can and do empathize from those who cannot—or choose not to. We have some control over when, and with whom, we empathize. This is a necessary thing. If we shared every form of suffering of every other human, we'd be wrecks. If I broke down every time I passed a homeless person sleeping on a subway grate, I couldn't teach my students or write an intelligible word. We must have the innate capability to select what we react to and, like a switch, give us the power to turn empathy off.

The primatologist Frans de Waal suggests that we (humans) who are free of psychiatric disorders manage our emotions through a "portal." When a situation occurs that typically triggers our emotions, we recognize it and open the portal.[35] We allow ourselves to be "triggered." The obvious portal for empathy is identification; we readily share this emotional process with someone we identify with, someone in our inner circle. But outside this circle everything is optional. It may depend on whether we can emotionally afford being affected (e.g., becoming upset every time I walk by a homeless person on the sidewalk) or simply on whether we want to be affected by so many empathy-inducing stimuli.

"The empathic understanding of the experience of other human beings is as basic an endowment of man as his vision, hearing, touch, taste and smell," noted the influential Austrian psychoanalyst Heinz Kohut.[36] The desire to be known, heard, and felt deeply never disappears. But for some, empathy can be the nonstop default way of relating. For them, psychological well-being erodes since always having the switch on to enter the portal is humanly unsustainable.

We have to strike a balance between emotion and thought and between ourselves and others. We can open the empathy portal and leave it that way. However, truly "grokking" another human being is both delicate and arduous work. To put ourselves in someone else's shoes we must find the healthy balance between emotion and logic and between self and other. Managing life in a world of mean men involves not only putting ourselves in someone else's place but also in finding the balance. Empathy can be a trap for the rest of us, and even if we are psychologically healthy, we may feel imprisoned by the feelings of others.

How we find our own "switch" requires dexterity in paying attention to someone else's needs while not ignoring our own. For those who can empathize deeply, it becomes apparent that others find this attention deeply rewarding. But it puts the responsibility on us to determine when to extract ourselves and close the portal. Highly empathic people can overlook their own needs in potentially destructive ways, so intertwined are they with the needs of others.

As people, we find it natural and necessary to put others first sometimes; it is equally part of the human experience that that selflessness is reciprocal. People in any relationship share power and move back and forth, giving and receiving it. If more of us are to learn how to navigate empathy effectively, we may need to dip back into the concept of gender and meanness. If I had difficulty finding mean women, could empathy be part of the explanation?

Researchers including de Waal have described men as generally more violent, territorial, and combative. While both genders are able to exhibit empathy, given those traits, men may be able to hold firmer boundaries in wanting to hold on to power than women, even at the expense of empathy. Global studies show that women are perceived as generally more empathetic; some theorists have posited that women are biologically hardwired for empathy in ways that men are not.

What we know for sure is that boys are less attentive to the feelings of others, more action- and object-oriented, and rougher in their play than girls. Even young girls are more prosocial than boys, that is, more interested in positive, relationship-building behavior. They read emotions better as a result of being better attuned to nonverbal cues like the sound of voices. Studies also show they are more remorseful after hurting someone and better at quickly taking another's perspective on an issue. University of Minnesota psychologist Carolyn Zahn-Waxler investigated gendered reactions toward distress and found that girls physically comforted those in need, connecting and checking in, reactions exhibited less often in the boys.[37]

"Today, neuroimaging studies support the idea that humans are biologically wired to respond in caring ways to the suffering of others," Zahn-Waxler says. "From our studies we had already learned that empathy and caring behaviors are present in the first years of life." She goes on to explain, "I saw that the question wasn't whether children had the capacity for empathy. The question was how far back in development can you trace it? Once this was known, we could then identify both biological factors (genes and temperament) and environmental processes (such as family life and socialization) that helped explain why some children reach out to those in need while others turn their backs."[38]

Though previously seen more as a women's thing, empathy is experiencing an academic renaissance that is flowing over into business, parenting, and popular culture. In my work, I've seen the business literature abuzz with the neuroscience of "mirror" neurons, which allow us to replicate in our heads what we see other people doing. Books such as Dev Patnaik's *Wired to Care* make a big deal about mirror neurons, amplifying not only the newness of these findings but the broader impact he believes they have in how organizations can better understand their customers and employees. But ultimately, and ironically, what Patnaik and others are advising leaders to do is, well, figure out how to care for other people's feelings. To step into other people's shoes more often. To engage in empathy.

STANDING UP TO MEAN

This book has been populated with examples of men behaving badly, men in position of power, authority, and influence. These men have not strayed from their path so much as followed a similar path to one another's, responding to their deepest core needs in ways that resist adaptation and ultimately do harm. In most cases, they end up losing—maybe their careers, their families, their status. Yet the connection between their downfall and their pathology is not often made. That's why I felt compelled to out some of the most outrageous behavior. While the cases may seem shocking or titillating, these are men that as a society we've allowed to act this way, if not outright reinforced their behavior. Some flaunted their meanness from the outset. But others maneuvered their meanness in Machiavellian ways that crept up on us . . . until they ultimately creeped us out.

On an individual level, we protect ourselves best by developing a situational awareness. We pay closer attention to our feelings, to the people around us, and to the events in our lives. Is someone making us more anxious than normal? Demeaned? Used? Do we find that we're particularly confused when dealing with this person? Are our feelings seemingly out of sync with the situation? Are the facts not what they seem to be, or what the other person is telling us? ("Gaslighting," a term taken from the movie of the same name from the 1940s, refers to the way others manip-ulate our environment and cause us to doubt our own perceptions. It is a predictable ploy of subclinical psychopaths.) Monitor your feelings more closely if you experience betrayal, callousness to you or others, decep-tion, or someone's inability to take responsibility or feel remorse for an obviously inappropriate act.

Once you've noticed, what then? Standing up to mean, something I have not taken lightly in this chapter, can be a scary proposition, but it is our only alternative if we are to begin to shift the tide. As an individual, you can now develop the skills to recognize mean for what it is, and not confuse it with healthy competition or dismiss it as revenue-maximizing behavior or even genius. When you see it, speak up. Talk directly to the mean man, and do it with care. Observe how the person you confront lis-tens to you and how they respond. Is their immediate reaction to flip into a defensive posture and outright deny your concerns, minimize them, or spin them around to blame everything on you? If you notice this, then it may verify you're in the presence of a subclinical psychopath, and admit-tedly, that's not good. But when you feel used or abused by someone and they listen and actively try to understand from your perspective, even if they do not share it, then you may be able to make progress and move into problem-solution mode. Since the ultimate goal is to solve a prob-lem, the means to achieving this is to have a real discussion. While these conversations may be difficult, what's important is the need and ability to exchange viewpoints and information.

A DIFFERENT PATH TO SUCCESS

"Psychopath and hero may be twigs on the same genetic branch," wrote the late David Lykken, a University of Minnesota professor of psychiatry and psychology.[39] But while both may be described as fearless, the hero is exposed to effective ways of being around people and adapts himself in ways the psychopath cannot. I have suggested in this book that the successful psychopath represents one important dimension of incivil-ity, specifically meanness, in America. And the culture's management of meanness seems to be taking a holiday. But the hero gives us insight into what it looks like to be "successful" in a society not dominated by mean.

We've seen organizations where meanness rules and no one takes action. We've seen the poisonous drip of toxic power run amok. But what does it look like when ambition is channeled appropriately? Where risk is part of the game but it's not everything? Where people are people, not things? Perhaps no one finds it stranger than I do that I found one example in the NFL.

What most people remember about the 2014 Super Bowl is one of two things, depending on which team you supported in the final. On the one hand, there is the play-offs' ball-deflating scandal that many say put an asterisk next to the Patriots' eventual win. On the other, there is that play by the Seahawks, an ill-advised pass caught by a rookie Patriot in the end zone that lost the game for the Seahawks in the final seconds. But more interesting to me than either of these is what brought one of those teams to the Super Bowl in the first place. While the Patriots' dynasty is linked to the physical prowess of their quarterback, the Seattle Seahawks have an organizational philosophy that more closely mirrors the culture and practices of the companies on *Fortune*'s 100 Best Companies to Work For list, hinting at a potential antidote for organizational meanness, regardless of its pervasiveness and tolerance in professional sports. The Seahawks are not composed of very many first-round picks, those players others have determined are the best and brightest coming out of college. *Sports Illustrated* is not alone in calling the highly competitive team "an island of misfit toys."[40] They don't often choose the stars, opting instead for players they believe have a depth of talent that simply needs development. When considering potential draft picks (job candidates), the Seahawks look at the language used by the players and cut from the pool those who lean on negative language or finger-pointing. They want a culture of accountability and optimism, and they start by getting the right people in the room.

The team's coach, Pete Carroll, seems the antithesis of many CEOs in a polite city that nevertheless mints hotheaded and successful leaders. The kinder, gentler Coach Carroll has a style that belies a ferocious commitment to winning, because it's all about encouragement, not about laying blame. He gives the individual men on the team the freedom to be themselves and sees himself on a continuous journey to identify and maximize the uniqueness of every player and coach. Is it weird to say that a professional football team offers a *nurturing* environment to its players? Maybe, but it seems that this one does, inspiring players to be accountable to the team and to themselves rather than demanding a certain level of play. In other words, the worth of the player is a composite of not only his performance on the field but the respect and trust he gives his teammates on and off the field. Angela Duckworth, University of Pennsylvania professor and author of *Grit*, traveled to study Carroll at his Renton, Washington, facility to see the effects of his leadership approach on the team. "I'm interested in how culture influences grit," she told *Sports Illustrated*. "And Pete has very deliberately created a culture that encourages passion and perseverance—the two components of grit."[41]

Tom Cable, former coach of the Oakland Raiders with a mean-man past, changed his coaching style after working with Pete Carroll as the assistant head coach and offensive line coach. According to Cable, "If I go ballistic on a guy because he dropped his outside hand or missed an underneath stunt, who is wrong? I am. . . . I'm attacking his self-confidence and he's learning that if he screws up, he is going to get yelled at. If you make a mistake here, it's going to get fixed."[42]

Also in the world of sports, there is Steve Kerr, former NBA star and the encouraging, diplomatic coach of the Golden State Warriors voted Coach of the Year in 2016. Kerr has a unique story with childhood challenges that might fairly have earned him the right to be a bitter, angry, vindictive man. And as Kerr tells it, as a child, anger did get the better of him. "When I was 8, 9, 10 years old, I had a horrible temper," Kerr said. "I couldn't control it. Everything I did, if I missed a shot, if I made an out, I got so angry. . . . I was such a brat."[43] But it was Kerr's father who helped him sort through the anger and find a better way. After Kerr had a chance to calm down, his father would casually bring up his observations about Kerr's reactions and have a conversation about them.[44] Then tragedy struck. It was 1984, Kerr was eighteen years old, and Lebanon was caught in the middle of a brutal power struggle between Syria and Israel. Kerr's father, Malcolm Kerr, was president of the American University of Beirut, and he was assassinated, shot twice in the back of the head. A group called Islamic Holy War took credit for the murder. The experience changed Kerr, but rather than turning to hate, he turned into a man who seeks to understand rather than judge, who advocates passionately on topics he cares about, from tolerance and common ground with the Islamic world to stemming gun violence. On the court, he's a competitive and winning coach, but he achieves his results through nurturing encouragement rather than by berating players for missteps. He seems, in fact, the living embodiment of a sentence his father once wrote related to the Middle East conflict: "The truly civilized man is marked by empathy."[45]

But Carroll and Kerr aren't the only examples—far from it. We just don't hear stories like this often enough. If we are to believe there is an alternative to the status quo, we must seek out these stories, share them, and lift them up. In fact, with as many mean men as I've encountered in my work, I've been pleasantly surprised over the years by entrepreneur clients' sensitivities to rooting out abusive behavior. It doesn't take a mean founder or CEO to create a toxic climate; certain whole industries and professions attract mean men like jackals to a fresh kill. But if the situation is flipped and we can admire and emulate good leadership, then it's the mean man who gets crushed.

I've spent more than a few pages thus far profiling tech entrepreneurs who fit the mean man profile, but even in this cutthroat industry we can find notable exceptions to the rule, such as Marc Benioff, founder, chairman, and CEO of Salesforce, the cloud computing company that posted $6.67 billion in revenue in 2016.[46] Benioff was groomed at Oracle, where Ellison's infamous mean-man style provided a cogent example of what *not* to do. Rather, Benioff based his company's culture on the Hawaiian word and concept of "mahalo," or gratitude. Salespeople who meet, not just exceed, their quotas are rewarded with trips to Hawaii. Benioff uses his platform to promote LGBTQ rights and gender equity. In 2015, the company spent $3 million in time and money analyzing seventeen thousand salaries and adjusting compensation where necessary to ensure women and men earned the same.[47] And Benioff took the best of his former workplace with him in focusing on philanthropy and using a "1-1-1" model. This translates into a company where 1 percent of equity is given to Salesforce's charitable foundation, 1 percent of every employee's time is spent in service volunteering for others, and 1 percent of profits goes to charity.[48]

Beyond the structure of his company, Benioff is active in calling for the benefits of tech to reach all and lift all boats, rather than increase income disparity. In a January 2017 leadership article in *Fortune*, Benioff argues for the four pillars of "Trust, Growth, Innovation, and Equality" to drive the "Fourth Industrial Revolution." Rather than choosing between innovation and quality, trust or growth, Benioff argues they all must be present for the world to truly progress. "A more equitable world, supported by living-wage job growth, transformed by phenomenal innovations will lead to a trust revolution that allows us to face the challenges of the Fourth Industrial Revolution in a responsible and responsive way. It's within our grasp to work together to create a better future."[49] The tech entrepreneur understands that not only is equity and trust moral—it makes for good business.

And for all those mean men who would say success depends on maximizing profit or winning at any cost? Who can't look past their own interests? Benioff says this: "You read all about these CEOs who are maniacally focused on shareholder value. Short-termism. But there's this theory that if you're going to successfully manage and lead a modern organization, you need to have a multistakeholder dialogue. You need to be able to bring in everybody and understand it's not just about one thing. When you're the CEO, you'd better have a big lens of everyone you're representing."[50]

In professional worlds where meanness is more than tolerated, leaders like Pete Carroll, Steve Kerr, and Marc Benioff give us hope for change. If a pro football team can make it to the Super Bowl on the tailwind of civility, if the NBA's Coach of the Year can be defined by empathy, if a multibillion-dollar empire can actively work to promote equality, equity, and trust, can't this model of leadership work in every sphere?

Though I've spent chapters laying out some of the more complex research, the results strike me as deceptively simple. In our lives and in our work, we want to feel valued. We want our bosses and colleagues and constituents to care about us. We want to forge professional and personal relationships with people who encourage us to develop and express our talents. We want the work we do to matter and our lives to have dignity. We want to matter. We crave to have our own identity recognized *and* to be part of a larger community engaged in a mission beyond ourselves.

These needs begin at the most formative stages of our lives. The development of a healthy persona requires feeling loved and cared for in our earliest months alive. Without it, we dramatically reduce our odds for a strong sense of security and trust throughout life—something the researcher and psychologist John Bowlby called "a secure base."[51] Yet we simultaneously have strong needs to separate and individuate—to establish our own identities. Psychologically healthy people find no conflict in the need for individuality coexisting with the need to be intimately connected with others and part of a larger community. In a fantasy, this is what we crave.

In the real world, beyond such a fantasy, our desire for independence and need for connection start to compete with each other. It's normal that we mature with varying degrees of insecurity about ourselves and our relationships. And all of this plays itself out in the workplace and in our communities. On a deeper, mostly unconscious level, those unmet needs from our childhood seep into and color our adult relationships. Feeling valued and valuable is not just "the soft stuff." One could say we don't need to "grow up" so much as we need to return to the basic lessons we hopefully learn as children, or extend what we most desire and need to others: respect, empathy, and love.

If this seems easier to read about in a book than to see played out in corporate boardrooms, maybe that's because the leaders getting airtime bear a closer resemblance to reality TV stars—or actually *are* reality TV stars—than to statesmen, or those heroes we are all yearning for. You've seen a lot of politicians in this book, a brand of entrepreneur that seems ever-more content deploying meanness as a primary strategy. Senator Ben Downing from Massachusetts is different. A state senator who until November 2016 represented the western section of the Commonwealth, Downing was the youngest ever to be elected to the role, and his constituents seem to feel he excelled far beyond any of his predecessors.

On the face of it, Downing could be characterized as an oddball politician. He ran for the state senate during the summer between his two years in graduate school at Tufts, with the expectation that he'd lose. Ready to regale his classmates with a what-I-did-this-summer tail of campaigning and loss, the story required a rewrite when he won—handily. But that's not the strange part.

Though he may not have expected to win, Downing hunkered down and got to work representing vastly diverse constituent needs. In fact, the guy seemed like a perpetual-motion machine, delivering consistently on thoughtful social, economic, and environmental initiatives. Rather than taking the spotlight and hogging media coverage on the ceremonial ribbon cuttings or even significant accomplishments, he instead kept his head down and worked collaboratively with colleagues. Most insiders considered him the key mediator in a number of high-profile conflicts that were successfully resolved, and he didn't take public credit for one. It's that attitude that saw him run unopposed from 2006 to 2016, when he decided not to run for reelection. He was so likable, so trustworthy, so respectful of anyone who may differ with him, and so effective in the job, that nobody wanted to take him on.

Downing was still a relative kid in the legislature when President Obama appointed US Senator John Kerry as secretary of state, vacating a US Senate seat. A flurry of politicos immediately expressed interest, but it was the state Democratic Party who moved Downing's name to the top of the list. But Downing demurred; he said he wasn't ready for the lift, wasn't ready for the heavy fund-raising required, and wasn't ready to give up his projects in western Massachusetts that his constituents needed. In January 2016, voters were shocked and saddened by Downing's announcement that he would not be seeking reelection in the Massachusetts Senate. He wasn't quitting to pursue a private-sector opportunity or to run for higher office. "It's been 10 years," he said. "I always said I wanted to do 10 years. It's just time for something new."[52]

If you think that the world of politics is nothing but a rarified bubble, what would you say if I showed you another leader who, like Downing, showed nothing but humble determination, even when becoming CEO of a century-old company so far in the red they were preparing to lose more than $12.7 billion in revenue that year alone? What if the reaction of the CEO who undertook that challenge had the following reaction and mind-set? "At the most fundamental level, it is an honor to serve—at whatever type or size of organization you are privileged to lead, whether it is a for-profit or nonprofit. It is an honor to serve."[53]

We've seen example after example of entrepreneurial CEOs who rained down profits but ultimately suffered, victims of their own hubris and psychopathy. We saw the ironfisted reign of Henry Ford and learned of the missed opportunities his lack of trust and inability to cede control led to. Well, the century-old company teetering on the brink referenced above is none other than the Ford Motor Company. And the man who feels acutely the responsibility and honor of leadership is Alan Mulally, former CEO of Boeing Commercial Airplanes and most recently of Ford, credited with performing nothing short of a miracle in turning Ford around when GM and Chrysler went on life support. One could imagine there were a few things wrong when he stepped through the door. So what was in his special sauce? According to Mulally, "It is important to have a compelling vision and a comprehensive plan. *Positive* leadership—conveying the idea that there is always a way forward—is so important, because that is what you are here for—to figure out how to move the organization forward. Critical to doing that is reinforcing the idea that everyone is included. Everyone is part of the team and everyone's contribution is respected."[54]

Now, Mulally wasn't an entrepreneur. Perhaps, you could argue, he didn't feel the unique pressures that a self-made man is subject to. Then what about Bob Chapman, owner and CEO of Barry-Wehmiller Companies. Chapman inherited the reins from his father, the founder, and took the once struggling company to the brink of $2 billion in annual revenue. He's also kept investors happy with a 15 percent compounded rate of return.

Chapman has also become a vocal supporter for "truly human leadership," which is focused on employee safety, health, and fulfillment. Chapman wrote a book detailing his personal and business transformation, *Everybody Matters: The Extraordinary Power of Caring for Your People Like Family*, in which he readily admits to being far less than a great leader.

"My business education had ignored the question of how my leadership would impact the lives of other people," he writes. "It was mostly about how to use people to further my own financial success. I was taught to view people as functions and objects to be used and manipulated to achieve my own goals rather than as full-fledged human beings with hopes, dreams, fears and aspirations every bit as legitimate as my own."[55] Chapman shared with the *New York Times* an aha moment that came as he walked past a storeroom full of inventory in one of his own factories—it was locked. "That practice said loudly to our people, 'We don't trust you.' It was humiliating."[56] He now says they "measure success by the way we touch the lives of people," turning on its head the familiar mean-men ethos not to trust anyone.[57]

His head of HR echoed Chapman's new philosophy, adding, "It's a fundamentally optimistic view of people and their possibilities. Trust is given here, not earned. It's our belief that given the opportunity, people want to do a great job and perform and make things better every day."[58]

During the Great Recession, Barry-Wehmiller took a hit just like so many other businesses. Instead of cutting staff, the company offered furloughs. The company employees took care of one another, with those in better positions to take a break from paid work doing so to support others without the means. The company didn't lay off a single individual.[59]

This is the major tenet in his factories—nourishing the humanity of each employee. While the salaries enjoyed by his workers aren't above average, the other perks are: flexibility, advancement opportunities, continuing education, and even time off for community work and service hours.

Chapman's behavior is inspirational to many, yet basic stuff. He doesn't just provide a paycheck but also enriches lives, his generosity begetting the same in his staff, as well as hard work and fierce loyalty.

A new model for leadership, one that eschews mean and builds on trust and collaboration and responsibility, is indeed what is needed. Let us start now.

ACKNOWLEDGMENTS

WE ALL HAVE ONE OR more pursuits in life that feel like one long strange trip. *Mean Men* represented one of those for me.

The kernel for the concept, and the resulting research it invoked, sprouted back in the 1990s and took me to places I could not have imagined when this project began. As I close in on the destination, I am reminded of the people who inspired and guided me to keep it flourishing. They get the credit. There were times I wanted to just pull off to the side of the road and end the journey, but their encouragement kept me moving.

For introducing me to the wonders and mysteries of psychoanalytic psychology, I thank my colleagues at the Austen Riggs Center in Stockbridge, Massachusetts. Jerry Fromm and Jane Tillman saw the potential and wide-ranging implications of the research underlying this project far more clearly than I could back in 2008. Ed Shapiro and Andrew Gerber, past and present medical directors and CEOs of Riggs, offered their unflagging support and genuine curiosity. Lee Watroba assured that my fellowship residency achieved its potential. They have since become strong allies and friends. I am indebted to all of the brilliant and caring clinicians at Riggs who offered their time and insight over the years that enabled me to unravel the intrapsychic dimensions of the mean man. Riggs transformed me intellectually, and because I remain in awe of the work they do to transform those who seek help there, I hope these friendships continue.

For sharpening my critical thinking, I am indebted to The New School. My colleagues not only in the graduate management programs but also in the psychology department and at Parsons School of Design provided insight that helped to shape ideas. The New School culture enabled me to take bold risks that other universities would dismiss. Its strong values have given me strength to stay focused on marginalized members of society, whether in organizations or society at large, and these values became a guiding light for this work. Enthusiastic support from students who learned of and worked on the research gave me a tailwind of encouragement. Andrew Gordon-Kirsch and Fernando Delgado were superb investigative researchers. Suzanne Bostwick has been a strong ally and resource for the length of this trip.

For supporting my research into Founders Dilemma, and its prevalence in the not-for-profit sector, I thank Ann Tenenbaum. Her generosity and confidence in my work led to significant empirical findings. And for underwriting our "Following the Founder" leadership development programs at The New School, Ann changed the lives of many.

For pushing me to question long-held assumptions about leadership, and CEOs in particular, I am indebted to colleagues Benjamin Finzi and Vincent Firth. Benjamin has been my most engaging intellectual sparring partner for the past eight years. His positive influence on this project and beyond helped to shape the new ways I look at CEOs and organizational strategy. My thanks also to the team that works with Benjamin and Vincent; they have been a joy to collaborate with, and I am grateful to be affiliated with them all.

For trusting me with the pain of their experiences, I thank the many employees, wives, children, and partners of mean men. Your stories moved and motivated me more than I can express.

For bringing a thrice-rewritten manuscript back to life, and for reawakening the original excitement and confidence I had when this effort started, I am indebted to Leslie Ann Miller, my editor, colleague, and co-provocateur for social good. Leslie (who prefers to go by "Lam") oozed ceaseless inspiration and a wicked-smart sense of the cultural landscape to "get" what I was trying to convey. Her expertise in all things editorial was the essential ingredient that brought the manuscript and this book to life. As cochief of Girl Friday Productions (GFP), Lam was able to marshal some of the most talented, professional, and reliable individuals I have ever worked with in the publishing world and beyond.

Others at GFP have been essential to assuring our collective standards of quality were met. Nicole Burns-Ascue, *Mean Men*'s special projects editor, has been relentless at getting us all to deliver on responsibilities and in only the best ways fed my neuroticism for commitment and timeliness. Meghan Harvey, executive editor for independent publishing, worked tirelessly to form and coordinate the team. Michael Trudeau as copy chief, Paul Barrett as art director, and Rachel Christenson and Devon Simpson supporting social media design and execution have been quintessential professionals. The cover materials were designed by Anna Curtis, and I am grateful for her patience and skill to accommodate my evolving concepts. Kristin Sheppard has been an insightful marketing strategist, intuiting and translating my goals for this project into actionable strategy. For meaningful support during the project's initial stages, I am grateful to Regina Maruca, David Callahan, and Andrew Stuart.

For insuring that *Mean Men* is as good a book as any great publishing house could produce, I thank my literary attorney, Jessica Friedman, for keeping me safe and honest. And my gratitude to the copyeditors and fact checkers who cut me no slack to assure accuracy and integrity.

And for the emotional sustenance required to keep me upright and moving day after day while I simultaneously spun so many professional plates, I am indebted to my loving partner, Valerie. You are my pillar of strength, my most trusted adviser, my talented personal editor, and the woman of my dreams.

NOTES

PROLOGUE

1. Ryan Tate, "Mark Pincus: The Facebook Desperado Making Off with Millions," *Gawker*, April 29, 2010, http://gawker.com/5527403/mark-pincus-the-facebook-desperado-making-off-with-millions.

2. Dean Takahashi, "How Zynga Grew from Gaming Outcast to $9 Billion Social Game Powerhouse," Venture Beat, December 12, 2011, http://venturebeat.com/2011/12/12/zynga-history/view-all/; Nick Saint, "Zynga's Secret to Success: Steal Great Ideas!" *Business Insider*, January 19, 2010, http://www.businessinsider.com/how-zynga-is-just-like-microsoft-2010-1; and Khondkar Faiaz Hasan and Mohammed Suhail Akhtar, "The Dark Side of Facebook Games: An Interactive Qualifying Project Report Submitted to the Faculty of Worcester Polytechnic Institute in Partial Fulfillment of the Requirements for the Degree of Bachelor of Science," April 27, 2010, https://web.wpi.edu/Pubs/E-project/Available/E-project-042710-133041/unrestricted/IQP_FinaL%5B1%5D.pdf.

3. Anonymous, "The Worst Possible Work Environment and Culture Imaginable," Glassdoor, April 27, 2013, http://www.glassdoor.com/Reviews/Employee-Review-Zynga-RVW2600413.htm.

4. Nellie Bowles, "Zynga in Deeper Chaos as CEO Mark Pincus Resigns Again," *Guardian*, March 1, 2016, https://www.theguardian.com/technology/2016/mar/01/zynga-ceo-mark-pincus-resigns-farmville-candy-crush.

CHAPTER ONE

1. A. O. Scott, "Review: *Steve Jobs*, Apple's Visionary C.E.O. Dissected," *New York Times*, October 8, 2015.

2. Why just *men*? For starters, a great many entrepreneurs are men, including those who are most successful and visible. As I noted earlier, I initially chose to focus this book only on men for one reason: most of the legitimate research underpinning my findings is overwhelmingly

biased toward using only men in the sample populations. I still cannot say definitively that the personalities—and potential personality disorders— are the same or different if we compare male and female entrepreneurs, though later in the book I make some observations related to what we reward in men and in women. Before I began writing, it was premature to generalize the story that would unfold as applicable across both genders. That said, every effort is made to make an evidence-based case; to introduce research results that are not as statistically robust would weaken my confidence—and ultimately yours—in the findings and the story that evolves here.

3. "Police Booking Photos: Mugshots of the Rich and Famous," Celebrity News, *Telegraph,* http://www.telegraph.co.uk/news/picturegalleries/ celebritynews/8523372/Police-booking-photos-mugshots-of-the-rich -and-famous.html?image=1.

4. Martin Obschonka et al., "Rule-Breaking, Crime, and Entrepreneurship: A Replication and Extension Study with 37-Year Longitudinal Data," *Journal of Vocational Behavior* 83, no. 3 (2013): 386–96.

5. Zhen Zhang and Richard D. Arvey, "Rule Breaking in Adolescence and Entrepreneurial Status: An Empirical Investigation," *Journal of Business Venturing* 24, no. 5 (2009): 436–47.

6. A big reason these iconic figures are so poorly understood is that the many research paths probing entrepreneurship have been distinctly separate for decades. They reside in different disciplines, including economics, psychology, and business strategy. Too often, academics in any one of those disciplines have struggled to draw on the knowledge that has been gathered in the others—a common story in the isolated world of academia. Business professors can't wrap their heads around studies by clinical psychologists, and vice versa. It seems no one has been able to gain traction in developing a big picture and multidisciplinary understanding of the entrepreneur.

7. Robert I. Sutton, *The No Asshole Rule: Building a Civilized Workplace and Surviving One That Isn't* (New York: Business Plus, 2010).

8. Daniel H. Pink, *Free Agent Nation: How America's New Independent Workers Are Transforming the Way We Live* (New York: Warner Books, 2001).

9. Adam Grant, "In the Company of Givers and Takers," *Harvard Business Review*, April 2013, https://hbr.org/2013/04/in-the-company-of-givers -and-takers.

10. Timothy A. Judge, Beth A. Livingston, and Charlice Hurst, "Do Nice Guys—and Gals—Really Finish Last? The Joint Effects of Sex and Agreeableness on Income," *Journal of Personality and Social Psychology* 102, no. 2 (2012): 390–407.

CHAPTER TWO

1. Jennifer Steinhauer, "Testing a Wider Concept of Sexual Harassment,"
    New York Times, March 27, 1997, http://www.nytimes.com/1997/03/27/
    business/testing-a-wider-concept-of-sexual-harassment.html.

2. Daniel Lyons, "The Crazy Genius of Brand Guru Peter Arnell," *Newsweek*,
    March 27, 2009, http://www.newsweek.com/crazy-genius-brand-guru
    -peter-arnell-76137.

3. Ibid.

4. Richard Linnett, "The Gospel of Peter: Arnell on a Mission,"
    AdvertisingAge, November 18, 2002, http://adage.com/article/news/
    gospel-peter-arnell-a-mission/50827/.

5. Ibid.

6. Steinhauer, "Testing a Wider Concept of Sexual Harassment."

7. Ibid.

8. Emily Gould, "New York's Worst Bosses: Peter Arnell," *Gawker*, March 15,
    2007, http://gawker.com/244608/new-yorks-worst-bosses-peter-arnell.

9. Peter Arnell, *Shift: How to Reinvent Your Business, Your Career, and Your
    Personal Brand* (New York: Crown Business, 2010), 22.

10. David C. McClelland, *Human Motivation* (Cambridge: Cambridge
    University Press, 1988).

11. Ibid.

12. Christopher J. Collins, Paul J. Hanges, and Edwin A. Locke, "The Relationship
    of Achievement Motivation to Entrepreneurial Behavior: A Meta-
    analysis," Cornell University ILR School, 2004, http://digitalcommons.ilr
    .cornell.edu/cgi/viewcontent.cgi?article=1841&context=articles.

13. Edwin A. Locke and J. Robert Baum, "Entrepreneurial Motivation," in *The
    Psychology of Entrepreneurship*, ed. J. Robert Baum Jr., Michael Frese, and
    Robert Baron (Mahway, NY: Lawrence Erlbaum Associates, 2010), 101.

14. Karen Horney, *Neurosis and Human Growth: The Struggle Toward Self-
    Realization* (New York: W. W. Norton & Company, 1991).

15. See Hermann Brandstätter, "Becoming an Entrepreneur—A Question of
    Personality Structure?" *Journal of Economic Psychology* (February 1997):
    157–77; Stanley Cromie, "Assessing Entrepreneurial Intentions: Some
    Approaches and Empirical Evidence," *European Journal of Work and
    Organizational Psychology* 9, no. 1 (2000): 7–30.

16. Andrew S. Grove, *Only the Paranoid Survive: How to Exploit the Crisis
    Points That Challenge Every Company* (New York: Random House: 2010).

17. David Carr, "In Media Moguls' Rarefied Realm, It's Like Father, Like Son,"
    New York Times, March 30, 2014, http://www.nytimes.com/2014/03/31/
    business/media/in-media-moguls-rarefied-realm-its-like-father-like-son
    .html?_r=0.

18. Ibid.

19. James Surowiecki, "Epic Fails of the Startup World," *New Yorker*, May 19, 2014, http://www.newyorker.com/magazine/2014/05/19/epic-fails-of -the-startup-world.

20. Frank H. Knight, *Risk, Uncertainty, and Profit* (Boston: Houghton Mifflin, 1921).

21. Surowiecki, "Epic Fails of the Startup World."

22. Gavin Cassar and Justin Craig, "An Investigation of Hindsight Bias in Nascent Venture Activity," *Journal of Business Venturing* 24, no. 2 (2009): 149–64.

23. Ibid.

24. James Surowiecki, "Do the Hustle," *New Yorker*, January 13, 2014, http:// www.newyorker.com/magazine/2014/01/13/do-the-hustle.

25. Manfred F. R. Kets de Vries, "The Dark Side of Entrepreneurship," *Harvard Business Review*, November 1985, https://hbr.org/1985/11/the -dark-side-of-entrepreneurship.

26. Roderick E. White, Stewart Thornhill, and Elizabeth Hampson, "Entrepreneurs and Evolutionary Biology: The Relationship Between Testosterone and New Venture Creation," *Organizational Behavior and Human Decision Processes* 100, no. 1 (2006): 21–34.

27. William B. Gartner, *Entrepreneurship as Organizing: Selected Papers of William B. Gartner* (Cheltenham: Edward Elgar Publishing, 2016), 268.

28. Mark Singer, "The Book Eater," *New Yorker*, February 5, 2001, 62.

29. It should be noted, the behavior of at least one man included in these pages, President Donald J. Trump, prompted a group of mental health workers to break the 1973 "Goldwater Rule," which cautions professionals against profiling the mental health of public figures. In a February 2017 letter to the *New York Times*, a retired Harvard psychiatry professor and a former research committee chair of the International Psychoanalytic Association, along with thirty-five other psychiatrists, psychologists, and social workers, call him unfit for office, citing among other reasons the fact that his "speech and actions demonstrate an inability to tolerate views different from his own, leading to rage reactions" and that "his words and behavior suggest a profound inability to empathize." See Lance Dodes and Joseph Schachter, "Mental Health Professionals Warn About Trump," *New York Times*, February 13, 2017, https://www.nytimes .com/2017/02/13/opinion/mental-health-professionals-warn-about -trump.html?_r=0.

30. Leander Kahney, *Inside Steve's Brain* (New York: Penguin Group, 2009).

31. Charles Arthur, "Steve Jobs: Smoke and Mirrors or iCon?" *Register*, May 20, 2005, http://www.theregister.co.uk/2005/05/20/jobs_biography/.

32. *The Search for the Self: Selected Writings of Heinz Kohut: 1950–1978*, ed.

Paul Ornstein, vol. 2 (London: International Universities Press, 1978).

33. Marc Galanter, "The 'Relief Effect': A Sociobiological Model for Neurotic Distress and Large-Group Therapy," *American Journal of Psychiatry* 135, no. 5 (1978): 588–91; Marc Galanter, Richard Rabkin, Judith Rabkin, and Alexander Deutsch, "The Moonies: A Psychological Study of Conversion and Membership in a Contemporary Religious Sect," *American Journal of Psychiatry* 136, no. 2 (1979): 165–70; M. Galanter, "Psychological Induction into the Large Group: Findings from a Modern Religious Sect," *American Journal of Psychiatry* 137, no. 12 (1980): 1574–9; M. Galanter, "Engaged Members of the Unification Church: Impact of Charismatic Large Group on Adaptation and Behavior," *Archives of General Psychiatry* 40, no. 11 (1983): 1197–202.

34. Ethel Spector Person, "Manipulativeness in Entrepreneurs and Psychopaths," in *Unmasking the Psychopath: Antisocial Personality and Related Symptoms*, ed. William H. Reid (New York: W. W. Norton & Company, 1986), 256.

35. Tom Toles, "The 'Normalization' of Donald Trump Is Already Complete," *Washington Post*, December 20, 2016, https://www.washingtonpost.com/news/opinions/wp/2016/12/20/the-normalization-of-donald-trump-is-already-complete/?utm_term=.aa1490f617dc.

CHAPTER THREE

1. Dov Charney, "Here's the Autobiography of the Controversial CEO American Apparel Just Fired," *Business Insider,* June 19, 2014, http://www.businessinsider.com/dov-charney-how-i-became-who-i-am-today-2014-6.

2. Ibid.

3. Ibid.

4. Jenna Millman, Sabina Ghebremedhin, and Lauren Effron, "American Apparel CEO Dov Charney: A Tarnished Hero?" *ABC News*, March 28, 2015, http://abcnews.go.com/Business/american-apparel-ceo-dov-charney-speaks-time-ouster/story?id=29923392.

5. Rebekah Kearn, "Fired Worker Calls Dov Charney a Wild Man," *Courthouse News Service*, December 3, 2012, https://www.courthousenews.com/fired-worker-calls-dovcharney-a-wild-man.

6. Anonymous, "Worst Corporate Environment, Terrible CEO," Glassdoor, January 2, 2014, http://www.glassdoor.com/Reviews/American-Apparel-Reviews-E18373_P13.htm.

7. Anonymous, "Good Way to Make Friends, Bad Way to Support Yourself," Glassdoor, December 11, 2013, http://www.glassdoor.com/Reviews/American-Apparel-US-Reviews-EI_IE18373.0,16_IL.17,19_IN1_IP13.htm.

8. Defendants' Trial Brief of American Apparel, Inc., Dov Charney and

Martin Baily, *Nelson v. American Apparel, Inc.*, No. BC 333028 (Superior Court of the State of California, for the County of Los Angeles, Central District) (filed January 9, 2008).

9. "Dov Charney—American Apparel," YouTube video, 5:32, from the Ernst & Young Entrepreneur of the Year awards ceremony, posted by "UndeMiThumbre," January 19, 2008, https://www.youtube.com/watch?v=_b-PW6Rurb0&feature=related.

10. Kimberly Phillips, "My Body Is a Sacred 'Garment'—Does the First Amendment Creative Expression Protection Shield Clothing Designers Who Work Naked," *Rutgers Law Record* 42 (2014–15): 85, http://lawrecord.com/files/42_Rutgers_L_Rec_82.pdf.

11. Ibid.

12. Cristina Alesci, "How Dov Charney Got Fired from American Apparel—Twice," *CNN Money*, December 30, 2014, http://money.cnn.com/2014/12/24/news/companies/dov-charney-american-apparel/.

13. Jessica DiNapoli and Lauren Hirsch, "Exclusive: Amazon, Forever 21 Vying for Bankrupt American Apparel—Sources," *Reuters*, January 5, 2017, http://www.reuters.com/article/us-americanapparel-m-a-idUSKBN14O281.

14. American Psychiatric Association, *Diagnostic and Statistical Manual of Mental Disorders: DSM-5* (Washington, D.C.: American Psychiatric Publishing, 2013).

15. Ruth Benedict, *Patterns of Culture* (New York: Houghton Mifflin, 1934).

16. Jim Edwards, "How a Sex Harassment Case Against American Apparel Could Lead to CEO's Fall," *CBS MoneyWatch*, March 16, 2011, http://www.cbsnews.com/news/how-a-sex-harassment-case-against-american-apparel-could-lead-to-ceos-fall/.

17. Theodore Millon et al., *Personality Disorders in Modern Life* (Hoboken: John Wiley and Sons, 2004), 290.

18. Ibid.

19. John M. Oldham and Lois B. Morris, *The New Personality Self-Portrait* (New York: Bantam Books, 1995), 21.

20. Olivia Zaleski, Peter Waldman, and Ellen Huet, "How Hampton Creek Sold Silicon Valley on a Fake-Mayo Miracle," *Bloomberg BusinessWeek*, September 22, 2016, https://www.bloomberg.com/features/2016-hampton-creek-just-mayo/.

21. "Hampton Creek, Named by Bill Gates as One of Three Companies Shaping the Future of Food, Debuts First Product at Whole Foods Market," *BusinessWire*, September 20, 2013, http://www.businesswire.com/news/home/20130920005149/en/Hampton-Creek-Named-Bill-Gates-Companies-Shaping.

22. "The Future of Food: Josh Tetrick at TEDxEdmonton," YouTube

video, 18:16, posted by "TEDx Talks," http://ccsubs.com/video/
yt%3AQVTkdpfeb8A/the-future-of-food-josh-tetrick-at-tedxedmonton/
subtitles.

23. Zaleski, Waldman, and Huet, "How Hampton Creek Sold Silicon Valley
on a Fake-Mayo Miracle."

24. Ibid.

25. Ibid.

26. Biz Carson, "Sex, Lies, and Eggless Mayonnaise: Something Is Rotten at
Food Startup Hampton Creek, Former Employees Say," *Business Insider*,
August 5, 2015, http://www.businessinsider.com/hampton-creek-ceo
-complaints-2015-7.

27. Sarah Buhr, "Our Lingering Questions for Hampton Creek,"
TechCrunch, August 30, 2015, https://techcrunch.com/2015/08/30/
haveyouseenthewarningletter/.

28. Hervey Cleckley, *The Mask of Sanity: An Attempt to Clarify Some Issues
About the So-Called Psychopathic Personality*, 5th ed. (self-published,
1988).

29. Robert D. Hare, *Without Conscience: The Disturbing World of the
Psychopaths Among Us* (New York: Guilford Press, 1999).

30. Willem H. Martins, "The Problem with Robert Hare's Psychopathy
Checklist: Incorrect Conclusions, High Risk of Misuse, and Lack of
Reliability," *Medicine and Law* 27, no. 2 (2008): 449–62, https://www.ncbi
.nlm.nih.gov/pubmed/18693491; Kathleen Wayland and Sean D. O'Brien,
"Deconstructing Antisocial Personality Disorder and Psychopathy: A
Guidelines-Based Approach to Prejudicial Psychiatric Labels," *Hofstra
Law Review* 42, no. 2 (2013): 519, http://www.hofstralawreview.org/wp
-content/uploads/2014/04/BB.6.Wayland-OBrien.final2_.pdf; J. R. Minkel,
"Fear Review: Critique of Forensic Psychopathy Scale Delayed 3 Years by
Threat of Lawsuit," *Scientific American*, June 17, 2010, https://www
.scientificamerican.com/article/critique-of-forensic-psychopathy-scale
-delayed-by-lawsuit/.

31. Mehmet Mahmut, Judi Homewood, and Richard J. Stevenson, "The
Characteristics of Non-criminals with High Psychopathy Traits: Are They
Similar to Criminal Psychopaths?" *Journal of Research in Personality* 42,
no. 3 (2008): 679–92, DOI: 10.1016/j.jrp.2007.09.002.

32. Michael H. Stone, *Abnormalities of Personality: Within and Beyond the
Realm of Treatment* (New York: Norton, 1993).

33. Jennifer L. Skeem and David J. Cooke, "Is Criminal Behavior a Central
Component of Psychopathy? Conceptual Directions for Resolving the
Debate," *Psychological Assessment* 22, no. 2 (2010): 433–45.

34. Heidi Noelle Strohmaier, "Successful Psychopathy: Do Abnormal
Selective Attention Processes Observed in Criminal Psychopaths

Replicate Among Non-criminal Psychopaths?" ProQuest Information & Learning (2016): AAI3708495.

35. Kate Pickert and John Cloud, "If You Think Someone Is Mentally Ill: Loughner's Six Warning Signs," *Time*, January 11, 2011, http://content .time.com/time/nation/article/0,8599,2041733,00.html.

36. James R. P. Ogloff, "Psychopathy/Antisocial Personality Disorder Conundrum," *Australian New Zealand Journal of Psychiatry* 40 (6–7) (June/July 2006): 519–28.

37. Catherine Tuvblad and Kevin M. Beaver, "Genetic and Environmental Influences on Antisocial Behavior," *Journal of Criminal Justice* 41, no. 5 (September/October 2013): 273–76.

38. Devon L. L. Polaschek, "Adult Criminals with Psychopathy: Common Beliefs About Treatability and Change Have Little Empirical Support," *Current Directions in Psychological Science* 23, no. 4 (2014): 296–301.

39. Theodore Millon, Erik Simonsen, and Morten Birket-Smith, "Historical Conceptions of Psychopathy in the United States and Europe," in *Psychopathy: Antisocial, Criminal, and Violent Behavior*, eds. Theodore Millon, Erik Simonsen, Morten Birket-Smith, and Roger D. Davis (New York: Guilford Press, 1998), 438.

40. Theodore Millon, *Disorders of Personality: DSM-III: Axis III* (New York: John Wiley and Sons), 183.

41. Millon, *Disorders of Personality: DSM-III: Axis III*.

CHAPTER FOUR

1. Maureen Dowd, "Who's Hormonal? Hillary or Dick?" *New York Times*, February 8, 2006, A21.

2. Daniella Diaz, "RNC Chief Critique: Clinton Didn't Smile During National Security Forum," CNN Politics, September 8, 2016, http://www.cnn.com/2016/09/07/politics/reince-priebus-donald-trump-2016 -election/.

3. Diaz, "RNC Chief Critique: Clinton Didn't Smile During National Security Forum."

4. Ryan Teague Beckwith, "Trump: Debate Moderator Had 'Blood Coming Out of Her Wherever,'" *Time*, August 7, 2015, http://time.com/3989652/ donald-trump-megyn-kelly-blood-wherever/.

5. "Trump to Clinton: 'That's Called Business, by the Way,'" *Washington Post*, September 26, 2016, https://www.washingtonpost.com/video/politics/ trump-to-clinton-thats-business-buddy/2016/09/26/81f0d5a0-845a -11e6-b57d-dd49277af02f_video.html.

6. Daniella Diaz, "Trump: 'I'm Smart' for Not Paying Taxes," *CNN Politics*, September 27, 2016, http://www.cnn.com/2016/09/26/politics/donald -trump-federal-income-taxes-smart-debate/index.html.

7. Dowd, "Who's Hormonal? Hillary or Dick?"

8. Victoria L. Brescoll and Eric L. Uhlmann, "Can an Angry Woman Get Ahead? Status Conferral, Gender, and Expression of Emotion in the Workplace," *Psychological Science* 19 no. 3 (2008): 268–75.

9. Lisa F. Barrett, "Hillary Clinton's 'Angry' Face," *New York Times Sunday Edition*, September 23, 2016; Lisa F. Barrett and Eliza Bliss-Moreau, "She's Emotional. He's Having a Bad Day: Attributional Explanations for Emotion Stereotypes," *Emotion* 9, no. 5 (October 2009): 649–58, http://www.affective-science.org/pubs/2009/shes-emotional-2009.pdf.

10. Eric Uhlmann, "Anger in the Workplace Men vs. Women: Unequal Rage?" *HEC Paris*, March 15, 2011, http://www.hec.edu/Knowledge/Strategy -Management/Leadership-Management/Anger-in-the-Workplace-Men -vs.-Women-Unequal-rage.

11. Leslie Kaufman, "Questions of Style in Warnaco's Fall," *New York Times*, May 6, 2001, http://www.nytimes.com/2001/05/06/business/questions -of-style-in-warnaco-s-fall.html.

12. Gene E. Landrum, *Profiles of Female Genius: Thirteen Creative Women Who Changed the World* (Amherst, NY: Prometheus Books, 1994), 363.

13. Kaufman, "Questions of Style in Warnaco's Fall."

14. Ibid.

15. Steve Forbes and John Prevas, "The Price of Arrogance," *Forbes*, June 18, 2009, http://www.forbes.com/2009/06/18/alexander-great-hubris -leadership-power.html.

16. Melissa J. Williams and Larissa Z. Tiedens, "The Subtle Suspension of Backlash: A Meta-analysis of Penalties for Women's Implicit and Explicit Dominance Behavior," *Psychological Bulletin* 142, no. 2 (February 2016): 165–97, http://dx.doi.org/10.1037/bul0000039.

17. Ronald C. Kessler, "Epidemiology of Women and Depression," *Journal of Affective Disorders* 74, no. 1 (2003): 5–13.

18. Janet Shibley Hyde, Amy H. Mezulis, and Lyn Y. Abramson, "The ABCs of Depression: Integrating Affective, Biological, and Cognitive Models to Explain the Emergence of the Gender Difference in Depression," *Psychological Review* 115, no. 2 (April 2008): 291–313.

19. Carol S. Aneshensel, "Social Stress: Theory and Research," *Annual Review of Sociology* 18 (1992): 15–38; Mary Clare Lennon, "Sex Differences in Distress: The Impact of Gender and Work Roles," *Journal of Health and Social Behavior* 28, no. 3 (September 1987): 290–305; Robin W. Simon, "Assessing Sex Differences in Vulnerability Among Employed Parents: The Importance of Marital Status," *Journal of Health and Social Behavior* 39, no. 1 (March 1998): 38–54; Robin W. Simon, "Revisiting the Relationships Among Gender, Marital Status, and Mental Health," *American Journal of Sociology* 107, no. 4 (January 2002): 1065–96; Robin W. Simon, "The Contributions of the Sociology of Mental Health

for Understanding the Social Antecedents, Social Regulation, and Social Distribution of Emotion," in *Mental Health, Social Mirror*, eds. William Avison, Jane McLeod, and Bernice Pescosolido (New York: Springer, 2007), 239–74; Debra Umberson et al., "The Effects of Social Relationships on Psychological Well-Being: Are Men and Women Really So Different?," *American Sociological Review* 61, no. 5 (October 1996): 837–57.

CHAPTER FIVE

1. Ted Morgan, "Intrigue and Tyranny in Motor City," *New York Times*, July 13, 1986, http://www.nytimes.com/1986/07/13/books/intrigue-and -tyranny-in-motor-city.html?pagewanted=all.

2. Davia Temin, "How a CEO Can Wreck a Brand in One Interview: Lessons from Abercrombie & Fitch vs. Dove," *Forbes*, May 13, 2013, https://www .forbes.com/forbes/welcome/?toURL=https://www.forbes.com/sites/ daviatemin/2013/05/13/abercrombie-and-fitch-v-dove-or-how-a -ceo-can-wreck-a-brand-in-1-interview-7-years-ago/&refURL=https:// www.google.com/&referrer=https://www.google.com/; Brian Sozzi, "3 Huge Reasons Abercrombie CEO Mike Jeffries Lost His Job," *The Street*, December 9, 2014, https://www.thestreet.com/story/12979205/1/3-huge -reasons-abercrombie-ceo-mike-jeffries-lost-his-job.html.

3. Elizabeth A. Harris and Steven Greenhouse, "The Road to Dov Charney's Ouster at American Apparel," *New York Times*, June 26, 2014, http://www .nytimes.com/2014/06/27/business/road-to-dov-charneys-ouster-at -american-apparel.html?_r=0.

4. Nicola F. Sharpe, "Questioning Authority: Why Boards Do Not Control Managers and How a Better Board Process Can Help," University of Illinois College of Law, Illinois Law, Behavior and Social Science Research Papers Series Research Paper No. LBSS12-02, 2012, April 16, 2012, https://papers.ssrn.com/sol3/Papers.cfm?abstract_id=2003010.

5. Jim White, "Alex Gibney Interview for *The Armstrong Lie*: 'I've Never Met a Better Liar than Lance,'" *Telegraph*, January 31, 2014, http://www .telegraph.co.uk/culture/film/10599723/Alex-Gibney-interview-for-The -Armstrong-Lie-Ive-never-met-a-better-liar-than-Lance.html.

6. Ibid.

7. Louis Jacobson, "Congress Has 11% Approval Ratings but 96% Incumbent Reelection Rate, Meme Says," *Politifact*, November 11, 2014, http://www .politifact.com/truth-o-meter/statements/2014/nov/11/facebook-posts/ congress-has-11-approval-ratings-96-incumbent-re-e/.

8. Jeffrey M. Jones, "Ahead of Midterms, Anti-incumbent Sentiment Strong in U.S.," *Gallup*, May 14, 2014, http://www.gallup.com/poll/168998/ ahead-midterms-anti-incumbent-sentiment-strong.aspx.

9. *StartUp*, Gimlet Media, season 4, episodes 4–10, 2016, https:// gimletmedia.com/show/startup/all/.

10. Jim Edwards, "American Apparel Founder Dov Charney Is Back with a New T-Shirt Business He Says Is Already Worth $30 Million," *Business Insider*, September 12, 2016, http://www.businessinsider.com/american -apparel-founder-dov-charney-is-back-thats-los-angeles-2016-9.

11. Christine L. Porath, "Emotional and Behavioral Responses to Workplace Incivility and the Impact of Hierarchical Status," *Journal of Applied Social Psychology* 42 (2012): E326–57.

12. Josephson Institute, "Josephson Institute's 2012 Report Card on the Ethics of American Youth," 2012, http://charactercounts.org/pdf/report -card/2012/ReportCard-2012-DataTables.pdf.

13. Harold Greenwald, ed., *Experimentation and Innovation in Psychotherapy* (New Brunswick: Aldine Transaction, 2010), 364.

14. Harold Greenwald, ed., *Active Psychotherapy* (New York: J. Aronson, 1974), 366.

15. Greenwald, *Experimentation and Innovation in Psychotherapy*, 364.

16. Ibid., 366.

CHAPTER SIX

1. David McClelland and David Burnham, "Power Is the Great Motivator," *Harvard Business Review* 73, no. 1 (1995): 126–39.

2. Nick Wingfield, "A Different Gates Is Returning to Microsoft," *New York Times*, February 5, 2014, https://www.nytimes.com/2014/02/06/ technology/a-different-gates-is-returning-to-microsoft.html.

3. Morgan Housel, "The Pain of Zynga's Brain Drain: How Compensation Can, and Can't, Motivate Executives," *Motley Fool*, September 19, 2012, https://www.fool.com/investing/general/2012/09/19/the-pain-of-zyngas -brain-drain.aspx.

4. Noam Wasserman, *The Founder's Dilemmas: Anticipating and Avoiding the Pitfalls That Can Sink a Startup* (Princeton, NJ: Princeton University Press, 2012).

5. Emily Landes, "Zynga's Mark Pincus Delists $18-Million Gold Coast Home," *SFGate*, April 9, 2015, http://blog.sfgate.com/ ontheblock/2015/04/09/zyngas-mark-pincus-delists-18-million-gold -coast-home/.

6. Donald Trump, "Exclusive: Donald Trump on Cabinet Picks, Transition Process," interview by Chris Wallace, *Fox News Sunday*, FOX News, December 11, 2016, http://www.foxnews.com/transcript/2016/12/11/ exclusive-donald-trump-on-cabinet-picks-transition-process/.

7. Alyson Shontell, "Why Businesses Succeed and Fail," *Entrepreneur*, January 12, 2011, http://www.entrepreneur.com/article/217843.

8. Matthew L. A. Hayward, Dean A. Shepherd, and Dale Griffin, "A Hubris Theory of Entrepreneurship," *Management Science* 52, no. 2 (2006):

160–72; Valérie Petit and Helen Bollaert, "Flying Too Close to the Sun? Hubris Among CEOs and How to Prevent It," *Journal of Business Ethics* 108, no. 3 (2012): 265–83.

9.   Wasserman, *The Founder's Dilemmas.*

10.   Michael Powell and Russ Buettner, "In Matters Big and Small, Crossing Giuliani Had Price," *New York Times*, January 22, 2008, http://www .nytimes.com/2008/01/22/us/politics/22giuliani.html?ex=1358658000& en=29fd0ff771df8a73&ei=5088&partner=rssnyt&emc=rss&mtrref=www .huffingtonpost.com&gwh=CDB6586DA3663D5B8E9C09203FE6A1B4& gwt=pay.

11.   Rudolph W. Giuliani with Ken Kurson, *Leadership* (New York: Hyperion, 2002).

12.   Powell and Buettner, "In Matters Big and Small, Crossing Giuliani Had Price."

13.   Ibid.

14.   Ibid.

15.   Errol Louis, "Rudy Giuliani's Obama Outburst Is Ugly, Divisive," CNN, February 20, 2015, http://www.cnn.com/2015/02/19/opinion/louis-giuliani-obama/.

16.   Darren Samuelsohn, "Giuliani: Obama Doesn't Love America," *Politico*, February 18, 2015, http://www.politico.com/story/2015/02/rudy-giuliani -president-obama-doesnt-love-america-115309.

17.   Peter Collier and David Horowitz, *The Fords: An American Epic* (San Francisco: Encounter Books, 2002).

18.   John Cunningham Wood and Michael C. Wood, *Henry Ford: Critical Evaluations in Business and Management*, (London: Routledge, 2004), 73.

19.   Ibid.

20.   Federica Pazzaglia et al., "The Dangers of Disgruntled Ex-Employees," *MIT Sloan Management Review*, June 18, 2013, http://sloanreview.mit .edu/article/the-dangers-of-disgruntled-ex-employees/.

CHAPTER SEVEN

1.   Roderick M. Kramer, "The Great Intimidators," *Harvard Business Review*, February 2006, https://hbr.org/2006/02/the-great-intimidators.

2.   Ibid.

3.   Timothy A. Judge, Ronald F. Piccolo, and Tomek Kosalka, "The Bright and Dark Sides of Leader Traits: A Review and Theoretical Extension of the Leader Trait Paradigm," *The Leadership Quarterly* 20, no. 6 (2009): 855–75.

4.   Walter Isaacson, *Steve Jobs* (New York: Simon & Schuster, 2011).

5.   Judge, Piccolo, and Kosalka, "The Bright and Dark Sides of Leader Traits."

6. Isaacson, *Steve Jobs.*

7. Kramer, "The Great Intimidators."

8. "Is *Lie to Me* Lying to You?" *Science of People,* http://www.scienceofpeople .com/2014/05/is-lie-to-me-true/.

9. Kevin Randall, "Human Lie Detector Paul Ekman Decodes the Faces of Depression, Terrorism, and Joy," *Fast Company,* December 15, 2011, https://www.fastcompany.com/1800709/human-lie-detector-paul -ekman-decodes-faces-depression-terrorism-and-joy.

10. Frederick James Billings, "Psychopathy and the Ability to Deceive," ETD Collection for University of Texas, El Paso, Paper AAI3125565 (January 1, 2004), 90–93, http://digitalcommons.utep.edu/dissertations/AAI3125565.

11. White, "Alex Gibney Interview."

12. Ibid.

13. Ibid.

14. Ibid.

15. Adam Grant, "The Dark Side of Emotional Intelligence," *Atlantic,* January 2, 2014, http://www.theatlantic.com/health/archive/2014/01/the-dark -side-of-emotional-intelligence/282720/.

16. Reed Albergotti and Vanessa O'Connell, *Wheelman: Lance Armstrong, the Tour de France, and the Greatest Sports Conspiracy Ever* (New York: Penguin, 2014), 142.

17. Kahney, *Inside Steve's Brain.*

18. Isaacson, *Steve Jobs.*

19. Pew Research Center, "2016 Campaign: Strong Interest, Widespread Dissatisfaction," July 7, 2016, http://www.people-press.org/2016/07/07/ 4-top-voting-issues-in-2016-election/.

20. Dolia Estevez, "Debunking Donald Trump's Five Extreme Statements About Immigrants and Mexico," *Forbes,* September 3, 2015, http:// www.forbes.com/sites/doliaestevez/2015/09/03/debunking -donald-trumps-five-extreme-statements-about-immigrants-and -mexico/2/#76ef99411715.

21. Walter Ewing, Daniel E. Martínez, and Rubén G. Rumbaut, "Special Report: The Criminalization of Immigration in the United States," American Immigration Council, July 13, 2015, https://www .americanimmigrationcouncil.org/research/criminalization-immigration -united-states.

22. AP, "Donald Trump Says Mexicans Are 'Killing Us' in Latest Inflammatory Speech," *Telegraph,* July 12, 2015, http://www.telegraph .co.uk/news/worldnews/republicans/11734214/Donald-Trump-says -Mexicans-are-killing-us-in-latest-inflammatory-speech.html.

23. Pew Research Center, "2016 Campaign: Strong Interest, Widespread Dissatisfaction."

24. Adam Grant, *Give and Take: A Revolutionary Approach to Success* (New York: Penguin Group, 2013).

25. C. Daniel Batson, "These Things Called Empathy: Eight Related but Distinct Phenomena," in *The Social Neuroscience of Empathy*, eds. Jean Decety and William John Ickes (Cambridge, MA: MIT Press, 2009).

26. Robert B. Cialdini, *Influence: The Psychology of Persuasion, Revised Edition* (New York: Harper Business, 2006).

27. Grant, "The Dark Side of Emotional Intelligence."

28. Ibid.

29. Vamik D. Volkan, *Enemies on the Couch: A Psychopolitical Journey Through War and Peace* (Durham, North Carolina: Pitchstone Publishing, 2013).

30. Ibid.

31. Paul Ekman, "Biological and Cultural Contributions to Body and Facial Movement in the Expression of Emotions," in *Explaining Emotions*, ed. Amélie O. Rorty (Berkeley: University of California Press, 1980), 73–102.

32. Betty Glad, "Why Tyrants Go Too Far: Malignant Narcissism and Absolute Power," *Political Psychology* 23, no. 1 (2002): 1–37.

33. Gordon Hodson, Sarah M. Hogg, and Cara C. MacInnis, "The Role of 'Dark Personalities' (Narcissism, Machiavellianism, Psychopathy), Big Five Personality Factors, and Ideology in Explaining Prejudice," *Journal of Research in Personality*, 43, no. 4 (2009): 686–90.

CHAPTER EIGHT

1. Michael A. Hiltzik, "The Twisted Legacy of William Shockley," *Los Angeles Times*, December 2, 2001, http://articles.latimes.com/2001/dec/02/magazine/tm-10501.

2. Joel N. Shurkin, *Broken Genius: The Rise and Fall of William Shockley, Creator of the Electronic Age* (New York: Palgrave Macmillan, 2006).

3. Hiltzik, "The Twisted Legacy of William Shockley."

4. Rachel Mendleson, "Larry Ellison: Why It Pays to Be a Jerk," *Canadian Business*, April 8, 2011, http://www.canadianbusiness.com/business-strategy/larry-ellison-why-it-pays-to-be-a-jerk/.

5. Christine L. Porath, Deborah J. MacInnis, and Valerie S. Folkes, "Witnessing Incivility Among Employees: Effects on Consumer Anger and Negative Inferences About Companies," *Journal of Consumer Research* 37, no. 2 (2010): 292-303.

6. Ibid.

7. Christine M. Pearson and Christine L. Porath, *The Cost of Bad Behavior:*

How Incivility Is Damaging Your Business and What to Do About It (New York: Penguin Group, 2009).

8. Ibid.

9. Evelyn M. Rusli, "Zynga's Tough Culture Risks a Talent Drain," *New York Times*, November 27, 2011, http://dealbook.nytimes.com/2011/11/27/ zyngas-tough-culture-risks-a-talent-drain/.

10. Ibid.

11. Ibid.

12. "Full Transcript: N.J. Gov. Chris Christie's Jan. 9 News Conference on George Washington Bridge Scandal," *Washington Post*, January 9, 2014, https://www.washingtonpost.com/politics/transcript-chris-christies -news-conference-on-george-washington-bridge-scandal/2014/01/09/ d0f4711c-7944-11e3-8963-b4b654bcc9b2_story.html?utm_term= .ce7242caaadb.ce.

13. Ezra Klein, "Chris Christie's Problem Is That He's Really, Truly a Bully," *Washington Post*, January 8, 2014, https://www.washingtonpost.com/ news/wonk/wp/2014/01/08/chris-christies-problem-is-that-hes-really -truly-a-bully/?utm_term=.58982e03923f.

14. Michael Barbaro, "With Bridge Case Charges, a Cloud Descends on Christie's White House Hopes," *New York Times*, May 1, 2015, https:// www.nytimes.com/2015/05/02/nyregion/charges-in-bridge-scandal -pose-trouble-for-chris-christie.html.

15. Nick Corasaniti, "2 Christie Allies Are Sentenced in George Washington Bridge Scandal," *New York Times*, March 29, 2017, https://www.nytimes .com/2017/03/29/nyregion/christie-bridgegate-baroni-bridget-anne-kelly .html.

16. Ibid.

17. Aliyah Frumin, "Bridgegate: Two Former Aides to Chris Christie Convicted in Lane-Closure Scandal," NBC News, November 4, 2016, http://www.nbcnews.com/news/us-news/bridgegate-two-former-aides -chris-christie-convicted-lane-closure-scandal-n678016.

18. Robert Costa, Philip Rucker, and Elise Viebeck, "Pence Replaces Christie as Leader of Trump Transition Effort," *Washington Post*, November 11, 2016, https://www.washingtonpost.com/news/powerpost/ wp/2016/11/11/pence-to-lead-trump-transition-effort/?utm_ term=.24021748f847.

19. Robert D. Putnam, *Bowling Alone: The Collapse and Revival of American Community* (New York: Simon & Schuster, 2000).

20. Ibid.

21. Christine L. Porath and Christine M. Pearson, "The Price of Incivility," *Harvard Business Review*, January–February 2013, https://hbr.org/2013/ 01/the -price-of-incivility.

22. Anonymous, "Fantastic Place to Work," Glassdoor, April 9, 2014, http://
    www.glassdoor.com/Reviews/Employee-Review-Facebook-RVW4029568
    .htm.

23. Alyson Shontell, "Why 'Arrogant Jerks' Become Rich and Successful
    in Silicon Valley," *Business Insider*, November 22, 2014, http://www
    .businessinsider.com/asshole-ceos-startup-founders-and-success-2014-11.

24. Ibid.

25. Andrew Kirtzman, "Revealing the Total Giuliani," *Washington Post*,
    March 18, 2007, http://www.washingtonpost.com/wp-dyn/content/
    article/2007/03/16/AR2007031602698.html; Jim Sleeper, "Rudy Giuliani's
    Sad Self-Destruction: How 'America's Mayor' Became Just Another
    GOP Sidewalk Lunatic," *Salon*, February 22, 2015, http://www.salon
    .com/2015/02/22/rudy_giulianis_sad_self_destuction_how_americas_
    mayor_became_just_another_gop_sidewalk_lunatic/.

26. Michael Grunwald, "Cruel to Be Kind," *New Republic*, January 15, 2001,
    https://newrepublic.com/article/95729/cruel-be-kind.

27. Brenden Beck and Amanda Matles, "We Need Fewer NYPD Officers—
    Not More," *AM New York*, June 24, 2015, http://www.amny.com/opinion/
    we-need-fewer-nypd-officers-not-more-1.10575625.

28. Michael Dobbs, "Most Revealing Fibs: Rudy Giuliani," *Washington
    Post*, December 16, 2007, http://voices.washingtonpost.com/fact
    -checker/2007/12/most_revealing_fibs_rudy_giuli.html.

29. Sam Roberts, "Infamous 'Drop Dead' Was Never Said by Ford," *New
    York Times*, December 28, 2006, http://www.nytimes.com/2006/12/28/
    nyregion/28veto.html.

30. Christine L. Porath and Amir Erez, "Does Rudeness Really Matter? The
    Effects of Rudeness on Task Performance and Helpfulness," *Academy of
    Management Journal* 50, no. 5 (2007): 1181–97.

31. Gérard Ouimet, "Dynamics of Narcissistic Leadership in Organizations:
    Towards an Integrated Research Model," *Journal of Managerial
    Psychology* 25, no. 7 (2010): 717.

32. Arijit Chatterjee and Donald C. Hambrick, "It's All About Me:
    Narcissistic Chief Executive Officers and Their Effects on Company
    Strategy and Performance," *Administrative Science Quarterly* 52, no. 3
    (2007): 351–86

33. Ibid., 362.

34. Ibid.

35. Aaron Blake, "Ted Cruz: Democrats Caused the Shutdown," *Washington
    Post*, January 26, 2014, https://www.washingtonpost.com/news/
    post-politics/wp/2014/01/26/ted-cruz-democrats-caused-the
    -shutdown/?utm_term=.2eb46b305e7d.

36. Matthew L. A. Hayward and Donald C. Hambrick, "Explaining the
    Premiums Paid for Large Acquisitions: Evidence of CEO Hubris,"

Administrative Science Quarterly 42, no. 1 (1997): 103–27.

37. James B. Stewart, "Steve Jobs Defied Convention, and Perhaps the Law," *New York Times*, May 32 2014, http://www.nytimes.com/2014/05/03/business/steve-jobs-a-genius-at-pushing-boundaries-too.html?_r=0.

38. Ibid.

39. Ibid.

40. Ibid.

41. Julia Preston, "Immigration Crackdown with Firings, Not Raids," *New York Times*, September 29, 2009, http://www.nytimes.com/2009/09/30/us/30factory.html.

42. Glassdoor, review, https://www.glassdoor.com/Salary/American-Apparel-Salaries-E18373.htm.

43. http://securities.stanford.edu/filings-documents/1045/APP10_01/2011429_f01c_10CV06352.pdf; https://www.sec.gov/Archives/edgar/data/1336545/000144530511000600/app12311010k.htm; http://www.americanapparelshareholdersettlement.com/media/76358/ameraprl_second_amended_complaint.pdf.

44. Porath and Pearson, "The Price of Incivility."

45. Hayward, Shepherd, and Griffin, "A Hubris Theory of Entrepreneurship."

46. Yoni Appelbaum, "'I Alone Can Fix It,'" *Atlantic*, July 21, 2016, https://www.theatlantic.com/politics/archive/2016/07/trump-rnc-speech-alone-fix-it/492557/.

47. Petit and Bollaert, "Flying Too Close to the Sun? Hubris Among CEOs and How to Prevent It."

CHAPTER NINE

1. Peter Biskind, "The Weinstein Way," *Vanity Fair*, February 5, 2011, http://www.vanityfair.com/news/2004/02/weinstein-miramax-200402.

2. Ibid.

3. Ibid.

4. Ibid.

5. Ibid.

6. David Carr, "The Emperor Miramaximus," *New York*, http://nymag.com/nymetro/news/people/features/5460/#comments.

7. Bryan Burrough, "How Harvey Got His Groove Back," *Vanity Fair*, February 3, 2011, http://www.vanityfair.com/news/2010/09/boardwalk-belles-201009.

8. Nadia Damouni and Jeffrey Dastin, "Exclusive: American Apparel Finds CEO Misused Funds; Helped Discredit Employee—Source," *Reuters*, June 21, 2014, http://www.reuters.com/article/2014/06/21/us-american-apparel-charney-idUSKBN0EW08B20140621.

9.   Michael Hiltzik, "American Apparel Saga: Why Did It Take So Long to Sack Dov Charney?" *Los Angeles Times*, June 20, 2014, http://www.latimes.com/business/hiltzik/la-fi-mh-dov-charney-20140620-column.html#page=1.

10. Ibid.

11. Troy A. Paredes, "Too Much Pay, Too Much Deference: Is CEO Overconfidence the Product of Corporate Governance?" Washington University School of Law Working Paper (04-08), 02, 2004, https://papers.ssrn.com/sol3/papers.cfm?abstract_id=587162.

12. Steve Blank, "Why Tim Cook Is Steve Ballmer and Why He Still Has His Job at Apple," *Business Insider*, October 25, 2016, http://www.businessinsider.com/tim-cook-is-steve-ballmer-2016-10.

13. Adam Lashinsky, "The Decade of Steve," *Fortune*, November 23, 2009, http://archive.fortune.com/2009/11/04/technology/steve_jobs_ceo_decade.fortune/index.htm.

14. Apple Press Info, "Apple's Special Committee Reports Findings of Stock Option Investigation," October 4, 2006, https://www.apple.com/pr/library/2006/10/04Apples-Special-Committee-Reports-Findings-of-Stock-Option-Investigation.html.

15. Carr, "The Emperor Miramaximus."

16. Andrew Rafferty and Alex Seitz-Wald, "Trump Revokes Washington Post's Press Credentials," NBC News, June 13, 2016, http://www.nbcnews.com/politics/2016-election/trump-revokes-washington-post-s-press-credentials-n591586.

17. Adam Liptak, "Donald Trump Could Threaten U.S. Rule of Law, Scholars Say," *New York Times*, June 3, 2016, http://www.nytimes.com/2016/06/04/us/politics/donald-trump-constitution-power.html.

18. Lyons, "The Crazy Genius of Brand Guru Peter Arnell."

19. Ibid.

20. Noreen O'Leary, "The Arnell Exodus," *Adweek*, February 13, 2011, http://www.adweek.com/news/advertising-branding/arnell-exodus-125734.

CHAPTER TEN

1.   Andrew Ross Sorkin, "Berkshire's Radical Strategy: Trust," *New York Times*, May 5, 2014, http://dealbook.nytimes.com/2014/05/05/berkshires-radical-strategy-trust/.

2.   Ibid.

3.   Ibid.

4.   Ibid.

5.   Ibid.

6.   Bo Burlingham, "Decades Later, the Owners of Ann Arbor's Iconic

Zingerman's Are Still at Odds Over Expansion," *Forbes*, October 20, 2016, https://www.forbes.com/sites/boburlingham/2016/10/20/what-price -growth/#67ed6f3832e8.

7. Jennifer Conlin, "At Zingerman's, Pastrami and Partnership to Go," *New York Times*, July 5, 2014, http://www.nytimes.com/2014/07/06/business/ at-zingermans-pastrami-and-partnership-to-go.html?emc=eta1&_r=0.

8. Ibid.

9. David Shepardson, "The Zingerman's Way: How a Small Ann Arbor Delicatessen Grew into a $35-Million Powerhouse by Teaching Its Employees to Comprehend a P&L Statement," *Dbusiness*, November 8, 2013, http://www.dbusiness.com/December-2008/The -ZingermansWay/#.WLDbnH_Jw2x.

10. Ibid.

11. Grant, "The Dark Side of Emotional Intelligence."

12. Erin McLaughlin, "An Emotion Business: The Role of Emotional Intelligence in Entrepreneurial Success" (unpublished doctoral dissertation, University of North Texas, 2012).

13. Marcus Ryu, "Authenticity as Competitive Advantage," *Management Innovation eXchange*, July 14, 2013, http://www.managementexchange. com/story/integrity-rationality-and-collegiality-ingredients-greatness.

14. Alex Taylor III et al., "6 Great Teams That Take Care of Business," *Fortune*, April 10, 2014, http://fortune.com/2014/04/10/6-great-teams-that-take -care-of-business/.

15. Ibid.

16. Guidewire Reviews, Glassdoor, https://www.glassdoor.com/Reviews/ Guidewire-Reviews-E122537.htm.

17. David Cohen, "Set Your Values Before Your Agenda," *Wall Street Journal*, February 7, 2013, http://blogs.wsj.com/accelerators/2013/02/07/set-your- values-before-your-agenda/.

18. Pamela Vaughan, "Boston Business Journal Names @HubSpot the #1 Best Place to Work," *HubSpot*, July 11, 2010, https://www.hubspot.com/blog/ bid/6082/Boston-Business-Journal-Names-HubSpot-the-1-Best-Place-to -Work.

19. Brian Halligan, "10 Keys to Creating a Great Company Culture: Free Beer, Unlimited Vacation & More," *Huffington Post*, May 25, 2011, http://www .huffingtonpost.com/brian-halligan/great-company-cultures_b_790613. html.

20. Ibid.

21. Ibid.

22. "100 Best Companies to Work for 2017," *Fortune*, http://fortune.com/ best-companies/.

23. "The World's Top 10 Employers 2016," Universum Global, http://
    universumglobal.com/insights/worlds-top-10-employers-2016/.

24. Press release, "Guidewire Named a 2016 'Best Place to Work in the
    Bay Area' by *San Francisco Business Times* and *Silicon Valley Business
    Journal*," Guidewire, April 25, 2016, https://www.guidewire.com/about
    -us/news-and-events/press-releases/20160425/guidewire-named-2016
    -%E2%80%98best-place-work-bay-area%E2%80%99-san.

25. Ryu, "Authenticity as Competitive Advantage."

26. Ibid.

27. Ibid.

28. Ibid.

29. Adam Bryant, "Finding Purpose in Tunneling Through Granite," *New York
    Times*, April 13, 2013, http://www.nytimes.com/2013/04/14/business/
    guidewires-chief-on-embracing-adversity.html?pagewanted=all&_r=0.

30. Ryu, "Authenticity as Competitive Advantage."

31. Ibid.

32. Benjamin R. Palmer and Gilles Gignac, "The Impact of Emotionally
    Intelligent Leadership on Talent Retention, Discretionary Effort and
    Employment Brand," *Industrial and Commercial Training* 44, no. 1
    (2012): 9–18.

33. Tony Schwartz and Christine Porath, "Why You Hate Work," *New York
    Times*, May 30, 2014, http://www.nytimes.com/2014/06/01/opinion/
    sunday/why-you-hate-work.html.

34. Yehuda Baruch et al., "Prosocial Behavior and Job Performance: Does the
    Need for Control and the Need for Achievement Make a Difference?,"
    Social Behavior and Personality 32, no. 4, 2004.

CHAPTER ELEVEN

1. Craig Welch, "The Rise and Fall of Mars Hill Church," *Seattle Times*,
   February 4, 2016, http://www.seattletimes.com/seattle-news/the-rise
   -and-fall-of-mars-hill-church/.

2. Ibid.

3. Ibid.

4. Dale Fincher, "Mark Driscoll and Christian Rape Culture," *Soulation*,
   August 1, 2014, http://www.soulation.org/freeatlast/2014/08/mark
   -driscoll-and-christian-rape-culture.html.

5. Welch, "The Rise and Fall of Mars Hill Church."

6. Lynda V. Mapes, "Mars Hill Protesters Call for Pastor's Resignation,"
   Seattle Times, August 4, 2014, http://www.seattletimes.com/seattle-news/
   mars-hill-protesters-call-for-pastorrsquos-resignation/.

7. Ibid.

8. Ruth Graham, "The Evangelical Celebrity Machine: Janet Mefferd Accused Pastor Mark Driscoll of Plagiarism Then Deleted All Her Proof. Why'd She Back Down?" *Slate*, December 11, 2013, http://www .slate.com/articles/life/faithbased/2013/12/mark_driscoll_plagiarism_ accusations_janet_mefferd_accused_the_seattle_pastor.html.

9. Welch, "The Rise and Fall of Mars Hill Church."

10. Mark Lipton, "When Clients Make You Crazy," *Journal of Management Consulting* 8, no. 4 (Fall 1995).

11. Martha Stout, *The Sociopath Next Door* (New York: Harmony, 2006).

12. Ibid.

CHAPTER TWELVE

1. Roy F. Baumeister, *Evil: Inside Human Cruelty and Violence* (New York: W. H. Freeman and Company, 1997).

2. Ibid.

3. Arendt, *Eichmann in Jerusalem* (New York: Viking Press, 1963).

4. "The Banality of Evil, Part II," Radio Open Source: Arts, Ideas, and Politics with Christopher Lydon, March 13, 2007, http://radioopensource.org/ the-banality-of-evil-part-ii.

5. Hannah Arendt, *Eichmann in Jerusalem: A Report on the Banality of Evil*.

6. Ibid.

7. Philip Zimbardo, "The Story: An Overview of the Experiment," Stanford Prison Experiment, 1999–2017, http://www.prisonexp.org/the-story/. http://www.prisonexp.org/.

8. Arendt, *Eichmann in Jerusalem*.

9. Richard W. Sonnenfeldt, *Witness to Nuremberg: The Many Lives of the Man Who Translated at the Nazi War Crimes Trial* (New York: Arcade Publishing, 2011).

10. Ben Jacobs, "D.C.'s Top Rabbi Is a Peeping Tom," *Daily Beast*, February 19, 2015, http://www.thedailybeast.com/articles/2015/02/19/d-c-s-top-rabbi -is-a-peeping-tom.html.

11. Ibid.

12. Michelle Boorstein and Pamela Constable, "Georgetown Rabbi Accused of Voyeurism Is Focus of Other Allegations," *Washington Post*, October 20, 2014, https://www.washingtonpost.com/local/national-rabbi-board -knew-of-misconduct-allegations-against-georgetown-rabbi-for-at-least -two-years/2014/10/20/f3c924ca-5865-11e4-bd61-346aee66ba29_story. html?utm_term=.0e4a196eb5bc.

13. Michelle Boorstein, "Prominent D.C. Rabbi Accused of Voyeurism Presents a Disturbing Paradox," *Washington Post*, November 8, 2014, https://www.washingtonpost.com/local/prominent-dc-rabbi-accused-of

-voyeurism-presents-disturbing-paradox/2014/11/08/ef1e63e6-5f71
-11e4-9f3a-7e28799e0549_story.html?utm_term=.86b689a6ee38.

14. Julie Zauzmer, "Victims of Rabbi Freundel, Who Videotaped Women,
    Ask for $100 Million in Lawsuit," *Washington Post*, August 16, 2016,
    https://www.washingtonpost.com/news/acts-of-faith/wp/2016/08/16/
    victims-of-rabbi-freundel-who-videotaped-women-ask-for-100-million
    -in-lawsuit/?utm_term=.72dd101f445f.

15. Josh Nathan-Kazis, "Did Rabbi Barry Freundel Treat Mikveh Like 'Car
    Wash' to Peep on Women?" *Forward*, December 24, 2014, http://forward
    .com/news/211529/did-rabbi-barry-freundel-treat-mikveh-like-car-was/.

16. Ibid.

17. Ibid.

18. Ibid.

19. Ibid.

20. Ibid.

21. Weber Shandwick, Powell Tate, and KRC Research, "Civility in America
    2014," 2014, https://www.webershandwick.com/uploads/news/files/
    civility-in-america-2014.pdf.

22. "The Art of Living Together," *Hedgehog Review* 15, no. 3 (2013), http://
    www.iasc-culture.org/THR/THR_article_2013_Fall_short_take_3.php.

23. Stephen L. Carter, *Civility: Manners, Morals, and the Etiquette of
    Democracy* (New York: Harper Perennial, 1998), 11.

24. Weber Shandwick, "Press Release: Poll Finds Americans United in Seeing
    an Uncivil Nation; Divided About Causes and Civility of Presidential
    Candidates," Weber Shandwick, January 23, 2017, http://www.
    webershandwick.com/news/article/poll-finds-americans-united
    -in-seeing-an-uncivil-nation-divided-about-cause.

25. Daniel M. Shea, "Nastiness, Name-calling & Negativity—The Allegheny
    College Survey of Civility and Compromise in American Politics,"
    Allegheny College, 2010, http://sitesmedia.s3.amazonaws.com/civility/
    files/2010/04/AlleghenyCollegeCivilityReport2010.pdf.

26. Porath and Pearson, "The Price of Incivility."

27. "76% Say U.S. Society Is Ruder, Less Civilized," *Rasmussen Reports*,
    October 29, 2012, http://www.rasmussenreports.com/public_content/
    lifestyle/general_lifestyle/october_2012/76_say_u_s_society_is_ruder_
    less_civilized.

28. Zygmunt Bauman and Leonidas Donskis, *Moral Blindness: The Loss of
    Sensitivity in Liquid Modernity* (Cambridge: Polity Press, 2013).

29. Shandwick, Tate, and KRC Research, "Civility in America 2014."

30. Ibid.

31. Deloitte, "Mind the Gaps: The 2015 Deloitte Millennial Survey, Executive

Summary," https://www2.deloitte.com/content/dam/Deloitte/global/ Documents/About-Deloitte/gx-wef-2015-millennial-survey -executivesummary.pdf.

32. Ibid.

33. Ibid.

34. Dorothy Rowe, "*Zero Degrees of Empathy* by Simon Baron-Cohen— Review," *Guardian*, April 15, 2011, https://www.theguardian.com/ books/2011/apr/15/zero-degrees-of-empathy-baron-cohen-review.

35. Frans de Waal, *The Age of Empathy: Nature's Lessons for a Kinder Society* (New York: Harmony Books, 2009), 213–15.

36. Robin Stern and Diane Divecha, "The Empathy Trap," *Psychology Today*, May 4, 2015, https://www.psychologytoday.com/articles/201505/the -empathy-trap.

37. Carolyn Zahn-Waxler et al., "Development of Concern for Others," *Developmental Psychology* 28, no. 1 (1992): 126–36; Soo Hyun Rhee et al., "Early Concern and Disregard for Others as Predictors of Antisocial Behavior," *Journal of Child Psychology and Psychiatry* 54, no. 2 (2013): 157–66.

38. Gayla Marty, "Origins of Empathy," University of Minnesota, College of Education + Human Development, October 2013.

39. David T. Lykken, *The Antisocial Personalities* (Hillsdale, NJ: Lawrence Erlbaum Associates, 1995).

40. Greg Bishop, "Pete Carroll, NFL's Eternal Optimist, Is Ready to Turn Heartbreak into Triumph," *Sports Illustrated*, July 28, 2015, http://www .si.com/nfl/2015/07/28/pete-carroll-seattle-seahawks-2015-season-super -bowl-xlix.

41. Ibid.

42. Alyssa Roenigk, "Lotus Pose on Two," *ESPN*, August 21, 2013, http:// www.espn.com/nfl/story/_/id/9581925/seattle-seahawks-use-unusual -techniques-practice-espn-magazine.

43. John Branch, "Tragedy Made Steve Kerr See the World Beyond the Court," *New York Times*, December 22, 2016, https://www.nytimes .com/2016/12/22/sports/basketball/steve-kerr-golden-state-warriors.htm l?=undefined&moduleDetail=section-news-0&action=click&content Collection=ProBasketball&region=Footer&module=MoreInSection& version=WhatsNext&contentID=WhatsNext&pgtype=article&mtrref= undefined&gwh=7F4570CAE50AD5CB1323AF234048BC60&gwt=pay.

44. Ibid.

45. Ibid.

46. "Salesforce.com Inc.," *Marketwatch*, http://www.marketwatch.com/ investing/stock/CRM/financials.

47. Claire Zillman, "Salesforce's Marc Benioff Urges His Fellow CEOs to Close the Gender Pay Gap," *Fortune*, January 18, 2017, http://fortune.com/2017/01/18/salesforce-ceo-marc-benioff-gender-pay-gap/.

48. "Mystic Marc's Guide to Success," *Economist*, November 24, 2009, http://www.economist.com/node/14953117.

49. Marc Benioff, "Salesforce CEO Marc Benioff: How Business Leaders Can Help Narrow Income Inequality," *Fortune*, January 17, 2017, http://fortune.com/2017/01/17/automation-workers-marc-benioff/?iid=sr-link2.

50. "Salesforce.com's Marc Benioff Focuses on Many Stakeholders," *Wall Street Journal*, October 26, 2015, https://www.wsj.com/articles/salesforce-coms-marc-benioff-focuses-on-many-stakeholders-1445911375.

51. John Bowlby, *A Secure Base: Clinical Applications of Attachment Theory*, (New York: Taylor & Francis, 2005).

52. Jim Therrien and Jenn Smith, "State Sen. Benjamin Downing Won't Seek Election This Fall," *Berkshire Eagle*, January 26, 2016, http://www.berkshireeagle.com/stories/state-sen-benjamin-downing-wont-seek-election-this-fall,172991.

53. "Notable & Quotable: Alan Mulally," *Wall Street Journal*, March 9, 2016.

54. "Leading in the 21st Century: An Interview with Ford's Alan Mulally," McKinsey & Company, November 2013, http://www.mckinsey.com/Insights/Strategy/Leading_in_the_21st_century_An_interview_with_Fords_Alan_Mulally?cid=other-eml-alt-mip-mck-oth-1311#sthash.ausO4of6.dpuf.

55. Tony Schwartz, "To Get More Out of Workers, Invest More in Them," *New York Times*, October 2, 2015, https://www.nytimes.com/2015/10/03/business/dealbook/to-get-more-out-of-workers-invest-more-in-them.html.

56. Ibid.

57. Ibid.

58. Ibid.

59. Ibid.

INDEX

ABOUT THE AUTHOR

Photo © Val Allard

MARK LIPTON IS GRADUATE PROFESSOR of management at The New School in New York City. For over forty years, he has been a trusted adviser to Fortune 500 corporations, think tanks, philanthropies, not-for-profits, and start-ups.

His diverse entrepreneurial client base includes founders of transformative start-ups in technology, manufacturing, media, education, health care, finance, and marketing. His coaching skills and leadership development programs are engaged by C-level executives across all sectors of the economy, and his development of corporate and nonprofit boards allows them to govern more effectively. In the not-for-profit realm, he has consulted to and led leadership development initiatives for organizations ranging from multibillion-dollar philanthropic game-changers to local community-based social service providers to the world's largest international NGOs. Much of his work to infuse progressive leadership practices into the NGO and not-for-profit world has been made possible by significant grants from the Ford, Rockefeller, Mott, and Charles H. Revson Foundations, among others.

His work as a consultant and professor has inspired his writing for such publications as *Harvard Business Review, MIT Sloan Management*

Review, and *Journal of Management Consulting,* as well as his previous book, *Guiding Growth: How Vision Keeps Companies on Course* (Harvard Business School Press, 2003). A leading authority on the founders' dilemma, the strong and often dysfunctional psychological forces that organizational founders experience when they are pressured to step down, Mark has been a frequent commentator on National Public Radio's *Marketplace* to discuss CEO transitions in the corporate sector.

Mark holds a PhD from the School of Management at the University of Massachusetts in Amherst and was an Erik Erikson Visiting Scholar-in-Residence in 2009 at the Austen Riggs Center. He lives in New York City and the Berkshires of western Massachusetts.